YOUR CAREER

in

TRAVEL AND TOURISM

By Laurence Stevens

Merton House Publishing Company,
Wheaton, Illinois

Revised 1979

ISBN Number: 0-916032-02-7
Library of Congress Catalog Card Number: 76-50938
Copyright © 1977 by Laurence Stevens

Merton House Publishing Company
937 West Liberty Drive
Wheaton, Illinois 60187

Manufactured in the United States of America

DEDICATION

Dedicated to the young men and women of America who aspire to professional travel careers, and to those educators who instruct and encourage them, by whose character and dedication the high professional standards of the travel and leisure industry are assured for the future.

ABOUT THE AUTHOR

Laurence Stevens not only writes about the travel industry—he has been part of it for more than twenty five years.

Born and educated in England, Mr. Stevens began his career in travel in 1950 with the Automobile Association in Leeds. When he moved to the United States in 1955 he immediately joined the travel division of American Express Company, His assignments with the company included travel sales positions in New York and Los Angeles, and he became district travel manager of Pasadena, St. Louis and Chicago. His management responsibilities included the sale and promotion of retail travel products and the training and development of staff.

Since 1972 Mr. Stevens has operated his own company which offers a variety of specialized services to the travel industry, including business consultations, and the sale and appraisal of travel related companies.

World-wide travel has been a part of the author's life. He has visited many parts of the world—either on one of his own exploration trips, conducting one of his many groups and conventions, or on seagoing assignments with the cruise staff of luxury cruise liners.

Other Merton House books by Mr. Stevens include *Guide to Buying, Selling and Starting a Travel Agency,* and volume 2 of The Travel Agency Management Library, *The Travel Agency Personnel Manual.*

TABLE OF CONTENTS

Establishing your career goals. Preparing yourself for the job hunt. How to complete an employment application and prepare a résumé. The personal call—your best approach. How to use the telephone and direct mail effectively. Preparing for the job interview. Your dress and grooming. How to conduct yourself during the interview.

The Federal Aviation Administration. The Civil Aeronautics Board. Opportunities with foreign airlines. Airline employee benefits. Pilots and flight engineers. Flight attendants. Technicians and maintenance staff. Airline food service careers. Sales, office, and ground staff. Airline salaries. Air traffic controllers.

Bus drivers. Hostesses. Information clerks. Mechanics. Ticket agents. Tour representatives.

Mechanics. Rental sales agents. Reservation agents. Sales representatives. Service agents. Utility workers.

Amtrak career opportunities: Reservation clerks. Passenger sales representatives. Sales representatives. *Other railroad careers:* Conductors. Brake operators. Engineers. Shop workers. Signal installers and maintainers. Station agents. Tower operators. Track workers. Clerical positions.

Deck officers. Engineer officers. Radio officers. Seamen and engine room ratings. Stewards. Training programs. Cruise staff opportunities.

FOREWORD

Traditionally we think of professions in terms of doctors, dentists, lawyers, or teachers. However, in the past decade the field of business has been increasingly recognized as one of the most challenging and stimulating of the professions. A business manager, for example, is truly a professional. According to the dictionary, a profession is "a calling in which one professes to have acquired specialized knowledge which is used either in instructing, guiding, or advising others." It is obvious therefore that management is of a professional nature.

The essence of the travel business is "advising of others." This is a business which provides competent, professional advice and service to those who are traveling or making travel plans. For example, a travel agency epitomizes all of the requirements for a stimulating professional-type business firm.

Tourism today is one of the world's largest businesses. It is made up of many segments, the principal ones being accommodations (food and lodging), transportation, shopping, and activities for vacationists such as providing cultural experiences, adventure, sports, entertainment, instruction, and similar pleasurable pursuits.

None of these activities would be possible without someone selling the services to interested would-be travelers. This is where the marketing and sales departments of travel companies come into the picture in a very significant manner. They make up the overall marketing structure for the travel industry—and a very important part indeed. For example, in the United States in one year, travel agents marketed about $11 billion worth of travel services. This is a remarkably large figure and represents about one sixth of all the dollars which are spent on travel in this country. There are more than 17,000 travel agencies in the United States and the number keeps growing yearly. Each of these agencies must have a capable staff and a competent manager who supervises the activities of those working in the agency. Every hotel, motel, restaurant, and transportation firm also has a marketing responsibility. Without this, no business can succeed for very long.

One of the most challenging things about the travel business is the broad scope of knowledge which must be acquired concerning every conceivable aspect of the traveler's anticipated pleasurable experience. One of the first fields of knowledge that we would recognize is geography. If someone wants to travel, we have to know where his destination is located and the mode of transportation and route by which it is reached. We also have to know about meteorolgy—the science of weather. No one will enjoy a trip to an area where rain falls every day for 20 days or where it is so hot or cold that a person is extremely uncomfortable. Some trips must be made at all times of the year but pleasure trips should be taken at times which are the most comfortable and pleasant for the traveler. Other fields of knowledge include communication, history, history of art,

VII

geology, fisheries and wildlife, botany and forestry, archeology, commercial geography, political science, preventive medicine, and laws or regulations for travelers. Of course, any travel counselor must be very knowledgeable concerning aviation, ships, buses, trains, helicopters, and other forms of transportation. Likewise, the counselor is expected to know ways of life of people in any country which the tourist may wish to visit.

From the above, you can see that this is a formidable list. It is certainly a most challenging one and requires a lifetime of study in order to be fully proficient. Furthermore, the travel aspects of any country change from time to time so that acquiring current knowledge is a constant upgrading process.

As previously mentioned, any travel business is a combination of a professional counseling service and a business organization. Some of the most important considerations of business management are the overall management process itself, office management, the management of personnel, reporting and communications, marketing management, financial management, legal aspects and insurance. All of these considerations require a depth of specialized knowledge. Such learning is mainly acquired through on-the-job training, formal courses, self-study, and attendance at seminars, meetings, short courses or other subject-type offerings which are available to travel people.

The most comprehensive educational preparation is enrollment in a four-year college or university course of study in Travel and Tourism Management or Hotel and Restaurant Management. Such curriculums are often part of a College of Business and offered by a number of prominent universities and colleges in the United States and Canada. Also available are two-year programs in community and junior colleges which have specialized courses in public hospitality, transportation, travel agency management, and closely related subjects. Throughout the United States there are technical institutes or specialized schools which offer intensified study leading to a diploma in travel industry related work. These schools are usually located in the larger cities and provide a basic education which anyone would need to enter this business. Knowledge is power and in this type of work an almost necessary power. As an example, it is difficult to obtain employment in travel agency work without formal training and education of some sort prior to embarking on the job. In rare cases, a person might be hired without any experience whatever. But immediately there would be a need for intensive in-depth, self-study and training.

Educational opportunities are constantly being offered by the public carriers—airlines, railroads, cruise lines, ship lines, and by the hotel and restaurant trade associations. These courses are well planned and expertly taught. Attendance at such schools is a regular part of the industry's educational program.

At the managerial level, the Institute of Certified Travel Agents, the Educational Institute of the American Hotel & Motel Association, and the National Institute for the Foodservice Industry offer educational programs leading to various certification designations. These Institutes hold short seminars in various parts of the country from time to time. Also, there are many study groups organized in various cities. However, whether a person desires to be a manager or not, a tremendous amount of good information can be obtained to increase ability by becoming a Candidate in one of these educational institutes.

After 40 years in the business, one highly competent travel executive told me, "there is always something new in this business and I never stop learning. If I did, it would be my undoing." So, there is plenty to learn in any aspect of the travel business. I trust that if you enter this business that you will enjoy it and that you will constantly search for excellence as you grow in experience and competence into a person recognized as a travel business authority.

Robert W. McIntosh, Ph.D.
Professor of Tourism
School of Hotel, Restaurant and Institutional Management
Michigan State University
East Lansing, Michigan

PREFACE

The travel industry has been an important and integral part of my life for more than 25 years. As I reflect I can safely say that it has been an extremely rewarding career, one in which I have experienced the personal fulfillment of helping people plan their vacations and enjoy the trips of their dreams. If I care to think about it long enough, the degree of trust, almost blind faith, placed in my knowledge and experience by thousands of unsuspecting travelers is almost frightening.

Ever since I arrived on these shores in 1955, I have been engaged in one facet or another of travel and tourism. During this time there have been enormous changes in modes of transportation and travel patterns. For example, during the 1950's and early 1960's, ocean travel was extremely popular; travelers had to reserve their accommodations a year in advance if they expected to cross the Atlantic by ocean liner during the peak travel months. A voyage on one of the fast, comfortable, trans-Atlantic liners was almost a vacation in itself — so much so that the advertising slogan of "Getting there is half the fun" used by the Cunard Line became a household expression. Today there are virtually no U. S. passenger ships plying the North Atlantic sealanes, and few foreign ships offer anything more than token sailings, and these only during the height of the European travel season. Passenger lines today offer cruise service, a type of vacation which has become immensely popular among modern travelers, and quite profitable for the companies.

Aviation has undergone drastic change too. The transition from piston-engine to pure jet propulsion first had to go through the chrysalis stage of the turboprop (a jet engine that spins a propeller). The British Vickers Viscount was the first airliner to make use of turbine power and it entered into service in 1953.

The pure jet era was ushered in by the British with the Comet, which went into operational service with B. O. A. C., (now British Airways) in 1952. In October of 1958, a Comet IV, operated by B.O. A. C., inaugurated the first trans-Atlantic jet service. Pan American followed a few weeks later with a Boeing 707 — the aircraft from which a whole range of transports have descended — on their New York-Paris route. The first domestic jet service was flown by National Airlines, and in early 1959, American Airlines operated the first transcontinental jet service between Los Angeles and New York.

Aviation is still in a state of evolution. The era of the jumbo jets arrived with the Boeing 747. The tendency is now towards wide-bodied equipment such as the Lockheed 1011 and the Douglas DC-10.

In mid-1976, two sleek, needle-nose aircraft landed almost simultaneously at Washington's Dulles airport, thereby introducing supersonic travel. The Concorde is the result of a joint development, at enormous cost, between the British and the French. The Concorde cruises at Mach 2, or about 1,400 miles-per-hour at 52,000 feet — twice the speed of sound. Such aircraft reduces the travel time from the east coast to London or Paris to about 3½ hours instead of the 7 or 8 it takes by conventional jets.

In 1965, the scheduled U.S. airlines operated 867 piston-engine aircraft and 1008 jets. By 1977, there were only 28 piston-engine aircraft in scheduled operational service, and the number of jet transports had risen to 2030.

What of the future? No one really knows, but the travel and leisure field is constantly changing. Indeed, change it must if it expects to keep pace with the tourism growth created by a more affluent and mobile society.

According to all current indicators, opportunities for a career in the travel, leisure, and hospitality field are likely to increase in the years ahead. Although it is impossible to predict precisely what opportunities will exist, the fact remains that tourism growth is expected to generate a wide range of available jobs *for those who are trained and prepared.*

A career in the travel and hospitality industry is as fulfilling and rewarding as many jobs, and perhaps more so than most. But the professional standards of the future are likely to be considerably higher than they have been in the past for many segments of the field. Only those who are prepared can expect advancement and a secure position in the industry of tomorrow. Whichever facet of this huge industry you decide to work in, remember — it is a *service* career, and the needs, desires, safety, and comfort of the traveler must always come first. It is your *job* to give the very best you have in serving others, for you are their dealer in dreams.

Whatever your field, it is also your responsibility to achieve as high a level of professional training and development as possible. Sooner or later, your education will be recognized as valuable and essential in employment consideration. Samuel Johnson, that great essayist, once wrote, "The future is purchased by the present." Your entire career, advancement, earning power, lifestyle, and professional status will depend to a very great extent on how well you plan and prepare yourself through balanced study and education.

This book is nothing more than an introduction to career opportunities in the travel field. The subject is so immense that each facet of the industry is worthy of its own guide. What I have attempted to do is to prepare a synopsis, and to offer an insight into the entire industry for those who are interested in exploring the possibility of a career in travel, transportation, leisure and hospitality.

Laurence Stevens

ACKNOWLEDGEMENTS

This book could not have been written had it not been for the cooperation of many people of the travel and tourism industry, and my sincere thanks go to all who provided me with information and photographs. I am especially grateful to the following companies and organizations: Air Canada; the *Air Line Pilot*; the Air Transport Association; American Airlines; Amtrak; the Association of American Railroads; Avis Rent a Car System, Inc.; Budget Rent a Car Corporation; Continental Trailways; *Cooking for Profit;* Discover America Travel Organizations, Inc.; the Educational Institute of the American Hotel and Motel Association; the Federal Aviation Administration; International Association of Amusement Parks and Attractions; National Institute for the Foodservice Industry; Office of Maritime Manpower, Maritime Administration, U. S. Department of Commerce; United Airlines. My thanks also to the Educational Institute for the American Hotel and Motel Association; the National Institute for the Foodservice Industry, and the Federal Aviation Administration for permission to reproduce and adapt information relative to careers and training in their respective fields. I must also acknowledge the use of material published by the U. S. Department of Labor relative to certain careers, statistics, and job descriptions. Credit for cover photos, from top right, and anti-clockwise: Prudential Lines; Santa Fe Railway; The Sheraton Corporation; Air Canada; American Airlines; North Central Airlines.

Chapter 1

BEARDING THE LION
THE JOB HUNT

Once you have decided that a career in travel is for you, the easiest part of the job-hunting process is over. The next step is to find a position compatible with your goals and ambitions and commensurate with your training.

Locating the right opportunity is not always easy. Job-hunting is not a particularly pleasant experience, and it can quickly shake your confidence after a day or two. If you are lucky the time spent in your search will be short, but if the process does take much longer than expected you cannot give up your efforts. The important thing to bear in mind is that somewhere within the travel industry, there is a place just for you. So avoid accepting a job just to get started; if you take a job merely to get your foot in the door, sooner or later, you will be unhappy. Starting off in the wrong job will waste valuable time you could have spent on finding or preparing yourself for the right position to begin your travel career.

KNOW WHAT YOU WANT

Each year, thousands of people seek travel-related employment without really knowing what it is they are looking for. All they know is that they want to work in travel. If you are to be successful in your job-hunting, you should realize that the key to achieving your goal is to know *exactly* what it is you want. So before doing anything else, answer the following questions:

(1) Which segment of the industry do you want to work in—airline, hotel, travel agency, railroad, etc.?
(2) Are you qualified for the job you want? Do you meet the eligibility requirements the company of your choice has set as minimum standards (education, certification, height, vision, etc.)?
(3) Do you fit the pattern of those currently employed in the field?
(4) Is the average starting salary for the job acceptable to you?
(5) Would you stand a good chance of getting the job?

Which segment of the industry will you work in? The first thing you must decide is whether you wish to work for an airline, railroad, steamship line, tour operator, travel agency, hotel, or a related business such as an amusement park. Once you have made that first, all-

1

important decision, you must decide on the type of job you want. Is it to be a flight attendant or a reservationist? A pilot or an engineer? A tour guide or a travel agent? When you have made this decision too, you will have established your goal and can then take very precise steps to achieve it. You can plan your education, training, and work experience to qualify you for your career.

Consider setting up a contingency plan in the event that your first choice of employment is not available. Establish, in order of preference, your second and third alternatives. For instance, if you want to be an airline reservationist, but the airlines are not hiring new employees at the time you apply, look at reservation positions with tour operators, hotels, or car-rental companies. The job functions are very similar to those of an airline reservation agent, so you will have an edge over other applicants when airline positions become available. In other words, allow a degree of flexibility.

Are you qualified? You must be certain that you meet the qualifications and eligibility criteria for the position you want. Is your education sufficient, and does your weight, height, vision, and age fall within company standards? If an airline specifies minimum and maximum height requirements, it means that applicants must fall between these extremes. If you are a fraction over the maximum or under the minimum, you will not qualify—no matter how good your other qualifications are. Waivers are not granted on any of the basic requirements.

Most larger companies have comprehensive standards which must be met by prospective employees. You will find the career section of this book helpful in determining the general eligibility requirements for specific jobs or branches of the industry. For more complete information, contact employers.

If you do not meet the minimum standards for the particular position in which you are interested, don't waste your time pursuing it, unless the requirements can be achieved through education or specialized training. Consider falling back on one of your alternative choices instead.

Do you fit the pattern? Don't expect to be considered for a flight attendant if you are semi-retired. Although age discrimination is illegal, most employers are seeking young people for their trainee and entry-level positions. Employers assume that a younger person is likely to be more flexible, quicker to learn new skills, and more easily trained than someone of more mature years. Conversely, they feel that an older person will probably be far more successful as a commissioned salesperson with a travel agency than would a younger candidate. So set your sights on a position you will be comfortable in, and for which you are likely to be hired.

Is the salary adequate? Be certain before you accept a position that the salary scale is adequate and meets your needs and budget. You should also know the company policy on salary increases. Although you may not be able to exist permanently on a starting salary, you may be able to make ends meet for a while if you know you can expect a review and increase by a specific date.

Are you likely to be hired? If you meet the minimum standards and qualifications required for a certain position, the likelihood of your being hired will depend on intangibles like personality and employer preferences.

Many positions in travel require heavy public contact, and employers make it clear that they prefer applicants who have friendly, outgoing personalities. This does not necessarily mean that a reticent person cannot find employment for there are many behind-the-scenes positions ideal for quieter people. You know your own self best, so only pursue those jobs that fit in with your overall personality.

Many positions do not require specialized training as a prerequisite to employment, since employers have their own training programs for all new employees. To be an airline reservationist, for example, requires successful completion of the airline's own training program, whether or not the applicant has attended an airline-type private training school. You would therefore be well advised to approach the airlines directly before signing up for any school training.

On the other hand, many travel industry organizations prefer to hire applicants who have graduated from good trade schools which include reservation techniques in their curriculum. Amtrak, hotel reservation services, tour operators, and car-rental companies all prefer travel-school backgrounds.

If you want a career in sales leading directly into management, you will certainly want to consider colleges and universities offering degrees in your field of interest.

Whether or not you are hired depends upon what the employer is looking for. Later chapters will detail the ways in which you can increase your chances for employment, through knowledge and preparation.

THE APPLICATION FORM

No matter where you apply for employment you will be required to complete an application-for-employment form. Even if you have taken the time to prepare a detailed résumé, you will still be asked to fill in the company's own application. Employment applications all follow the same general format, though there may be minor variations from one company to another. If you are applying for a position which has very precise eligibility requirements (pilot, mechanic, flight attendant), you

may be asked to complete a preliminary application to assure the
employer that you meet all necessary conditions for the job. It is
necessary for many airlines to prescreen job applicants. Then, if the
company finds the requirements are met, the applicant is asked to
complete the regular application.

How to complete an application Many otherwise satisfactory
applicants are rejected simply because their applications are slovenly.
The employment application is a reflection of you—your education, your
experience, your desires and goals—reduced to a page or two of paper;
how well (or badly) you project yourself in written form has a forceful
impact on the interviewer.

Read through the application. Be certain that you understand the form
itself. If you have the good fortune of being able to complete it at your
home, you can use a typewriter; however, most interviewers prefer that it
be handwritten. Print clearly, using a blue or black ball-point or fountain
pen.

If you are filling out the form on company premises, work as quickly,
neatly, and accurately as you can. If you have prepared a résumé you can
transfer the information to the application. Don't ask questions. Many
interviewers begin evaluation of an applicant as soon as the application
form has been transferred. How quickly it is completed with a minimum
of questions may well be part of your appraisal. Just answer each
question as straightforwardly as you can.

Be scrupulously honest. If you can type at only 35 words per minute,
don't put down 50. If you are asked which languages you can speak
fluently, list only those in which you are fluent. Include all previous
employers and *never* falsify or omit information relative to previous
employment, work experience, health, disabilities, or other such data.
Most employers conduct a careful investigation of anyone they hire.
Airlines and other major employers will also require you to submit to a
physical examination. False information will almost always result in
immediate termination, if for no other reason but that the applicant lied.

Personal In this section you will be asked for your name, address,
telephone number, social security number, and similar data. You may
also be asked to answer questions relating to age, marital status, vision,
height, weight, and citizenship status if such information is required to
determine eligibility for the job. Applicants are protected from discrimination at both the federal and state levels; it is illegal for an
employer to discriminate against an applicant because of his age, race,
ethnic background, sex, etc.

Education Here is where you will list your education from grade school
through college. This is also the place to record specialized training such

as vocational or trade schools, correspondence courses, business or language instruction.

Business skills Include here your typing speed, the business machines with which you are familiar, and other business skills.

Employment history All prospective employers will want to know where you have worked. If you held any part-time jobs while in high school or college, by all means list them. If you are applying for a flight attendant's position, experience in a people-oriented job such as work in a nursing home, hospital, or restaurant, will be an asset. Such experience could even make you a prime candidate. You will also be required to list each full-time employer, the dates of employment, the beginning and final salary, and the reasons for leaving the company. You will be asked for the names of your supervisor or another reference.

HOW TO PREPARE A RÉSUMÉ

A well-prepared résumé is a necessary document for almost anyone who is actively seeking employment. Many small companies will ask an applicant to submit a résumé. You can also use your résumé as a preliminary application to companies which interest you.

Putting together a résumé is an excellent way to examine your credentials and learn more about yourself. A résumé is nothing more than a summary of your qualifications and credentials. Many people tend to make their résumés too lengthy; a busy employer does not have time to read through a long-winded résumé. All an employer expects is a summary; if he needs amplification or clarification, he will ask for it during the interview. Unless you have had a number of positions, one page should be adequate. Explain your accomplishments in simple terms and keep your remarks brief. Remember that the résumé is simply an outline intended to interest the employer in you as an applicant.

A typical résumé incorporates the following information: personal (name, address with zip code, telephone number, place and date of birth, marital status), educational background and honors, employment history, military service, personal and professional references, and individual interests. If you are applying for a specific position you may also wish to include a statement of objectives. For entry-level positions, however, goals are too confining and should be omitted.

If you prepare your résumé yourself, type it on an 8½" x 11" page, using an electric typewriter with a carbon (one time) ribbon. Read it carefully, and check for spelling mistakes and other errors. Better still, have someone else check it for you.

Since a résumé is an investment in your future career, don't spoil it by poor reproduction. Have the résumé printed by a good offset printer. This is much more economical than photocopying. Even in a major city, 100 copies (one side) will usually cost less than $4.00 on a good quality sulphite paper, and only a couple of dollars more for an impressive rag-bond.

You can also have your résumé prepared by companies specializing in résumé preparation, though it is hardly necessary if you are seeking an entry-level position. If you take care in its preparation, you can do a creditable job of preparing a résumé that will be quite acceptable.

STARTING THE JOB HUNT

Up to this point you have been establishing your goals, preparing your résumé, and planning the strategy that will, hopefully, result in obtaining the job you want. It is now time to put all of your plans into action and begin the search. It is during the actual job-hunting process that many people become discouraged and quit. However, if you persist long enough you will achieve your objective. Even in the depths of the 1974-75 recession, vacancies existed throughout the entire travel industry.

Several years ago, while one major airline was laying off many of its employees, it was also conducting interviews to fill hundreds of flight-attendant positions. If you hear that job prospects are bleak, don't believe it until you have personally checked the report for yourself.

Decide on location The first thing you must determine is the community, city, or general area where you would prefer to live and work. In smaller communities, and even in some suburbs of large cities, you will be limited to a few local travel agencies, and will find that it is difficult to locate potential openings. If you own a car, or have access to good public transportation, and are willing to travel a number of miles to and from your place of work, you can job hunt in a much larger area. If you live in a rural area, you will have to consider relocating to an area with more career opportunities. Don't expect to be considered for a position unless you are already living in the vicinity. Although there are exceptions, most companies do not hire applicants who say they will move if they get the job.

If you wish to work for an airline as a flight attendant, you will have to be governed by the route structure and base cities of the airline involved. Your willingness to relocate will probably be a prerequisite for employment.

Using the Yellow Pages The classified section of your telephone directory is an excellent starting place. Look up listings under airlines, travel agencies (or travel bureaus), car rental companies, hotels, etc. Such a study will give you an idea of the number and type of potential travel employers in your area.

The direct approach Once you have located a potential employer, the most effective approach is a personal visit to the company. If you telephone ahead, it is easy to be put off. Some airlines have a standard recorded message to the effect that they are not hiring. But if you show up on the doorstep with résumé in hand, ready to complete an application and prepared for an interview, it will be harder for the company to turn you away or deny you an interview. Many positions have been filled simply because an applicant appeared when a vacancy had suddenly become available in a company that was "not hiring." In other words, being in the right place at the right time can make all the difference in your career.

Even if the company is not hiring when you apply, you can fill out the application or leave a résumé. Always be certain to get the name and title of the interviewer.

Using the telephone If you are some distance from employers, or don't have the time to pound the pavement, then by all means start calling those companies that interest you. If it is a large organization, ask for the personnel department and request to talk with a personnel representative. Don't allow a secretary or clerk to put you off by telling you there are no openings; you have the right to insist on speaking with someone who is responsible for doing the interviewing or hiring. If you are calling an independent travel agency, or some other small company, ask to talk with the office manager.

If the interviewer is interested in talking with you further, you will be invited to visit the office, complete a form, and undergo an interview. If there are no openings when you call, you may be asked to mail your résumé for future reference.

A well conducted telephone campaign will give you an idea of hiring trends and the number and type of opportunities available. But it is not likely to be as successful in actually getting a job as the direct approach.

Applying by mail The least satisfactory approach (unless you are applying for a flight-attendant position) is by mail. If this is the only option available to you, write a covering letter addressed to the director of personnel. Your letter should be brief, and state that (1) you are enclosing a copy of your résumé, (2) you are interested in exploring employment opportunities, (3) you will call the company within a given number of days. You can then follow up your letter with a telephone call.

If you are applying for a flight attendant position, it is customary to write a letter to the airline and request an application. If the airline is hiring, you will receive information on the eligibility requirements and an application, which you then complete and return. If the airline thinks you are a serious candidate you will be invited for an interview.

Following up If you have been asked to leave your résumé, or if you have completed an application for an active file, you may expect to be contacted automatically if an opening occurs. Not so! Airlines are inundated with applicants, and many employers assume that if there were no openings when you file the application, there will be no interest on your part several months later. The reasoning on the part of the employer is that you needed a job at the time you applied, and presumably will have found something else two or three months later.

Be sure to get the name and telephone number of your interviewer and call two or three times a month. Let the interviewer know that you are serious and that you are interested in working for the company. Persistent enthusiasm on your part will keep your name prominent and will single you out from applicants who assume that "they'll call me if they need me." Unfortunately, this just is not so, there are far too many people looking for travel-industry openings.

Newspaper advertising Due to the number of people seeking employment in the travel industry, advertisements in the help-wanted columns for entry-level positions are rare. In most instances, employers have all the applicants they need without having to resort to newspaper advertising.

Employment agencies There are very few employment agencies specializing in travel-industry placements; those that do exist usually accept only experienced and qualified travel staff.

Employment agencies always charge a fee for their services and, depending upon the policy of the agency, the fee may be charged either to the applicant or the employer, or divided equally between the two. In an agency specializing in one particular field, however, all fees are generally borne by the employer who retains the agency to recruit key staff. Because of the large number of applicants seeking entry-level positions, travel-industry employers are quite unwilling to assume a fee to fill their trainee openings. Some airlines will not interview or hire any applicants who have been referred by an employment agency.

You should be cautious in dealing with some general employment agencies. Unethical agencies may advertise such glamour positions as "Travel Trainee" or "Travel Reservationist." Frequently, the positions do not exist, but the advertising does produce a steady flow of applicants. The glamour appeal of the travel industry is like a magnet, and by the time the applicant has reached the agency, completed the application, and signed a contract, the job has been mysteriously filled. The applicant may then be informed of openings in insurance offices, banks, or other businesses. He may end up in something far removed from travel, or from the advertised job he went to the agency for, and may have to pay a fee as well.

General employment-agency counselors know little, if anything, about the travel industry and cannot provide the proper counseling or advice that may be needed by someone contemplating a career in travel. If you do decide to work with an agency, only do so with one specializing in the field for which you seek employment. *Always* read the contract before you sign it; make certain that you understand what it is you are signing and what obligations you are under if you accept a job. Better still, do your own job hunting. Once you have gained experience in your field and decide to change jobs, you can use the services of one of the specialized travel employment services. You will find them to be most helpful, professional, confidential, and interested in your career.

THE JOB INTERVIEW

The interview itself is really nothing more than two people getting together to look one another over, and to gain information. Nevertheless, it can be a nerve-wracking experience for those who are not used to interviews, or for those competing for a limited number of positions.

The impression you make during the job interview will determine whether or not you get the job you want. Try to bear in mind that the interview will be governed by how well you prepare for it and how you conduct yourself. In most instances, you will have about twenty or thirty minutes to convince the employer that you are the applicant for the job. There are no second chances, so it makes good sense to take the time to prepare properly for an encounter which will influence your entire career.

Your dress and grooming The first thing the interviewer will observe will be your clothing and grooming. Many applicants are ideal in every respect, yet they lose job opportunities because they are sloppy in their grooming. Many positions in travel require heavy public contact, so you must try to fit the image the employer wants to project to his clients or passengers. Dress should be conservative, but as smart and stylish as you can afford. Remember that you will not be judged on how much you pay for your clothes, but on how well you wear and care for them.

Run your eyes over the clothes you intend to wear a week or two in advance of the interview date. Look for missing buttons, loose hems, etc., and arrange for the necessary cleaning or repairs. If you expect to be going on a series of interviews, you should have at least two complete sets of interview clothes so that you can keep them fresh and in good condition.

Your hair should be neat, natural-looking, and conservatively styled. Give special attention to your make-up. It should be applied to create the fresh, natural, appearance the airlines are looking for—especially in flight attendants. Have your nails manicured and wear unobtrusive nail polish. Any evidence of bitten nails will mean instant disqualification for consideration as a flight attendant or other public-contact position. If you use perfume or after-shave, it should be subtle.

Before you leave for your interview take a last look at yourself in a full-length mirror. Better still, have a friend or a parent look you over; their advice and help could be invaluable.

Be on time The business world is extremely time conscious, and busy interviewers and managers operate on a strict appointment basis. If you arrive late, the interviewer has a choice of either cutting your interview short or delaying all of his other appointments for the rest of the business day.

Being late creates a poor impression. It indicates to the employer that you may also have a habit of arriving late for work. Of course, if there is a valid reason, then you should explain the reason for the delay. Most employers will understand if it is something beyond your control. But don't lie. Interviewers have been known to take the time and trouble to check out reasons given by an applicant who is of serious interest to them.

Be prepared with information Unless you have mailed your application or résumé to the company in advance, you will be asked to complete the form when you arrive for the interview. Make certain that you have all of the information you need to complete the form properly. Be sure to carry one or two ballpoint pens that work.

Try to relax This is easier said than done. It is quite understandable that you will be nervous, even apprehensive, when you go on a job interview. A good interviewer will recognize a tense applicant and will always try to make allowances. Nevertheless, try to maintain a relaxed but alert attitude at all times. Sometimes the wait can be worse than the interview itself. You can spend the time reading a book or magazine. Some employers will purposely keep applicants waiting to see if they are easily upset. Don't ever resort to tranquilizers or heavy medication of any type when you go on a job interview.

Starting the interview The interviewer may first attempt to put you at ease by talking about almost anything other than the reason you are there. Talking about the weather or your hobbies is designed to make you feel comfortable in strange surroundings and a tense environment. Although such conversation will not go on for very long, it is an excellent way of breaking the ice.

During the interview Be alert for signals of who should take the initiative. It is customary to let the interviewer set the tone and guide the interview. Some interviewers tend to talk a lot and will judge you by your reaction. Others will allow you to talk first in an attempt to discover how outgoing you are. Be prepared to follow the lead of the interviewer.

A good interviewer will be skilled at asking questions which call for more than a yes or no answer. They are designed to draw you out. Answer all questions as directly and to the point as you can while giving complete answers. If you are too long-winded, the interviewer will become bored. Avoid all sarcastic, cute, or flippant answers.

Be prepared to answer questions about your previous employment. You will probably be asked what you did, how well you carried out your responsibilities, and how well you got along with your colleagues and supervisor. One of the most important questions you will be asked will be your reason for leaving your last job or wanting to leave your present one. Have good explanations ready. It could be that your job was too far from your home, the public transportation was inadequate, there was a lack of potential or adequate salary. These are all valid reasons for leaving. If you were ever fired from a job, you should explain the reason for termination.

Many travel employers ask applicants such questions as to why they want to work in the travel industry. Many applicants say something to the effect that they enjoy traveling or they want the benefits of cheap or free travel. These are the wrong reasons for wanting to enter travel. Your response should be in terms of the work: "I want a lifetime career in a growing industry." "I enjoy working with people," etc.

Ask questions Satisfactory employment is two-sided, and if a job-match is to be successful, it must be compatible for both parties.

Do some research on the company so that you know something about it. If it is an airline or other major corporation, try to obtain a copy of the most recent annual report. Many airlines publish brochures listing possible employment opportunities. Study such pamphlets in advance of the interview.

Don't ask too many questions about all of the benefits and travel privileges that go with the job. If company benefits are not outlined in a brochure, ask the employer to spell them out for you, but don't dwell on them too much; otherwise the employer might think that you are far more concerned about the benefits than you are in job performance.

Indicate that you can get along with people Because of the nature of most positions, the ability to get along with people is essential. A flight attendant who cannot get along with her colleagues won't last very long. Many travel agencies are so small that everyone must get along if the business is to grow. When employers check references, one of the first questions they ask of a previous employer is, "How did he get along with other people?" You must be able to convince the interviewer that you can relate with others, both those with whom you work and the passengers or clients.

Display your abilities Try to indicate that you have self-confidence. Let the employer know that with suitable training, you can handle the job, whatever it is.

If you are applying for a flight attendant's position and your previous experience includes work in a nursing home, or other people-oriented job, explain how much you enjoyed working with and helping others. Show enthusiasm not only for the job you are applying for, but those you held previously. Always stress your experience and qualifications, your education, and your interests.

Other things Get to know the interviewer's name and use it during the interview. Always be yourself. The interviewer has been at his job long enough that he will be able to detect any lack of sincerity. When you leave, thank the interviewer and ask him how long it will be before you expect to hear fom him.

After careful analysis of your goals, thorough research of job opportunities, and meticulous preparation for the interview itself, you will become a strong competitor in the travel industry job market. Locating just the right job is not easy and the task will be time-consuming, but the opportunities are there for those who are persistent.

Chapter 2

AVIATION

THE FEDERAL AVIATION ADMINISTRATION (FAA)

The FAA traces its ancestry back to the Air Commerce Act of 1926, which led to the establishment of the Aeronautics Branch of the Department of Commerce. This branch of government had the authority to certificate pilots and aircraft, promote safety, and develop air navigation facilities.

The Civil Aeronautics Act of 1938 created the Civil Aeronautics Authority, an agency empowered to supervise safety and economic growth in the industry.

By 1940, another reorganization was needed, and the responsibilities of the CAA were assigned to the new Civil Aeronautics Administration, headed by an Assistant Secretary in the Department of Commerce.

In 1958, jet-powered transports were introduced into civil aviation, and Congress passed the Federal Aviation Act, thereby creating the independent Federal Aviation Agency which was vested with the authority to regulate civil aviation. In April, 1967, the Federal Aviation Agency became the Federal Aviation Administration, a segment of the newly formed Department of Transportation.

The FAA's major responsibility today is the safety and regulation of civil aviation, which includes operating and maintaining the world's largest and most advanced air traffic control and air navigation system; planning the expansion and modernization of airports; protecting the environment by controlling engine noise and emission; maintaining security; testing and certificating new aircraft; investigating accidents; and certificating and licensing instructors, pilots, mechanics, and technicians.

Because of its size and scope, the FAA employs thousands of people in a wide range of technological fields. For more information on career potential and job openings with the agency, contact the Personnel Division, Department of Transportation, Federal Aviation Administration, Washington, DC 20591.

THE CIVIL AERONAUTICS BOARD (CAB)

The United States Civil Aeronautics Board is an independent regulatory agency which was originally established under the Civil

Aeronautics Act of 1938, and continued by the Federal Aviation Act of 1958. The function of the CAB is to regulate and promote air commerce within the United States and between the United States and foreign countries.

Until 1978 no airline could engage in servicing a new route until it had been granted permission to do so by the CAB. If an airline wanted to start a new route it had to prove that it had the equipment and personnel to operate the service; that the proposed route was needed, would generate revenue, and would be economically feasible; and that if any other carrier was servicing the route, additional competitive service would not be a destructive factor to both carriers.

Under the Airline Deregulation Act of 1978, many of the rules have been relaxed or amended. Deregulation of the airline industry is intended to give the airlines more freedom in establishing or discontinuing routes and setting fares.

The CAB may grant subsidies to air carriers to finance the costs of providing air service to communities where the volume of traffic is insufficient to meet the costs of such service. The public interest is served by providing air transportation to small communities which would otherwise be without such service. The annual subsidy to eligible air carriers amounts to more than $70 million.

The Board is empowered to issue regulations which have the force of law. The CAB Bureau of Enforcement investigates reported violations, obtains voluntary corrective action when possible, and institutes proceedings of cease-and-desist orders and civil or criminal penalties when necessary. Investigatory areas include such matters as fare discounting, and charter violations by both foreign and domestic air carriers, tour operators and travel agents; passenger and freight tariff violations; unfair and deceptive practices; unauthorized air transportation; and illegal political contributions by air carriers.

For more information on career potential and job openings with the Board, contact the Officer of Personnel, Civil Aeronautics Board, Washington, DC 20428.

AIRLINES

During the last two decades, the airline industry has experienced tremendous growth. The development and evolution of civil aviation has created thousands of well-paying career opportunities in an industry in which more than 500,000 men and women are employed. The future employment picture is a healthy one, and indications are that the number of employees working in the field is expected to increase well into the mid-1980's.

Quite apart from the enormous inventory of equipment, people are, and always have been, the most important asset of the airline industry.

Without skilled, highly trained people, aircraft could not be loaded or flown.

The range of airline positions is broad and requires the specialized skills and training of many people in dozens of different departments. Each activity plays an essential role within its own sphere of responsibility, yet each department depends upon all of the others. The marketing department is responsible for generating passengers and freight—it must develop aggressive promotional campaigns to induce potential passengers to choose the service of its airline over a competitor's. Highly trained reservationists help people plan their trips with the best and most convenient flights. These people, in turn, must be backed up by others who issue tickets, handle baggage, and perform boarding procedures. Ground operations staff handle the loading and unloading of the aircraft, as well as fueling arrangements.

The modern aircraft is a highly complex and sophisticated piece of machinery, so it takes a whole army of unseen, skilled technicians and mechanics to maintain it in a safe and airworthy condition. Weather experts, communications personnel, and flight dispatchers are responsible for planning the flight and providing the necessary information about weather conditions along the route.

Finally, there are the captains and flight crews who operate the aircraft itself, and the flight attendants who tend to the needs and comfort of the passengers.

Not every airline job is listed in this chapter; the job descriptions are only a sampling of typical jobs available. Keep in mind that job titles vary from one airline to another. A Reservation Agent for one airline may have the same job functions as a Passenger Agent for another.

There is a wide range of career opportunities within civil aviation, and because of the size and scope of the airline industry, thousands of positions become available each year. No matter what your background, you are almost certain to find a position to fit your personality, training and goals.

OPPORTUNITIES WITH FOREIGN AIRLINES

In considering an airline career, do not limit yourself to American carriers, since more than 80 foreign airlines maintain office and service facilities in the United States.

If an airline is not "on line" (does not operate service to the United States), the office may be staffed by only a manager or representative, and perhaps a secretary. The function of this office is to "show the flag" of the country and generate business for the airline from other carriers who operate flights to the country.

On the other hand, some of the foreign airlines have a substantial network of sales and reservation offices. Thousands of American citizens and permanent aliens are employed by the national airlines of other countries.

Compared to domestic airlines however, the choice of positions is somewhat limited. It is impossible to become a pilot or a flight attendant for a foreign airline since their crews are nationals of the country to which the airline belongs. Home base is London, Tokyo, Sydney, or some other foreign city; an American city is the turnaround point for the aircraft and crew.

However, other opportunities exist for those who are seriously interested in employment with a foreign carrier. Positions include mechanics and maintenance staff, ramp agents and ground service crew, reservation agents, sales representatives, and many office positions. For some positions preference may be given to those who are fluent in the language of the country to which the airline belongs.

The Appendix contains a list of the main U.S. office of most foreign airlines. To determine if there is an office near you, check the pages of your local telephone directory.

AIRLINE EMPLOYEE BENEFITS

The salary and wages paid to airline employees are only a portion of the total compensation package. The following employee benefits are somewhat typical of the industry.

Vacations Two weeks vacation is usually granted after one year of service. The amount of vacation time is increased with length of service up to a specific maximum.

Insurance This usually includes company-paid accident and sickness insurance, dental insurance, and life insurance.

Retirement plan Most airlines now have pension plans to cover regular full-time employees who qualify by reasons of age or tenure. Some airlines require no contribution from employees in their pension programs, while others require some degree of employee participation.

Stock purchase plan Many airlines now have payroll-deduction plans whereby their employees can acquire stock in the company without incurring a financial burden.

Credit Union This allows employees the opportunity to establish a savings program, or to borrow money at moderate interest rates.

Travel privileges Pass and travel privileges vary depending upon the policy of the airline. In most cases, a new employee becomes eligible for reduced-rate travel after 30 days of employment and free travel after 6 months with the company. Sometimes there may be a small service charge. Travel privileges are also extended to the employee's immediate family. Travel is on a "space available" basis, which means that no reservations can be made and in the event the flight is fully booked, fare-paying passengers always take precedence. Airline employees can also travel "space positive" thereby increasing their chances of getting space on the desired flight.

In addition to travel over its own routes, each airline has interline agreements with other carriers, both domestic and foreign, thereby enabling employees of all airlines to travel to most parts of the world at greatly reduced prices.

Airline employees can enjoy reduced and special airline rates at hotels and resorts, discount rental cars, and many other benefits. There are also frequent low-cost interline tours and packages to many parts of the world, designed specifically for airline staff who prefer to travel on a structured basis or with a group.

PILOTS AND FLIGHT ENGINEERS

The commercial airline pilot profession is a highly skilled and technical one demanding nothing less than the highest degree of proficiency. The pilot of a modern jet transport is fully responsible for the aircraft itself (which is worth up to $50 million) and the safety of the passengers, crew, and cargo. The potential pilot must exhibit unusually high personal standards, show strong leadership qualities and sound judgment, possess the ability to think clearly in times of stress, and be able to make split-second decisions.

Many hours must be spent in classroom and private study as well as in gaining the necessary hours of actual flight time required to attain the FAA certificates and ratings. The would-be airline pilot must successfully pass a whole series of examinations and proficiency tests before he can even apply for a job.

After a pilot has been hired by an airline, he must participate in a comprehensive training program so that he is able to meet the airline's standards and earn a rating for the type of aircraft he will be flying.

EMPLOYMENT OUTLOOK

According to the statistics prepared by the U.S. Department of Labor, pilot employment is expected to increase at a faster than average rate through the mid-1980's. In addition to the jobs created by industry growth and expansion, many of the pilots who joined the airlines following World War II will be reaching the mandatory retirement age of sixty during the 1978-81 time period. As copilots and flight engineers are upgraded, there will be openings for new pilots. Competition for available jobs will be intense, however, because the number of qualified pilots seeking jobs is expected to exceed the number of openings.

More than half of the anticipated openings will occur outside the airlines. Companies are expected to increase the number of planes they operate and the number of pilots they employ to transport executives and cargo to communities without scheduled air service. Additional jobs will result from the need for more flight instructors to train new pilots and to insure that qualified pilots meet FAA proficiency standards.

The expected growth of airline passengers and cargo traffic will create a need for more aircraft and more pilots to fly them. However, for the next few years airlines will be able to transport more people by buying larger planes rather than more planes. Since the number of aircraft is not expected to increase immediately, opportunities with the airlines should be limited with many available positions being filled by experienced pilots on furlough.

Recent college graduates who have experience in flying large, multi-engine aircraft and who possess a commercial pilot's license and a flight engineer's license can expect first consideration for jobs with the airlines. Some airlines may accept and train those who have only a commercial license. Other companies usually have fewer formal education and experience requirements than the airlines. However, these companies prefer applicants with flying experience in the type of aircraft they will be flying on the job.

There are a number of factors that will have a bearing on airline hiring policies in the years ahead. These include: (1) long term impact of fuel prices. (2) Economic impact of fuel prices. (3) Increased use of smaller (or larger) aircraft. (4) The freedom of the airlines to set their own routes and fares (deregulation). (5) International travel trends. (6) The business and economic climate of the country.

All factors considered, the future hiring trend is one of cautious optimism on the part of many airlines.

EARNINGS AND ADVANCEMENT

Salaries for airline captains range from about $38,000 to $85,000; for copilots, $10,000 to $58,000; and for flight engineers, $10,000 to $48,000. Salary is determined by seniority and type of aircraft flown.

New airline pilots start as flight engineers with airlines who use aircraft requiring a three-man crew, or as a first officer if an airline has smaller equipment requiring only two men in the cockpit. Flight engineers must be qualified pilots.

Depending on the airline, it may be 5 to 10 years before a flight engineer advances, on the basis of seniority, to copilot, and another 10 to 20 years before promotion to captain.

While the starting salary of an airline pilot is low, good annual salary increases are the norm of the industry. As the pilot gains in seniority, his salary increases automatically.

EDUCATION AND FLIGHT TRAINING

Because of the time required to earn the FAA certificates and ratings, it is necessary to prepare for a pilot's career as early as possible; ideally, you should begin your studies while in high school.

The pilot must have a thorough grasp of aerodynamics, aeronautical navigation, aeronautical engineering, and meteorology. High school studies should encompass the basic sciences with a strong emphasis on mathematics and physics. Such subjects as chemistry, radio, mechanics, engineering and electricity should be considered mandatory; geography, social studies, history, economics and political science are also helpful.

While most airlines specify that the minimum educational requirement is a high school diploma, preference is usually given to those with a college background. Some airlines will require a four-year degree. The more training, flight time, certificates and ratings you can acquire the better chance you will have for employment when the right time comes.

There are several methods of acquiring flight training. These include: (1) An FAA certificated ground and flight school. (2) A professional aviation degree from a university. (3) The military.

Flight schools If you want to get into aviation for pleasure only almost any flight school will be able to help you earn your private pilot's license. However, if you are seriously interested in an aviation career, you should look for a school which is FAA approved, and can provide the necessary training to take you through instrument, commercial, multi-engine, and other advanced ratings. Not every flight school is FAA approved. The FAA has established minimum standards, and if these standards are not maintained, the FAA can revoke or suspend the certificate until the deficiencies are corrected.

Flight schools are private enterprises, and depending upon the school, it will cost approximately $1,000 to acquire a private pilot's license. By the time you are through with your instrument rating and commercial license, it will have cost you about another $4,000. Learning to fly is an expensive proposition, so you should exercise considerable care when choosing a school. Look at several before you make the final decision. Check that the school is FAA approved, that the percentage of students passing FAA examinations is in the 80-90 percent range, that the school has adequate training facilities and equipment, and that its insurance policy covers collision and personal liability for students using the school's aircraft.

For a free list of FAA approved schools, request a copy of *List of Certificated Pilot Flight and Ground Schools*. This is available from:

Department of Transportation, Federal Aviation Administration, Office of General Aviation, Washington, DC 20591.

Universities There are now many colleges and universities offering degree programs in aviation. Some are two-year courses and others are for four years, leading to a baccalaureate and higher degrees. These programs are comprehensive, and some are tailored for those desiring a career as an airline pilot. In some cases flight training is offered by the college itself, or contracted out to fixed-base operators, or provided by a campus flying club.

For further information you should request a copy of *Directory of Aviation and Transportation Majors and Curricula Offered by Colleges and Universities,* available free from: Department of Transportation, Federal Aviation Administration, Office of General Aviation, Washington, DC 20591.

The Military This is an excellent way to get the necessary training and flight time and be paid for doing it. You will not only receive thorough training in all aspects of aviation, but at the same time you will have the opportunity to receive training on large multi-engine jet aircraft. For years the military has been a prime source of pilots for the airlines, and because of the quality and duration of the training, many airlines will give preference to candidates who are military veterans.

The Air Force draws its pilot trainees from Air Force Academy graduates or from ROTC programs. Both the Navy and Marine Corps require a degree to enter Officer Candidate School, plus completion of an aptitude test to be considered for pilot training. The Army has a program that does not require a college degree, and trainees are considered from those who have a high school diploma, pass an aptitude test, and complete a review by a board of officers. Other possibilities are the Coast Guard and the Civil Air Patrol.

Since programs and requirements change from time to time, you should always take time to thoroughly investigate before you sign up. Satisfy yourself that you will get the training you need to prepare yourself for an aviation career.

WHO'S WHO ON THE FLIGHT DECK

The Captain The captain has spent many years with his airline, and put in a great deal of time acquiring the skills and experience necessary to properly handle his aircraft in any weather or emergency situation likely to be encountered in commercial flying. Like the captain of a ship, an airline captain is responsible for the safety of his aircraft, his passengers, the crew, and the cargo.

In a marginal weather situation the captain is the only one who can decide if conditions are safe enough to attempt a landing, or whether it would be more advisable to seek an alternative airport. Although he is constantly in touch with ground control, he must still make the final decision.

The captain sits in the left seat in the cockpit and is identified by four stripes on his uniform jacket.

The First Officer Also referred to as the copilot, he too is an experienced airman and must be as skilled as the captain in flying the aircraft. He assists and relieves the captain in the operation of the aircraft and handles his share of take offs and landings. He sits in the right-hand seat, and is provided with a set of controls and instruments identical to those of the captain.

In those airlines which operate smaller aircraft requiring two-man crews, a pilot begins his career, after training, as a first officer. As he gains seniority and service time, he can eventually be upgraded to captain. He wears three stripes on his uniform jacket.

The Flight Engineer Also known as the second officer, this position is usually the first rung of the ladder leading to copilot and captain. In many of the larger airlines, this is where the new pilot starts his professional flying career. He must work his way, through experience and seniority, to the higher grades.

His main responsibility is the engine and other mechanical equipment on board the aircraft. During the flight he monitors engine operation, fuel flow and consumption, temperature, and electronic and hydraulic systems. He must be completely familiar with all working systems, have the ability to diagnose trouble with the operation of the engines and other systems, and be able to make in-flight adjustments as necessary.

The flight engineer must also be able to fly the aircraft should the captain and copilot be unable to do so for any reason. He must possess an FAA flight engineer's license, a commercial license, and a rating for the type of aircraft he is assigned to.

His position in the cockpit is behind the first officer and in front of a console or panel containing a myriad of instruments. He is recognized by having two stripes on his uniform jacket.

AIRLINE ELIGIBILITY REQUIREMENTS

While the basic requirements for new pilots are the same for all airlines, each carrier may have its own specific standards which may exceed those required by FAA certificates or ratings.

This section includes requirements general to the airline industry. Information about a specific airline's requirements may be obtained by contacting that particular airline.

Age Generally speaking, airlines prefer applicants from twenty-one to thirty years of age. Some airlines have set a minimum of twenty-three years since this is the minimum age required to qualify for the FAA airline transport pilot rating.

Sex Until quite recently there were very few women in the cockpits of commercial aircraft. There are several reasons for this situation, the main one being that since the airlines hire a large percentage of military veterans, there are few women who are able to meet the flight time and ratings requirements.

1976 was a landmark year for women in commercial aviation. Frontier Airlines upgraded a female copilot to captain status.

As women acquire the necessary flight time and training, more of them will be hired as pilots; but expect the competition to be keen.

Height Height and reach should be sufficient for full operation of all controls. 5 ft. 6 in. to 6 ft. 4 in. seems to be the range that most airlines prefer.

Weight Must be in proportion to height.

Vision Usually 20/20 in each eye separately is the norm. Minor astigmatic errors will sometimes be considered. Generally, for young pilots to be considered for employment, it should not be necessary at the time of hiring for them to wear glasses.

Health There is probably no other career where the physical demands are as stringent as they are in flying, especially in the case of an air transport pilot or a business pilot with an ATR rating. The Air Line Pilots Association strongly recommends that before beginning pilot training, all aspirants should obtain a first class FAA medical certificate. The acquisition and maintenance of this certificate is the key to a professional flying career.

Certificates Airlines require all applicants to have an FAA first class medical certificate without waivers, restrictions, or limitations of any kind. Other licenses required are a valid FAA commercial pilot's license, multi-engine and instrument ratings, and an FCC Restricted Radiotelephone Permit.

Experience This depends upon the airline. One major airline requires a minimum of 1000 hours of combined first pilot and copilot experience in jet or multi-engine equipment. Other airlines look for 1500 hours, and others will not consider applicants with less than 2500 hours. However, requirements may change at any time depending upon the availability of qualified candidates.

TRAINING

The initial training period after hiring varies with the airline, but averages about three months. Training involves ground school, simulators and actual inflight experience. Upon successful completion of the course, the new pilot is assigned to line duty either as a flight engineer or first officer.

Training never ceases, and all flight crews are continually kept abreast of new developments and equipment changes. All pilots must successfully pass proficiency checks at regular intervals, and undergo transition training to new aircraft.

OTHER INFORMATION

Flying hours Most airline pilots fly no more than 80 hours each month. Even though this does not include time spent on layovers, most pilots have an abundance of free time at their disposal. Many pilots operate small or part-time businesses to help supplement their airline pay.

Union membership Most pilots are required to belong to the union representing pilots of the airline employing them. Most airline pilots belong to the Air Line Pilots Association (ALPA). Founded in 1931, the ALPA represents the professional interests of the flight deck crew members of 32 airlines. An affiliated organization represents the flight attendants of 20 airlines. The ALPA is affiliated with the AFL-CIO.

The ALPA is more than a labor union. It is also a professional association which makes substantial contributions to the public interest through its air safety and flight-security programs, to which it devotes a considerable portion of its attention. It constantly monitors the safety scene, points out shortcomings, and makes recommendations to ensure that adequate standards and margins of safety are maintained.

Retirement Under FAA regulations the retirement age for an airline pilot is sixty. He is, of course, subject to early retirement if he is unable to successfully pass a medical examination at any time prior to the mandatory retirement age.

THE FAA CERTIFICATES AND RATINGS

FAA regulations change from time to time, so before you commence your training you should check the up-to-date specifications which can be obtained from the FAA.

There are four main pilot categories: (1) Student Pilot. (2) Private Pilot. (3) Commercial Pilot. (4) Airline Transport Pilot. In addition to the pilot categories there are also ratings applicable to private and commercial pilots:

(1) *Category ratings* Airplane, rotorcraft, glider.

(2) *Class ratings* Single-engine land; multi-engine land; single-engine sea; multi-engine sea.

   (3) *Type ratings* Requires a proficiency test in the type of aircraft for which the rating is sought. That is: Boeing 727, Douglas DC-10, Convair 340, etc.

(4) *Instrument ratings*

Several combinations of pilot certificates and ratings are available to the individual pilot. For example, an ATR pilot would be a commercial pilot with a rating on airplane or rotorcraft (helicopter). It may multi-engine or single-engine; an ATR would normally hold a certificate on a specific type of aircraft, such as Douglas DC-8, Boeing 727, etc.

Student pilot In order to obtain a student pilot's license, it is necessary to be sixteen years of age and able to read, write, and understand English. This latter requirement is essential because all air traffic control instructions are transmitted in English, and other vital information is written or spoken in English.

It is also necessary to obtain an FAA third class medical certificate by passing a physical examination conducted by an FAA Authorized Medical Examiner (AME). The AME is authorized to issue a combined medical/student certificate upon successful passage of the medical examination. Directories listing the approximately 7,000 AME's are available at all FAA offices and at many airports. Student pilot certificates are also available at all FAA General Aviation District Offices.

Solo flight requirements In order to operate an aircraft in solo flight, the student pilot must first be instructed by a qualified flight instructor on flight preparation procedures. These include preflight inspection and powerplant operation; ground maneuvering and runups; straight and level flight; climbing, turns, and descents; flying at minimum controllable air speeds; stall recognition and recovery; normal take offs and landings; airport traffic patterns; collision avoidance precautions and wake turbulence; emergencies, including elementary emergency landings, and visual flight rules.

Flights are restricted to local airports, and student pilots are also prohibited at high density airports, and from carrying passengers.

Endorsement by a rated instructor is required for the student to be considered competent to make a solo flight. Qualification for cross-country flying requires additional instruction in crosswind landings, climbing and gliding turns, cross-county navigation, air traffic control, radio and lights, and simulated emergencies. In order to retain solo privileges, a student pilot certificate must be endorsed by a flight instructor every 90 days.

Private pilot Applicants must be seventeen years old. All other requirements are the same as listed for student pilot. A private pilot may not carry passengers or freight for hire.

Aeronautical knowlege Must pass an oral and written test covering FAA regulations, air traffic rules, cross-country planning, radio communications and weather evaluation.

Aeronautical experience Must have a valid student pilot's license and a total of at least 40 hours certified flight time, including 20 hours solo and 10 hours cross-country solo.

Aeronautical skill Must demonstrate knowledge of preflight procedures; planning cross-country; straight and level flight; climbing and gliding turns; stall recovery; cross wind take offs and landings; night flying; and simulated aircraft and component malfunctions.

Commercial pilot Must be eighteen years old and have an FAA second class medical certificate.

Aeronautical knowlege Oral and written examinations include questions on FAA regulations; meteorology; navigation; loading and balance computations; and aircraft operations, including high altitude flight; and use of flaps and retractable landing gear.

Aeronautical experience Must have logged at least 250 hours of flight time, including 100 as pilot-in-command, 50 hours cross-country, 10 hours instrument, and 5 hours of night flying.

Aeronautical skill More complex demonstration of maneuvers similar to those required of a private pilot.

Airline transport pilot The minimum age requirement is twenty-three years. The FAA also requires that applicants have a high school diploma (or its equivalent), and an FAA first class medical certificate.

Aeronautical knowledge Must have a commercial pilot certificate with an instrument rating.

Aeronautical experience At least 1500 hours of flight time as a pilot, 500 hours cross-country, 100 hours of night flying, and 75 hours of actual or simulated instrument flying of which 50 hours are in actual flight. Also, the applicant must have 250 hours of flight time as pilot-in-command, or as a copilot performing the functions and duties of a command pilot under the supervision of a pilot-in-command, at least 100 hours of which are cross-country and 25 hours are night flying.

Aeronautical skill Must demonstrate satisfactory ability to pilot an aircraft under a complex list of maneuvers applicable to airline-type flying.

Instrument rating This rating is available to private, commercial, and ATR pilots.

Aeronautical knowledge FAA regulations as applicable to instrument flight rules (IFR), radio, navigation, and meteorolgy.

Aeronautical experience Commercial pilot, or private pilot who meets the requirements of commercial pilot; 40 hours of instrument time, not less than 20 in flight, 10 of instruction, and the rest may be simulated.

Aeronautical skill Must be able to execute flight maneuvers by reference to instruments—plan and conduct simulated instrument flight, flight planning procedures, radio navigation, instrument approaches, and recovery from emergency situations.

FLIGHT ATTENDANTS

More than any other employee, the flight attendant is the representative of the airline who is responsible for maintaining the corporate image and building good will. Passengers spend more time with flight attendants than with anyone else connected with the airline, and the service they receive while on board an aircraft will largely determine whether or not they remain customers of the line. Because of the importance of the job, it isn't really surprising that the eligibility requirements and standards are so high that only a limited number of people can meet them. One airline even states that only one person out of twenty-five can qualify for the job.

The job requires people who can work under stress, who are calm and even-tempered, and who enjoy serving others. Living out of a suitcase and serving hundreds of meals each day tend to remove much of the glamour, so before you make a final decision, consider all of the demands of the job itself.

Apart from being good-will ambassadors, flight attendants are expected to provide courteous and efficient inflight service. They welcome passengers as they board the aircraft; help them find their seats and hang up their coats; ensure that carry-on luggage is stored correctly (either in special compartments or under the seat); see that all passengers are wearing their seat belts when necessary; make pre- and post-flight announcements; point out the location of all emergency exits and demonstrate how to use oxygen masks should it be necessary to do so; serve beverages and meals; answer questions concerning schedules, connections, and other similar services; and pass out pillows, blankets and reading material. They must also be prepared to provide emergency first-aid treatment when necessary and must be thoroughly knowedgeable about emergency exit procedures and safety equipment of the aircraft in which they are flying.

Flight attendants must work hard, frequently under pressure and stress conditions. Dealing with a planeload of thirsty and hungry passengers is not easy even in the best of flying conditions. Add to this a weather or mechanical delay, or turbulence, and you have a situation requiring endless patience and tact on the part of the flight attendant.

EMPLOYMENT OUTLOOK

According to the U.S. Department of Labor, employment of flight attendants is expected to increase through the mid-1980's. Openings will occur not only because of industry growth, but because of the need to replace experienced attendants who retire. Job opportunities may vary because air travel is sensitive to the ups and downs of the economy, and applicants can expect keen competition for any available jobs since the number of applicants is expected to exceed the number of openings. Applicants with two years of college and work experience, or other experience in dealing with the public, have the best chance of being hired.

EARNINGS

Each airline has its own salary structure. According to the Air Transport Association, in 1979, the salary range for flight attendants was from $9,000 to $18,000 per annum. Starting salary varies from airline to airline.

At most airlines the trainee flight attendant receives no salary during the training period and is placed on the payroll upon successful completion of the training course. She must then undergo a six month probationary period before being considered a permanent employee. Permanent employee status is no guarantee that a flight attendant will not be furloughed (laid off) should it be necessary for the company to reduce staff for economic or seasonal purposes. Furloughs are made on a seniority basis, with the juniors (in order of employment, not of age) being released first. When this happens, many flight attendants take part-time or temporary jobs in retail stores or offices until called back by the airline.

For those who remain on the job, there are excellent possibilities for advancement to a supervisory position.

EDUCATION

A high school diploma, or its equivalent (General Educational Development Rating), is the minimum educational requirement by all airlines. Two years of college training is a decided asset, and will improve your chances of employment.

If you are still in high school the following subjects will be helpful in preparing you for a career as a flight attendant: psychology, English grammar and vocabulary, sociology, languages, home economics/nutrition, geography, art, music, public speaking, speech, hygiene, first-aid, physiology, current events, and physical education. Many airlines, especially those with routes over a large expanse of water, require that their flight attendants have good swimming skills.

The ability to communicate with people is a prerequisite for the job, so give special attention to learning how to speak clearly and grammatically. All too many otherwise desirable applicants are rejected because of poor communications skills or inferior grammar.

Although it is not always a condition of employment, most airlines flying within the United States and Canada (domestic carriers) recognize that an applicant's knowledge of a foreign language is an asset. Such an applicant will usually have an edge over those with no language skills, providing that all other eligibility requirements are equal. Some airlines demand fluency in at least one foreign language.

French and Spanish should be your first and second choices, German a close third. It is far better to learn to speak one language fluently than to dabble in two or three without becoming proficient in any.

If you live in Canada, you know that both English and French are official languages, and fluency in both is usally a requirement for most Canadian carriers. Air Canada also states that fluency in German, Czech, Danish, Flemish or other languages improves a candidate's competitive position.

If your goal is employment with an airline flying international routes, you will almost certainly be required to demonstrate conversational ability in at least one other language such as French, Spanish, or German. Additionally, fluency in the language of the country served in a route is frequently necessary, i.e., Japanese, German, Danish, Russian, Greek, Arabic, Hebrew, Portuguese, etc.

Your college courses should encompass the humanities. Be sure to continue studying your language(s) at the college level.

There are a number of two-year programs which provide flight attendant preparatory courses. These programs provide an orientation to the airline industry while giving the student a liberal education. Successful completion of such a course will in no way, however, guarantee employment as a flight attendant.

The Federal Aviation Administration publishes a directory of colleges and universities offering aviation and transportation majors which includes those junior colleges offering courses for flight attendant preparation. *Directory of Aviation and Transportation Majors and Curricula Offered by Colleges and Universities* is available free from: Department of Transportation, Federal Aviation Administration, Office of General Aviation, Washington, DC 20591.

It is not necessary to attend a vocational or private commercial school to prepare for a career as a flight attendant. Several airlines stress in their literature that they do not recommend independent airline training schools and do not give preferential consideration to applicants from these schools. Employment by all airlines is always based upon the availability of positions, a personal interview, and an exhaustive investigation into an applicant's background. All necessary training is provided by the airline after hiring.

WORK EXPERIENCE

If you do not attend college, two years of experience in a public-contact job will qualify you as a desirable applicant. Jobs in retail sales, travel agencies, reservation services, restaurants, and hospitals provide good background for airline work. Be certain to study a foreign language at the advanced level by attending adult extension courses at a local junior college or high school.

If you have been employed in another field for several years and wish to switch careers, you must meet all the eligibility requirements of the airline. Although you will have the same opportunity as younger candidates, your starting salary may be considerably less than your present compensation. If your previous field involved public contact, your experience will be helpful in this new career.

ELIGIBILITY REQUIREMENTS

Each airline has established its own eligibility requirements; the following standards are generally applied throughout the industry.

Appearance, grooming and health Applicants for the position of flight attendant must always appear neat, attractive, natural, and conservative. Hair should be conservatively styled, and if tinted, the treatment should be unobtrusive. If dental work is required, have it performed well in advance of sending in your application. Good posture and graceful movement should be developed. Speech should be clear and well modulated.

Male applicants should have a clean-cut appearance, with well-trimmed hair and sideburns no lower than mid-ear. Although mustaches are permitted by most airlines, a goatee or beard will disqualify you.

All applicants must have a consistent record of good health and be able to pass a rigid company medical examination. Many hours are spent walking or in a standing position, so there can be no history of back or foot problems. If you seek employment with an airline flying on international routes, you must be able to accept inoculations and immunizations without allergic reaction.

You must have the stamina to work long hours while maintaining a fresh and cheerful appearance. No airline wants a tired and irritable flight attendant looking after the welfare of its valuable passenger.

Age Twenty years of age at the time of employment is the minimum age most airlines specify for flight attendants. At some airlines, the minimum age is nineteen, at others it is twenty-one. Airlines do not list maximum age limits; all will consider any qualified applicant.

Height Most airlines specify a height of 5 ft. 2 in. as the minimum for female applicants; male applicants should be slightly taller. Maximum height is usually 6 ft. Height is measured in stocking feet with the hair pressed down on the head. If you are a fraction under the minimum or over the maximum you will not qualify. Waivers are not granted on any of the basic eligibility requirements.

Weight Some airlines are specific in their weight requirements. American Airlines states that for female applicants whose height is from 5 ft. 5 in. to 5 ft. 6 in. the maximum weight must be no more than 128 lbs. At United, the maximum weight at 5 ft. 6 in, is 131 lbs. Virtually all airlines insist that weight be in proportion to height. For example if you are tall and thin, you could be disqualified if you appear lanky, even though your weight is well within the acceptable range. The same would apply if you were short and stocky.

Vision Each airline has its own vision requirements; 20/50 uncorrected (without glasses) vision in each eye separately is generally the minimum acceptable. If vision does not meet this standard, correction must be used to attain it. Many airlines allow conservatively styled glasses, but some state that glasses are not permitted. Most airlines will allow their flight attendants to wear contact lenses to attain company vision standards, providing the applicant has been wearing them successfully for at least six months, and can do so without signs of eye irritation for a minimum of ten hours a day. If you are uncertain of your vision, it is a good idea to have it checked by a qualified professional well in advance of sending in your employment application.

Marital status Until quite recently it was the policy of airlines to hire only single females; those who married during employment were immediately "grounded." This rule prompted many to keep the knowledge of their new status from their employers; consequently, hundreds of clandestinely married stewardesses continued to fly.

Today, airlines will retain a flight attendant who marries during employment, and many airlines consider married applicants.

More and more young men are now being hired as flight attendants, or stewards, as some airlines prefer to call them.

Citizenship Due to immigration laws, applicants must be citizens of the United States (Canada for Canadian resident), or if an alien, must have a permanent immigration visa. Aliens must already live in the country before they can apply or be considered for employment.

For domestic airlines serving foreign countries, preference may be given to U.S. or Canadian citizens because of the complexity of visas and international travel requirements for aliens.

TRAINING

After an applicant is selected for flight attendant training, she must successfully complete a comprehensive and intense training course before becoming an employee of the airline. Since extreme care is taken in selecting applicants, the failure rate is low.

Each airline operates and maintains its own flight attendant training facility. Some facilicities are like college campuses. Others are less pretentious, and the trainees reside at local motels or hotels. The length of the training course varies from four to six weeks.

All airlines conduct extensive safety training during which the trainee learns the emergency procedures for every type of aircraft flown.This includes how to activate and operate evacuation chutes, life jackets, emergency exits, oxygen masks and other equipment. Students are also given instruction in first-aid procedures and maintenance of composure and self-control in an operational emergency, or in a confrontation with a disagreeable passenger.

A major responsibility of the flight attendant is to serve beverages and meals. A great portion of the training course covers inflight meal service and the correct method of mixing cocktails and serving meals. Much of this instruction takes place in mock-up aircraft interiors as well as on observation and training flights.

Because all airlines place such a heavy emphasis on grooming and appearance, there are instruction sessions and workshops in grooming and make-up application, fashion, and figure control.

Since flight attendants must also be "people conscious," training is given in passenger awareness—how to be alert to the needs and desires of the passenger.

During the training period, the student is closely watched and evaluated on how well he or she assimilates training and takes direction; and on emotional stability, self-confidence, organizational ability, and enthusiasm for the job.

When graduation day arrives, a new person emerges with the skills and poise to be a true profesional. This is the day trainees long await; on this day each person becomes a fully-fledged flight attendant. There is usually a ceremony which includes a graduation dinner, during which the new flight attendants receive their wings and a diploma. Within a day or two each one will be at his or her base, ready to assume a place in aviation.

OTHER USEFUL INFORMATION

Domicile (base) As a prerequisite to hiring, all applicants must indicate a willingness to relocate to any base city on the system of the airline. Large airlines with extensive route structures may have as many as nine or ten base cities, while smaller carriers require only one or two.

New flight attendants do not usually have too much choice of first base assignments since the airline will assign them where vacancies exist. After a specific period of time, a flight attendant can apply, or "bid," to transfer to another base. Most airlines will help their employees locate suitable living quarters, but the actual transfer and relocation expenses must be paid by the employee requesting the transfer.

Should the company request a flight attendant to transfer to another domicile, the company assumes all costs incurred.

Layovers The frequency and duration of layovers will depend upon the routes of the airline and the length of the flight. With the advent of jet-powered transports, less time is spent on layovers than during the era of propeller-driven aircraft.

On many domestic flights, and even on some short international routes, the turnaround and return to base may be accomplished in one day. On long domestic flights and on most international flights, layovers are at least 12 hours and frequently longer. On some international routes, flight crews are away from their home base for a week or longer, and lay over at several cities along the route. All layover expenses are always paid by the airline.

Uniforms Each airline has its own distinctive uniform. Frequently, uniforms are designed by leading fashion houses, and include a variety of styles. All airlines change their designs periodically to stay abreast of the current fashion, or to enhance a fresh, new, corporate image.

The new flight attendant pays the cost of the first uniform and accessories, and the company pays for all replacements. All airlines have a payroll deduction plan so the cost of the initial uniform can be covered in a series of easy payments, over a period of months. There are a few airlines that provide uniforms at no cost to the employee.

When an airline redesigns its uniforms, it pays the entire cost of any change or replacements necessary.

Some airlines also pay for the actual cost of uniform maintenance; others grant a monthly allowance for the same purpose. Other airlines assume that the cleaning and maintenance of uniforms and accessories is the personal responsibility of the employee.

Union Membership in one of the unions representing flight attendants is usually mandatory and is a condition of employment.

HOW TO APPLY

Write to those airlines which interest you and request information on their eligibility requirements and an application form. When you receive the information, the first thing to do is to determine if you meet the basic requirements. If you do, you can then complete and return the form as quickly as possible. If you find that you do not meet one or more of the requirements, you have the choice of checking with other airlines, or of forgetting the whole idea of becoming a flight attendant. Waivers are not granted to those who do not meet the requirements, no matter how small the deviation.

When the airline receives your completed application, someone in the personnel department will review it. If the company is hiring, and if you meet the requirements, arrangements may be made for a personal interview. Because of the large number of applicants, it is impossible for an airline to interview every eligible applicant who returns an application.

If the airline is not hiring new flight attendants at the time you apply, you will receive an acknowledgement with the suggestion that you apply at a later date.

The Appendix contains a list of the home office of each airline. Since foreign airlines do not hire Americans for flight attendant positions, don't waste your time contacting them; concentrate only on the domestic carriers. Many airlines also have hiring offices in other parts of the country, so check your local telephone directory to see if there is a personnel office near you.

MECHANICS, TECHNICIANS, AND MAINTENANCE STAFF

In order to keep aircraft in peak operating condition, skilled mechanics specialize in preventative maintenance. Using a schedule which is based on the number of calendar days, and/or flight hours, aircraft are inspected and the necessary maintenance is performed.

Mechanics may take engines apart, measure the parts for wear, check for invisible cracks with X-ray and magnetic inspection equipment, and replace parts as needed. They also may repair sheet metal surfaces, measure the strength of control cables, check the instruments and radio equipment, or check for rust and cracks on the fuselages or wings. After completing inspections or making repairs, mechanics test the equipment to make sure that the repairs were made properly.

Some mechanics specialize in repairing broken equipment. After obtaining a description of the problem from the pilot, mechanics locate and correct the faulty equipment. For example, as the captain and first officer are performing their preflight check, they may discover a mechanical malfunction which must be corrected before the aircraft can leave. After being informed of the problem, mechanics make the necessary tests to locate the source of the trouble and correct it as quickly as they can. They work as fast as safety permits so that the aircraft can continue on its way.

About 120,000 airplane mechanics were employed in 1979. This figure does not include about 30,000 employed to assemble airplanes in aircraft manufacturing firms. Over one-half of the mechanics worked for the airlines, and about one-third worked for the Federal Government. The rest were general aviation mechanics, most of whom worked for small repair shops and companies that operate their own planes transporting executives.

PROFILE OF A MAINTENANCE BASE

There are many different departments, or "shops," in the maintenance base of an airline. The following is a description of a typical maintenance base of a large airline:

Overhaul docks A large jet can be completely overhauled in less than a week. The airplane is stripped of all removable units which are then refurbished, reassembled, checked, tested, and inspected. The cabin areas are completely redecorated and the exterior of the airplane is painted.

Turbine engine maintenance shop The jet engines are broken down and all parts are cleaned and inspected. If suitable for re-use, parts are reconditioned to like-new specifications. Extreme care is taken to perfectly fit and balance all rotating parts. After being reassembled, the engines are tested in test cells to assure their complete functional reliability before being replaced on an airplane.

Sheet metal shop The sheet metal shop is responsible for a wide variety of airplane parts, from simple clips and brackets to complete control surfaces, such as ailerons and rudders. The shop also overhauls jet-engine pod parts and makes patterns and casts dies for stamped contoured parts.

Cabin equipment shop This shop performs its work in five different sections. The main shop produces seat upholstery and covers, seat belts, window curtains, carpeting, and many other items found in the passenger cabin. The seat shop strips, inspects, repairs, refinishes, and reinstalls all seats while the aircraft is being overhauled. The plastics shop manufactures and repairs items made of reinforced plastics and other plastic materials. The paint shop handles all necessary painting, both within and outside the aircraft. And the survival gear shop is responsible for survival gear tests and maintains all inflatable life vests and rafts carried on overwater flights.

Accessories shop Repairs and overhauls all hydraulic and fuel-handling components, the hydraulic units used to power landing gear retraction, and the cabin air compressors which pressurize the aircraft for high-altitude flying.

Machine shop This shop serves the entire maintenance base with precision lathe work, grinding, milling, drilling, heat treating, grit blasting, etc.

Electric shop Repairs, overhauls, and tests all electrical units such as generators, motors, valves, actuators, relays, thermoswitches, fire detectors, and all other electric components on board the aircraft—even the coffee-making equipment.

Instrument shop All of the indicators, gauges, meters, and other instruments used by pilots and flight engineers are cared for in the instrument shop. These include gyro horizon, altimeters, air speed and rate-of-climb indicators, tachometers, fuel-flow meters, temperature indicators, compasses, pressure gauges, and many other types of instruments. This shop also maintains oxygen systems and data recording equipment.

Radio shop The radio shop services the electronic equipment such as communications transmitters and receivers, weather-mapping radar, navigational radio (VOR), and radar (Doppler), distance measuring equipment (DME), inertial guidance equipment, the auto-pilot system, and music reproducers.

EARNINGS AND EMPLOYMENT OUTLOOK

In 1979, airline mechanics earned from $18,000 to $25,000 a year, depending on experience and responsibility.

According to the Aviation Maintenance Foundation, job opportunities for airplane mechanics are expected to be good. Apart from airline growth, the number of aircraft used by companies for executive transportation is expected to grow, thereby increasing the demand for mechanics.

Competition for airline jobs is expected to be keen because the high wages and excellent benefits attract many qualified applicants. However, airline deregulation, airline growth, and the retirement of many mechanics from the World War II era is expected to create a demand. About 12,000 mechanics retire or leave from all types of aviation each year.

EDUCATION AND TRAINING

The FAA requires that anyone who is directly involved in the maintenance and repair of aircraft have a valid certificate from the FAA. The FAA also licenses mechanic schools and the instructors who teach in these institutions.

Training for this career usually starts in high school. Courses in mathematics, physics, and chemistry, and experience in automotive repair or other mechanical work are helpful. Aviation mechanic courses are offered in many high schools, in adult education training centers, in private trade and technical schools, and in various junior colleges and universities.

Many aviation mechanics acquire their skills and experience in the military. Those who have done so usually have earned credits toward an apprenticeship. Military veterans who have experience as an aviation mechanic in the Armed Forces, and who were working on airframes, powerplants, or both, should present their credentials to an FAA maintenance inspector for evaluation. He will then advise the most direct course of action to obtain the necessary ratings.

Courses in private trade schools last about two years and provide training with the tools and equipment used on the job. Such training may be substituted for work experience when applying for the FAA license. However, these schools do not guarantee that students will pass the FAA examinations, or that they will be able to get a job.

Some mechanics gain experience through apprenticeship programs or on-the-job training. Some of the large airlines train apprentices in carefully planned two- or four-year programs which include both classroom and work experience.

The FAA lists the following basic qualifications for those who are interested in working as aviation mechanics: (1) Mechanical ability and aptitude. (2) A desire to work with tools. (3) An interest in aviation. (4) The temperament to do thorough and accurate work. (5) A responsible nature.

(6) A desire to continue learning and remain current with the changing aviation technology. Constant changes are normal in aircraft maintenance work, and the A & P mechanic must keep abreast of technological changes and must continually update his past training with experience on new equipment, new aircraft, and new engines.

THE FAA RATINGS

Aviation mechanics are maintenance airmen who are certificated by the FAA. There are two ratings available to certificated mechanics: A—Airframe, or P—Powerplant; or a combined Airframe and Powerplant—A & P—rating. Specific knowledge, experience, and skills are required for each.

To be eligible for a mechanic certificate and rating, the applicant must be at least eighteen years old, and be able to read, speak, write, and understand the English language. He must also be a graduate of an FAA certificated mechanic school or course, or submit satisfactory evidence of at least 18 months practical experience for either an airframe or powerplant rating, or 30 months experience for both the airframe and powerplant ratings.

To obtain an inspector's license, a mechanic must have held an A & P license for at least three years. Applicants for all licenses must pass written and oral tests and give practical demonstrations of their ability to perform the work authorized by the license.

FOR MORE INFORMATION

The FAA has several publications available to help those who are interested in a career as an aviation mechanic. A directory of FAA approved colleges and vocational schools offering training programs is also available. Request *Directory of FAA Certificated Aviation Maintenance Technician Schools* from Department of Transportation, Federal Aviation Administration, Office of General Aviation, Washington, DC 20591.

For information on apprenticeship programs and job opportunities, contact the personnel department of those airlines that interest you. See the Appendix for addresses of main offices.

OTHER USEFUL INFORMATION

Applicants must be in good health, and must successfully pass a company physical examination. Many airlines require experience closely related to the job to which the applicant will be assigned. In many cases, it is necessary for a mechanic to own a complete set of hand tools. A valid driver's license is also usually required. Since maintenance procedures sometimes continue around the clock, it is necessary to be able to accept shift work.

A wide range of advancement possibilities exist for those employees who demonstrate the necessary capabilities.

TYPICAL JOB DESCRIPTIONS

Aircraft Cleaner Duties include cleaning, washing, and polishing the interior and exterior of airplanes, ramp and automotive equipment, hangars and shops, and cleaning and stripping paint from aircraft and engine parts. Cleaners also place and arrange in the aircraft all passenger-service equipment, including first-aid and oxygen equipment.
Electrical Accessories Mechanic This job involves the maintenance of electrical systems on the aircraft, which includes electrical accessories and wiring. It is necessary to be familiar with generators, relays and starters, etc.
Instrument Technician Installs, tests, repairs, and overhauls all aircraft instruments, including altimeters, airspeed and rate of climb indicators, navigation instruments, engine instruments, compasses, pressure gauges, and many others. Must have an FAA instrument technician license.
Line Maintenance Mechanic Performs duties required in the maintenance and repair of the aircraft. Diagnoses trouble on the aircraft and carries out major and minor aircraft checks and repairs. Airframe mechanics (A license) work with the skin, frame, wings, fuselage, wheels and brakes. Powerplant mechanics (P license) maintain aircraft engines, including dismantling, inspecting, assembling and testing. Most airlines prefer their mechanics to hold both A & P ratings.
Machinist The trade of machinist as related to aircraft maintenance covers a wide variety of machine tools, working to fine tolerances. Previous experience should include the set-up of all machine tools, the ability to work from blueprints and drawings, and the use of such specialized instruments as calipers and micrometers.
Maintenance Inspector Checks the work done by mechanics and other specialists, and must give his final approval before an aircraft is released for operational activities.
Mechanical System Mechanic Performs shop maintenance functions on units and parts related to aircraft fuel, hydraulic and pneumatic systems.
Painter Functions include the paint work relating to the aircraft engines, also units and group equipment. Applicants for this job should have the ability to do layout work and lettering and sign painting, using both brush and spray gun and baking techniques.
Plumber Is responsible for the maintenance of all aircraft plumbing fixtures, including fabrication, repair, testing, fitting, and installing.

Radio Technician Installs, maintains, repairs, and tests all aircraft radio equipment. An FCC license is required.

Sheet Metal Mechanic Maintains the aircraft structural components and parts. Applicants in this trade must be able to fabricate these components using blueprints and drawings, operate hand and power tools for filing, drilling, shaping and riveting both aluminum and stainless steel.

Upholstery Mechanic Maintains the aircraft furnishings, including seats, carpets, drapes and paneling. Must be able to fabricate replacement coverings and parts as required, and repair damaged and worn areas. It is necessary to be experienced in working with foam rubber, springs, paneling, carpeting, and sewing.

Welder Is responsible for the welding of aircraft components, engine parts and related repair work. Applicants must be familiar with welding methods applicable to aircraft structure materials.

Wheel and Rubber Mechanic Maintains the aircraft wheels, brakes, and tires. Other units such as oxygen masks, life preservers, rubber rafts, and evacuation chutes are also the responsibility of this mechanic.

GROUND SERVICE EQUIPMENT FACILITIES

In addition to all of the foregoing skilled trades which are related directly to the aircraft itself, there are also many other mechanics and other specialists responsible for the repair and maintenance of ground equipment and supporting facilities.

Mechanics repair and perform overhaul work on all ground equipment, including trucks, tractors, carts, building, heating and ventilations system, electrical services, etc. Experience in the particular field is usually necessary, though some airlines will provide the required training. A valid driver's license is also necessary.

FOOD SERVICE

Airline inflight food service has come a long way since the days of early commercial aviation. The stewardess carried lunch boxes, filled with such gourmet delights as fried chicken and cold sandwiches and served them picnic style; passengers used their laps for tables.

All airlines recognize that the variety and quality of meals served in the air are important factors in attracting passengers. Many airlines stress in their advertising and promotional campaigns the features of the meals served on-board their aircraft. Many foreign airlines serve indigenous dishes, and passengers experience a bit of another country as soon as they step on-board the aircraft.

Passengers expect to be fed, and even if a flight is operating outside of normal mealtimes, the passengers are generally offered beverages and a light snack.

United Airlines inflight food service operation is a good example of how the service works. United's food service division's 3,000 employees prepare or handle 29,000,000 meals a year from 18 flight kitchens across the United States. Each year, United uses approximately 5,328,000 one-half pints of milk, about 820,000 pounds of lettuce, and 1,287,000 pounds of tomatoes.

United also prepares a wide variety of specially requested meals, including kosher, vegetarian, bland, diabetic, high protein, low cholesterol, low sodium, Hindu, Moslem, Oriental, soul, infants' and children's meals.

Not every airline has its own food service, and many carriers arrange for private caterers to prepare their inflight meals. United's food services division contracts with other airlines and caters meals for 28 U.S. and foreign airlines.

Food service occupations are frequently overlooked by those who are interested in an airline career, yet a variety of both entry-level and skilled positions do occur from time to time.

ELIGIBILITY REQUIREMENTS

Most airlines prefer applicants who have had educational training in food service, or practical experience in the hotel or restaurant fields. Candidates for entry-level positions should have at least an eighth grade education. Applicants should be in good health and be able to successfully pass a company physical examination. On-the-job training is conducted for all entry level positions. There are ample opportunities for those employees who are interested in advancement, and who demonstrate the potential to assume positions of greater responsibility.

FOOD SERVICE POSITIONS

Many of the positions in airline flight kitchens and food services are identical to those described in the food service chapter of this book.

HOW TO APPLY

Contact the local employment office of those airlines in your area and see if they handle food preparation locally.

SALES, OFFICE AND GROUND STAFF

This section encompasses a whole army of employees who require varied degrees of training and background. If you do not qualify or are not interested in any of the positions described so far, you may find what you are looking for here. Even if you don't see something you believe you would be qualified for, you should take the time to check with the airlines themselves, since not every job is described here.

Apart from those employees engaged strictly in airline functions, there are also many positions of a general or clerical nature. These include typists, file clerks, computer-operator personnel and many others.

In addition to entry-level positions, highly skilled candidates are occasionally required to fill management positions such as architect, draftsman, lawyer, financial analyst, engineer, translator, statistician, and many others.

EMPLOYMENT OUTLOOK

Because of the anticipated growth of the airline industry it is expected that opportunities for reservation agents, ticket agents, freight agents, and many other office positions will be excellent through the mid-1980's. However, opportunities for employment may fluctuate from year to year since the airline industry is affected by the economy of the country. All applicants can expect to find considerable competition for many openings because a large number of people are attracted to airline jobs.

EARNINGS

Beginning salaries vary widely from airline to airline, but all airlines pay well, and all employees enjoy merit and cost-of-living increases. For more information on airline salaries see the chart at the end of the airline section.

EDUCATION

All airline jobs require a high standard of personal qualifications and development. A sound education is essential, and the minimum requirement for employment consideration for most jobs is a high school diploma or its equivalent (General Education Development Rating). For those who want to advance into any type of management position, two years of college, a degree, or a license may be required. A degree in business with a travel and tourism major will be most helpful for those who want to enter in a management training program or marketing job.

Your ability to qualify and get the job you want may be governed by your educational background. Generally speaking, your high school studies should include business courses, supplemented by geography, political science, and speech.

Many airlines require candidates to have at least some business or work experience, especially if they do not have a college background. For some specialized positions, it is necessary to have experience in that particular field.

TRAINING

Airlines do not recommend any independent airline-type training schools nor is preferential consideration or treatment given to their graduates. Training is always given to newly hired employees, and many positions combine on-the-job training with classroom instruction. All employees involved with reservations and similar airline functions are required to attend refresher courses from time to time in order to remain current with new equipment, fares, routes, and procedures.

OTHER USEFUL INFORMATION

The average minimum age for consideration for employment is nineteen. Some airlines will accept applicants who are eighteen, while others will not hire anyone under twenty. Many positions require that employees be able to accept shift work. Good health is essential, and all airlines require new employees to successfully pass a physical examination. Depending upon the position, it also may be necessary for applicants to meet height, weight, and vision requirements. Applicants must be citizens, or registered aliens. Many airline employees are represented by a union, and applying for union membership may be a condition of hiring.

SOME TYPICAL POSITIONS

Accountant Uses airline accounting procedures to keep records, equipment and maintenance. Applicants should have a degree in accounting, or at least one to two years experience in the field.
Auditor Field auditors have the responsibility of safeguarding the assets of the company, and of providing management with meaningful reports. Requirements for this position usually call for an accounting degree and public accounting or auditing experience.
Clerk (general) General clerks perform many clerical duties which include typing, maintaining office records and files, recording statistics, and operating a wide variety of business machines. While some airlines will accept those without previous work experience, the majority of airlines look for at least some experience, or graduation from a business school.
Communications Agent Operates several different types of message-sending equipment. These include computerized telecommunications machines, teletype, cathode-ray tube equipment with typewriter keyboard, radio telephone, and copy machines. Some of their duties include sending and receiving messages, maintaining contact with pilots, and updating the closed circuit television information system on flight operations. Applicants must have a minimum typing speed of 45

words per minute and a restricted FCC Radiotelephone Operators Permit.

Computer Operator Data processing equipment is used to convert information from passenger tickets, air-cargo bills, payroll statistics, and various other functions. Applicants should be graduates of a data processing school, or have a minimum of six months to one year experience on equipment similar to that of the airlines.

Computer Programmer All airlines operate sophisticated computerized systems used in a variety of functions. Included are reservations, accounting, payroll, maintenance parts inventory, purchasing and supply, the scheduling of manpower and aircraft equipment. A degree is preferred, plus one or two years of programming experience.

Customer Service Representative (inflight) Typical duties include booking onward flight reservations, securing hotel and car rental reservations, and ticketing passengers in flight. Qualifications call for those of a Passenger Service Representative. This is not an entry level position, and requirements include previous experience in reservations or a ticket office.

District Sales Manager Adminsters the District Sales Office and supervises other sales staff such as Sales Representatives. The responsibilities include generating and promoting passenger and cargo sales in the district in accordance with company policies and procedures. In most cases it is the District Sales Manager who is the representative of the airline in the community. A degree in marketing or travel and tourism is usually required. This position is attained through experience as a Sales Representative; promotion depends upon motivation and ability.

Flight Dispatcher He is responsible for authorizing all flight departures for his airline and monitoring them to their destination. Duties include maintaining records of cargo, number of flight hours flown by each aircraft, the flying hours of flight crews; and meeting with flight crews prior to departure to help decide on the best route and altitude for the flight and alternative routes in the event of adverse weather conditions. While no license is required for assistant dispatcher positions, that of the Flight Dispatcher requires an FAA Flight Dispatcher Certificate. This is obtained after passing a written examination on meteorology, air traffic control, FAA regulations, air navigation and radio procedures, aircraft payloads, takeoff weights, cruising and landing speeds, etc. Two years of college is a minimum requirement; a degree in meteorology, mathematics, or physics is preferred. There are a number of FAA licensed college courses and private schools offering training in this field. It is expected that entry into this area of aviation will be somewhat limited in the future.

Freight Sales and Operation Agent Must be completely familiar with freight tariffs and rules governing the acceptance of various types of freight. They quote rates and advise on necessary documentation required for international shipments. They are also responsible for processing and routing of shipments, and arrange for pick up and delivery. A typing speed of 40 words per minute is required, and two years of college or equivalent business experience is helpful.

Ground Serviceman Duties include driving all types of trucks, tractors, and other automotive equipment; servicing aircraft with fuel, oil, and water; and other miscellaneous functions related to the aircraft and ground equipment. Must have a driver's license and be willing to work outside in all weather conditions. While previous experience is not essential, a mechanical background is helpful. All training is provided by the airline after hiring.

Passenger Service Agent Duties include assisting customers at airport locations; answering general inquiries about fares, accommodations, and schedules; selling and writing tickets; confirming reservations and making changes in reservations through the computerized reservation system. Agents also keep records of tickets sold, weigh, tag, and route baggage; and provide boarding services at the gate. For qualifications for this position refer to Reservation Sales Agent.

Passenger Service Representative (ground) This is a challenging position requiring a great deal of tact and patience. Responsibilities are varied, with heavy public contact, and include assisting passengers by providing information; arranging for ground transportation; directing passengers through customs and immigration services on international flights; providing special attention to the elderly, handicapped, disabled, or those having language difficulty; assisting parents traveling with young children. The basic requirements are similar to those of a Reservation Sales Agent plus previous public contact work. Anyone being considered for this job would have to have a pleasant and outgoing personality, a liking and concern for people and their needs, and an impeccable appearance. Promotion to this position is usually made from within the company from among those employees with reservation experience, and preference is generally given to those candidates possessing two or more languages.

Personnel Representative Interviews applicants for airline positions and employs qualified applicants as needed. Also undertakes career counseling and assists in on-the-job training programs and with matters dealing with labor and industrial relations. A degree in personnel administration plus work experience in the personnel field are the best credentials for consideration for this position.

Public Relations Representative Is employed in the advertising and public relations department of an airline. Works closely with the advertising agency, advertising programs, and with all types of communications media such as newspapers, magazines, radio, and television. Education and experience in journalism, advertising, and the public relations field are necessary.

Ramp Agent The work consists of loading and unloading cargo, mail, baggage and food supplies from the aircraft. Through the use of hand signals, assists pilots to safely and properly park aircraft at designated gate positions. He must also operate many different types of automotive and sophisticated baggage-handling equipment. Applicants must have a valid driver's license and a good driving record, must obtain an FCC Restricted Radiotelephone Operators Permit, and be willing to work on a shift basis out-of-doors in all weather conditions.

Reservation Sales Agent The men and women who are employed in reservations are usually the first contact a prospective passenger has with the airline, so virtually all airlines exercise extreme care when hiring applicants for this position. Reservation Sales Agents must be knowledgeable and skillful in making reservations through the airlines' computerized reservation system. They also quote fares, help passengers choose the most appropriate or convenient flight, give flight arrival and departure information, and reserve hotels and car rentals. All this must be handled over the telephone, through which the agent is required to project the image and personality of the airline. This position is also a prime training ground for promotion to ticket offices, ticket counters at the airport, customer service jobs and sales representatives. The training period is from three to four weeks duration, depending upon the airline. It is also necessary to accept shift work. Other qualifications include a typing speed of 40 words per minute, good speech qualities and the use of correct English, a pleasant telephone voice, a good personality, confidence, health and maturity. A college background will also be a decided asset as would two year of equivalent business experience.

Reservation Service Agent The service agent performs many of the behind-the-scenes functions so necessary for the smooth operation of any airline. Responsibilities include completing and maintaining passenger records, contacting passengers to confirm reservations or provide schedule change information, computing rates and constructing fares for complex itineraries, and providing special assistance to other units and departments. For qualifications of this position refer to Reservation Sales Agent.

Sales Representative Responsible for promoting and selling passenger and cargo services through retail travel agents and corporate clients. Duties include calling on travel agents and companies using airline services. It is a heavy public contact job requiring good communication skills, sales ability, an outgoing personality, and the ability to induce clients to use the services of the airline represented. This is an extremely responsible position in that the representative is instrumental in generating sales for the airline. The openings are very competitive, and airlines look for a degree in sales and marketing or travel and tourism, an in-depth knowledge of the travel industry and the route and fare structure of the airline. This position is good training for management for those who demonstrate leadership and management potential.

Stenographer Candidates for stenographic positions should be able to type accurately at 50-60 words per minute and take shorthand at 100 or more words per minute. Familiarization with dictating and transcribing equipment also may be necessary.

Ticket Sales Agent Involved in a great deal of public contact work, the Ticket Sales Agent must possess the same technical skills and competence as a Reservation Sales Agent. Experience in reservations is a prerequisite for promotion to this position. Duties, which are performed in city ticket offices or at the airport, include making reservations, issuing tickets, and giving out information on flights and tours. An agent is usually required to wear the company uniform and to work on a shift basis. The qualifications are similar to those of a Reservation Sales Agent, however, more emphasis is placed on physical appearance and grooming.

Teletype Operator Sends and receives messages over a teletype machine. Should be able to type at 60 words per minute. Previous business experience will be helpful.

Tour Sales Agent Almost every airline has a complete series of tours and packages available to key resort destinations along its routes. Depending upon the route structure of the airline, tours may range from a two- or three-day package to Las Vegas to a one-month Grand Tour of Europe. Tour Sales Agents may work over the telephone or occupy a desk in the ticket office. Because of the in-depth knowledge required, previous experience in reservations or in the ticket office is necessary. A Tour Sales Agent functions somewhat in the same manner as a travel agent by helping the passenger select the right tour or package and reserving hotels, car rentals, and sightseeing tours in the cities served by the airline. Promotion to this position takes time, and is usually achieved by spending time as a Reservation Sales Agent or as a Ticket Sales Agent.

HOW TO APPLY

Contact the local office of those airlines in which you are interested.

DOMESTIC AIRLINE SALARIES

The salaries listed here should be considered approximate. The actual salary for the job depends upon the airline, experience and seniority. These salaries do not include fringe benefits such as group insurance and pensions.

Flight Operations		
	Captain	$38,000 to $85,000
	First Officer	$10,000 to $58,000
	Flight Engineer	$10,000 to $48,000
	Flight Attendant	$ 9,000 to $18,000
	Flight Dispatcher	$25,000 to $32,000
	Meteorologist	$19,000 to $28,000

Maintenance	A and P Mechanic	$18,000 to $25,000
	Carpenter	
	Drill Press Operator	
	Electrician	
	Inspector	
	Instrument Technician	$16,000 to $25,000
	Machinest	
	Painter	
	Sheet Metal Worker	
	Upholsterer	
Office and Sales	Accountant	$14,000 to $22,000
	Air Freight Agent	$13,000 to $19,000
	Business Machine Operator	$ 8,000 to $12,000
	District Sales Manager	$25,000 to $50,000
	File Clerk	$ 6,500 to $11,000
	Passenger Service Agent	$12,000 to $18,000
	Personnel Representative	$15,000 to $24,000
	Programmer	$15,000 to $24,000
	Public Relations Representative	$18,000 to $28,000
	Reservation Agent	$11,000 to $18,000
	Research Analyst	$15,000 to $24,000
	Sales Representative	$16,000 to $25,000
	Secretary	$ 9,000 to $15,000
	Teletypist	$ 9,000 to $14,000
	Typist	$ 7,000 to $12,000

AIR TRAFFIC CONTROLLER

The air traffic control system in the United States is the most modern and efficient in the world. It consists of an extensive network of facilities located in all 50 states, and in such far-flung places as Guam and American Samoa to the west, Panama to the south and Puerto Rico in the Caribbean.

The system includes 25 air-traffic-control centers, over 400 airport-control towers, more than 300 flight-service stations, over 1,000 radio-navigation aids, nearly 500 instrument-landing systems, and some 250 long-range terminal radar systems. An air traffic controller could be assigned to almost any one of these facilities.

All air traffic control functions are the direct responsibility of the FAA, and more than half of the FAA's total complement of more than 50,000 people are engaged in traffic control. Additionally, 10,000 technicians and engineers are involved in the installation and maintenance of the system.

AIR ROUTE TRAFFIC CONTROL CENTERS

The 25 centers are responsible for handling enroute aircraft operating under instrument flight rules (IFR) between two airports. The typical center supervises more than 100,000 square miles of airspace. They maintain a check of all aircraft movements in the area; assign proper separation of aircraft; issue clearances to higher or lower altitudes; provide pilots with current weather conditions; and in the event of an emergency, activate search and rescue procedures.

The controller staff, depending upon the size of the center, can range from 300 to 700, with more than 150 on duty at any one time during peak periods. The Washington Center, located approximately 40 miles west of the capital, is responsible for more than 140,000 square miles of airspace, and 20,000 miles of airways over all or parts of six eastern states. On any given day, it will handle more than 3,500 flights.

At the Washington Center there are 34 radar sectors. Each sector represents a specific block of airspace over a particular geographical area. At least two, and as many as four, controllers work at each sector position. The pilot is in communication with the radar controller, who maintains the scope to keep traffic safely separated. Next to him sits the handoff controller who handles the transfer of flights between sectors or between traffic control centers. When traffic is light, these two may be sufficient for safe and efficient operation. During peak traffic periods, one or two assistants may be needed to handle clerical and other duties.

AIRPORT CONTROL TOWERS

The controllers in the control towers direct the movement of aircraft on the ground and in the vicinity of the airport. In addition to directing takeoffs and landings, approximately 150 of the 400 FAA-run control towers also provide radar approach and departure control services to IFR aircraft using not only the primary airport, but many secondary airports in the terminal and approach control area.

The size of the tower facilities can range from the familiar cupola to the free-standing structure several hundred feet high. Staffing can be as small as three or four controllers to a workforce of more than 150, working shifts around the clock.

FLIGHT SERVICE STATIONS

There are more than 300 of these facilities at airports around the country, and they are used primarily by private and general aviation pilots. Skilled staff provide information on weather conditions, navigation, winds aloft, preferred routes, and other essential data. They also are available sources of information and assistance to pilots who are lost or in distress, and will activate search and rescue procedures to locate overdue or downed aircraft.

ELIGIBILITY REQUIREMENTS

Age The FAA advises that all qualified applicants who have not yet reached their thirty-first birthday by the time of initial appointment will be considered for appointment to towers and centers. Applicants of thirty-one years or older are only eligible for assignment to flight service stations.

Education A bachelor's degree is preferred as the minimum requirement. If you are still a student, you may be offered a job if you expect to complete your course work within nine months of filing your application. All work must be completed before you can start work.

General experience Graduation from a four-year college will satisfy the general experience requirements. In the event that you do not have a degree, a minimum of three years experience in technical or administrative work will be necessary. You should have progressed in your job and demonstrated a potential for learning the controller's work. A combination of college and work experience will also satisfy the eligibility requirements.

Specialized experience This must include experience in either military or civilian air traffic control, or something comparable, which shows that you possess the knowledge, skills, and abilities to perform the work.

Personal characteristics You should be of a calm disposition, yet have the ability to make fast, accurate decisions when it is necessary to do so. The job requires working under a great deal of stress and pressure, and you will be required to demonstrate that you have the ability to work under these conditions without showing outward signs of excitement or pressure. Your speech must be clear, precise, and well modulated.

Health All candidates must successfully pass a rigid medical examination administered by the FAA. Vision should be correctable to 20/20.

Written examination and interview All applicants must successfully pass a competitive written test administered by the Civil Service. An interview is also required, and candidates will be expected to show that they possess the motivation and personal characteristics required of a controller.

TRAINING

The training period lasts approximately ten weeks at the FAA Academy in Oklahoma City. The curriculum includes FAA regulations, controller equipment used on the job, the air traffic control system, aircraft performance characteristics, and radar. On-the-job training is also part of the program. According to the FAA, it takes anything from two to three years to become a fully qualified controller. Those who fail to maintain the standards during the training period are liable to be dropped from the program.

ADVANCEMENT

Depending upon proven ability and motivation, controllers can advance to the position of chief controller or regional controller. There are also opportunities for advancement into administrative jobs within the FAA. Every controller is evaluated twice each year on his job performance, and must also undergo a physical examination once a year.

EARNINGS AND EMPLOYMENT OUTLOOK

In 1979 the trainee controller earned $13,000 to $16,000 a year; the average earnings for controllers was $34,000. Controllers work a basic 40-hour week; however, they may work additional hours for which they receive overtime pay or equal time off. Because control towers and centers operate 24-hours-a-day, 7-days-a-week, controllers are assigned to night shifts on a rotating basis.

Controllers also are entitled to receive from 13 to 26 days paid vacation time, paid holidays, paid sick leave, and have the benefits of insurance and retirement programs.

It is expected that the need for controllers will increase in the years ahead. New airport towers are scheduled to be built, and it is anticipated that there will be moderate growth in both private and commercial air travel. It is expected that the competition for jobs will be keen because the number of qualified applicants is expected to exceed the number of available openings.

HOW TO APPLY

A pamphlet providing general information about controllers and instructions for submitting applications is available from any U.S. Civil Service Commission Job Information Center. Check your telephone book for your local office and telephone number. If no number is listed, ask the operator to give you the toll-free number of the U.S. Civil Service Commission Job Information Center for your location.

You can also contact the nearest FAA office to ascertain if they are accepting applications.

Chapter 3

BUS COMPANIES

Intercity bus lines are an integral part of the transportation system of the United States. Intercity bus services reach towns and communities that are too small to justify or support air service and are far away from railroad passenger services. In many cases, buses provide the only public transportation between communities. In addition to carrying passengers, many intercity buses also transport express (freight) and offer speedy delivery of small packages to rural areas and small communities.

Today's modern long-distance bus is luxurious compared with its predecessor. It offers reclining seats, rest rooms, air conditioning, large windows, and soundproofing; some models even have an upper deck so that riders enjoy an unobstructed view of the passing scenery. Traveling by bus today is a relaxing method of getting from one city to another.

There are many small companies operating intercity buses, but most long-distance bus transportation is handled by the two nation-wide bus companies, Continental Trailways and Greyhound Lines, Inc. These companies not only operate scheduled services, but also offer a selection of escorted and independent bus tour programs.

Gray Line Sightseeing Companies Associated, Inc., as the name implies, is an organization specializing in sightseeing tours. The association consists of more than 150 independently owned-and-operated companies which operate both long-distance and local sightseeing tours as well as bus charters.

Because of competition from airlines, railroads, and private automobiles, intercity bus travel is not expected to grow significantly. However, should government energy policy make gasoline for automobiles very expensive or difficult to obtain, many persons may choose to ride buses rather than drive their own cars.

HOW TO APPLY

Inquiries about employment may be made at the nearest terminal or at the personnel department of the company's home office. For more information about possible openings with sightseeing companies, you should check with one of the member companies.

SOME BUS COMPANY POSITIONS

Bus Operator (Driver) This position requires a high degree of driving skill, good character, and the ability to communicate well with people. Intercity bus drivers must meet qualifications established by the U. S. Department of Transportation. Drivers must be at least twenty-one years old and be able to read, write and speak English well enough to communicate with passengers and complete reports. They must also have good hearing and have at least 20/40 vision in each eye, with or without glasses. In addition, they must take comprehensive written examinations which test their knowledge of Department of Transportation and State motor vehicle regulations. They must also take a driving test in the type of bus they will operate. Many intercity bus companies have considerably higher requirements. Most prefer applicants who are at least twenty-five years of age, and many prefer applicants who have bus- or truck-driving experience.

Drivers represent their companies, and must be courteous and tactful. Even temperaments and emotional stability are important qualifications because driving buses in heavy, fast-moving traffic and dealing with passengers can be demanding.

Most intercity bus companies conduct training programs for new drivers. These programs, which usually last from two to six weeks, include both classroom and driving instruction. In the classroom, trainees learn about rules of the company and the U. S. Department of Transportation, State and municipal driving regulations, and safe-driving practices.

After completing classroom work, trainees ride with regular drivers to observe safe-driving practices and other aspects of the job. They also make trial runs, without passengers, to improve their driving skills. After completing the training, which includes final driving and written examinations, new drivers begin a "break in" period during which they work under close supervision.

When drivers report to the terminal they inspect their buses carefully to make sure the brakes, steering mechanism, windshield wipers, lights, and mirrors work properly. They also check the fuel, oil, water, and tires, and make certain that the buses are carrying safety equipment such as fire extinguishers, first-aid kits, and emergency reflectors.

Although drivers must always be alert in preventing accidents, they must be especially careful in fast-moving highway traffic. They must operate the bus at safe speeds and must cope with adverse road conditions. Before arriving at major terminals, they announce the stop and the scheduled departure time. At some small stations, drivers stop only if they see passengers waiting or if they have been told to pick up or deliver freight. Drivers also regulate lighting, heating, and air-conditioning equipment.

Upon arriving at their final destinations, drivers may unload or supervise the unloading of baggage and freight. They prepare reports for their employers on mileage, time, and fares, as required by the U. S. Department of Transportation. They also report on the malfunctioning of any equipment which must be repaired before the buses are used again.

The wages of intercity bus drivers typically are computed on a mileage basis, but short runs may be on an hourly rate. Most regular drivers are guaranteed a minimum number of miles or hours each pay period. Drivers employed by large intercity bus companies are well compensated, and annual earnings average more than $16,000.

Driving schedules may range from six to ten hours a day. However, Department of Transportation regulations require that drivers shall not drive more than ten hours without having at least eight hours off.

Dispatcher This position requires knowledge in the movement of buses from one point to another. Dispatchers maintain records of buses and operators under their control and dispatch the equipment to terminals or other pick-up points on time. Dispatchers are often former drivers, mechanics, or other employees who perform other duties in the maintenance area or in the terminal.

Hostess Continental Trailways employs hostesses who serve the passengers on the company's luxury buses much in the same manner as airline flight attendants. Applicants for this position must be eighteen years of age, personally presentable, and have the personality and desire to meet and assist people.

Information Clerk This position normally exists in large terminals, and can be either a telephone information clerk, or at an information desk in direct contact with the public. All information clerks must possess a good telephone manner, be accurate in reading schedules and quoting fares, and have the ability to perform public contact work. Information clerks can advance to ticket agents, tour representatives, or other administrative and clerical positions.

Mechanic Most bus companies have their own maintenance departments. Continental Trailways performs all its own maintenance, from re-building engines to upholstering seats. Applicants must have a high mechanical aptitude and basic mechanic skills, which can be acquired in high school. Experience in an automotive repair shop will also be helpful. Younger employees who do not meet the age requirements for bus operator often start their careers as mechanics.

Ticket Agent A ticket agent must be able to meet and work with the public. Ticket agents should be high school graduates. They must be responsible with money, be able to read time tables, and act as salespersons. At Continental Trailways, training to be a ticket agent usually consists of working as a telephone information clerk.

Tour Representative Many bus companies operate comprehensive tour programs. Tour representatives should be high school graduates, have the ability to work with people, have a knowledge of world geography, and be willing to travel, since they may be called upon to escort tours.

Other Positions Apart from the positions relating directly to bus transportation, there are many other jobs available similar to those in any large company. These include accountants, secretaries, typists, sales representatives, file clerks, personnel interviewers, advertising and public relations specialists, and many others.

Chapter 4

CAR RENTAL COMPANIES

The United States is the most mobile society in the world; one where the private automobile is considered not a luxury, but a necessity in almost every household.

The private automobile provides almost complete independence from public transportation, and because so many Americans enjoy this freedom, a growing number of travelers look for the same autonomy when they are away from home. The rental car offers travelers a pleasant alternative to the rigid day-by-day schedule of an organized, pre-planned tour; it permits them to proceed at their own pace and to explore areas not included in many standard tour itineraries. Some of the most popular packages on the market today are fly/drive tours, where the air transportation, car rental, and sometimes hotel accommodations are all included in the package price. Business travelers find that flying to their destination and then renting a car gives them the mobility they need to conduct business.

Many car rental companies offer other rental services in addition to passenger cars, including trucks and chauffeur-driven automobiles.

The car rental field is a large one and offers excellent career opportunities for those who possess the necessary training and qualifications. In some cities, the operation is leased to independent investors and businessmen; at others, the location is entirely company-owned. Opportunities exist in both leased and company locations.

SALARIES

Entry-level salaries depend upon the company and its location in the United States. Rental Agents, Reservationists and Service Agents earn between $500 and $750 a month. Sales Representatives can earn between $8,000 and $13,000 a year, depending upon their sales performance. Employees in other positions are paid according to their specializations. However, most employees of car-rental companies are well compensated.

CAR RENTAL COMPANY POSITIONS

Mechanic Performs repairs and service as necessary. Must have the ability to diagnose and repair almost any mechanical malfunction. May also spend time in regular maintenance and service functions such as oil

55

changes and lubrication, engine tune-up and brake work. Applicants are preferred who have one to two years of automotive mechanical experience.

Rental Sales Agent Works at the counter of airport and city offices. Rental Sales agents greet customers and help them select a car suitable for their needs and commensurate with their budgets. They assist customers in completing rental agreements, obtain credit-card information for billing purposes, and accept payment from customers who return cars. Since this is heavy public contact work, car-rental companies look for applicants who are well-groomed, mature, and have outgoing personalities. It is also necessary to have a good working knowledge of the local areas, traffic laws, hotel and restaurant accommodations, and similar customer-service knowledge. Applicants should be high-school graduates, and most companies prefer applicants who are at least twenty years old and have several years of business experience. Successful completion of a travel course using an airline-type reservation system is preferred by some employers. After hiring, the training period lasts approximately two weeks; training is given in the use of computerized reservations, good telephone techniques, and customer relations.

Reservation Agent The reservation systems of all of the major car rental companies are now computerized. Reservation Agents work over the telephone directly with travel agents, airlines, and the public. When customers call to make a reservation, Reservation Agents check the availability of cars in the city requested. They also obtain the customer's name, flight arrival information, the length of the rental, the location to where the car will be returned, and credit-card information. Most reservation systems are centralized. For example, Avis maintains its reservation office in Tulsa, Oklahoma, and Budget Rent-a-Car is located in Omaha, Nebraska. Applicants should be high-school graduates and have basic business skills such as a typing speed of at least 40 words per minute. Car-rental companies prefer applicants who have attended an airline-type school where instruction is given in computerized reservations.

Sales Representative The responsibilities of this position are similar to those of Sales Representatives employed by airlines, hotel organizations, and tour operators. Sales Representatives who are assigned to commercial duties call on business accounts and sell the company services to the business travel market. The travel industry Sales Representative deals with travel agents and airlines with the intention of increasing sales in the tourist and tour markets. Avis states that although a college degree is helpful, it is not mandatory for this position. The prime qualities are maturity, salesmanship, business acumen, and promotional ability.

Service Agent The major duties of this position are the preparation of the vehicles for rental. This includes checking the oil, gasoline, windshield wipers and brakes; cleaning the cars; and perhaps making minor repairs and adjustments. Service Agents also transport cars from the maintenance facility to the rental area. Applicants should be high-school graduates, have a driver's license and a good safety record.

Utility Worker Employees move cars from one rental point to another. Examples would include transferring a car left at the airport to the downtown center, and from one city to another. Although there is no age limit, those who are twenty-one years old are preferred. Applicants must also have a driver's license and a good safety record.

Other Positions Since most car rental companies are large corporations, there is usually a wide range of positions covering a variety of skills and training. These include personnel workers, public relations specialists, secretaries, data processing staff, marketing and finance specialists, accountants, and many more.

Chapter 5

RAILROADS

AMTRAK

Throughout most of the 1950's and virtually all of the 1960's, the quality and frequency of passenger rail travel in the United States gradually deteriorated to the point where, unless something was done, and quickly, there would be no passenger train service remaining in operation.

While the railroad systems of Europe, Japan, and many other countries were being expanded and modernized, America's was in its death throes. Railroad executives overlooked the fact that hundreds of thousands of people preferred traveling at 70 miles-an-hour on ground level to being whisked along at close to the speed of sound, four or five miles up in the air. Assuming that passenger train transportation was a thing of the past, management concentrated on the more lucrative freight. A head of lettuce, an orange, a piece of lumber, a farm implement, or even an automobile was treated with much greater courtesy and concern than any human being.

Now, there is a new look for the railroads; rail travel is making its comeback. In 1971, by Congressional mandate, the passenger service on 13 major railroads was united under a single national intercity system, under the National Railroad Passenger Corporation — better known as Amtrak. The goal of Amtrak was to halt the downward trend in rail travel by improving and developing fast, comfortable, and convenient intercity transportation.

While Amtrak has most assuredly experienced growing pains in its attempt to renew public confidence in rail transportation, it is achieving many of its goals. Old cars are being refurbished and new, comfortable equipment is gradually being introduced. Day coaches have roomy, two-abreast seating; most long-distance overnight coaches feature reclining seats and leg-rests; slumber coaches offer economical sleeping accommodations for overnight travel. First-class accommodations feature swivel armchairs; bedrooms, roomettes, and suites come in various sizes. Meals have been improved too; today's passenger has a choice of almost anything, from light snacks and beverages to sumptuous dinners that compare favorably with many fine restaurants.

58

Famous trains such as the Broadway Limited, Silver Meteor, Sunset Limited, Empire Builder, etc. are still running, but there are newcomers to the field. The metroliner operates fast trips on the New York — Washington route, and turbo-powered trains capable of speeds up to 125 miles-an-hour run between such important cities as Boston and New York, Chicago and Detroit and Milwaukee.

In addition to good point-to-point transportation Amtrak offers, in conjuction with a number of leading tour operators, a variety of rail vacations and tour packages to popular destinations.

CAREER POTENTIAL WITH AMTRAK

Opportunities appear to be excellent because of anticipated growth and expansion. When Amtrak hires new employees, it does so with careful consideration for the future and looks for applicants who demonstrate management and leadership qualities. Many people begin their career in Amtrak's modern, computerized reservation and ticketing department.

ELEGIBILITY REQUIREMENTS

Age Applicants in the 24-38 age bracket are preferred, but both younger and older persons are eligible for employment if they meet the requirements.

Education A high school diploma, or its equivalent, is essential for most entry level positions. Two years of college will also be helpful. Graduation from a travel school which includes computerized reservation procedures in its curriculum will qualify you as a desirable candidate.

Work experience Previous office experience is preferred.

Training Amtrak has a comprehensive training program which lasts four weeks; three weeks cover reservation procedures, fares, ticketing, telephone techniques, etc. One week is devoted to sales functions.

BENEFITS

Salary Starting salaries at Amtrak are above average for the travel industry. in 1979 reservationists started at $50.92 per day. Employees are automatically progressed at six, twelve, and eighteen month intervals at which point maximum salary for the job is reached.

Vacation and holidays Amtrak has an excellent vacation policy, and all employees enjoy a number of paid holidays each year.

Insurance All employees are covered without cost by comprehensive health, accident, and life insurance.

Pension Employees participate in the well-known Railroad Retirement program.

Travel benefits Free transportation is granted to all employees. If sleeping accommodations are required, the employee pays a fee for such accommodations.

Union The new employee is on probation for the first sixty days of employment, after which seniority status is achieved and union membership becomes compulsory.

JOBS WITH AMTRAK

Reservation Clerk Reservation clerks handle telephone reservations from the general public and travel agents. Reservation centers are located in Chicago; New York City; Bensalem, Pennsylvania; Los Angeles; and Jacksonville, Florida. Reservation clerks can also be assigned to such responsibilities as checking passengers in at the station and staffing information desks.

Positions in City Ticket Offices and Station Ticket Offices are open on a "bid" basis to qualified and experienced personnel. Transfer and promotion to the marketing or operation departments are possible, as is promotion to a supervisory position. As in any company, progress is determined by the attitude and performance of the individual.

Passenger Service Representative The passenger service representative functions in much the same manner as a flight attendant or inflight service representative with the airlines. He or she is usually chosen for personality and ability and is specially trained in railroad functions. They look after the needs of passengers.

Sales Representative Openings in sales are available from time to time, and preference will usually be given to those applicants who have been employed in a similar position with an airline, tour operator, hotel, or related company. Sales representatives call upon travel agencies and other clients of the company. A degree in sales and marketing or travel and tourism is helpful, as is some sales experience.

OTHER POSITIONS WITH AMTRAK

Amtrak is responsible for all personnel dealing with passengers. This includes reservations and sales staff, cooks, porters, waiters and car attendants. There are also a wide range of office positions, including clerks, secretaries, accounting clerks, computer operators, key punch operators, receptionists and many others.

Specialized management and supervisory positions include sales managers and sales representatives, personnel representatives, computer programmers, and others.

HOW TO APPLY

Contact the nearest Amtrak Personnel office. Offices are located in Washington, DC; Boston; Chicago; New York; Jacksonville, Florida; Philadelphia, and Los Angeles.

OTHER RAILROAD CAREERS

The railroads carried over one and one-half billion tons of freight in 1978 and 281 million passengers. With more than 530,000 workers, the railroads are one of the Nation's largest employers.

Railroad workers are employed in every state except Hawaii. Large numbers are employed at terminal points where the railroads have central offices, yards, and maintenance and repair shops. Chicago has more railroad employees than any other area, while New York, Los Angeles, Minneapolis, Philadelphia, Pittsburgh, and Detroit are also large centers of employment.

Railroad occupations can be divided into four main groups:

Operating employees They make up almost one-third of all railroad workers. This group includes locomotive engineers, conductors, and brake operators. Also included are switchenders who help conductors and brake operators by throwing track switches in railroad yards and hostlers who check fuel and check and deliver locomotives from the engine house to the crew.

Station and office workers One-fourth of all railroad workers are station and office employees who direct train movements and handle the railroads' business affairs. Professionals such as managers, accountants, statisticians, and systems analysts do administrative and planning work. Clerks keep records, prepare statistics, and handle business transactions such as collecting bills and adjusting claims. Agents manage the business affairs of the railroad station. Telegraphers and telephoners pass on instructions to crews and help agents with clerical work.

Equipment maintenance workers This group comprises about one-fifth of all railroad employees. They service and repair locomotives and cars. Included are car repairers, machinists, electrical workers, sheet-metal workers, boilermakers, and blacksmiths.

Property maintenance workers They make up about one-sixth of all railroad employees; build and repair tracks, tunnels, signals, and other railroad property. Track workers repair tracks and roadbeds. Bridge and building workers construct and repair bridges, tunnels and other structures along the right-of-way. Signal workers install and service the railroads' extensive network of signals, including highway-crossing protection devices.

EMPLOYMENT OUTLOOK

According to the U. S. Department of Labor, the decline in railroad employment is expected to continue through the mid-1980's, but at a slower rate. However, the same source indicates that thousands of job opportunities will develop each year as the industry replaces experienced workers who retire, die, or transfer to other fields of work.

Most railroad employees work a 5-day, 40-hour week, and receive premium pay for any overtime. Operating employees, such as station agents, and telegraphers and telephoners often find it necessary to work nights, weekends, and holidays. Extra board workers may be called at any time. Bridge and building workers, signal installers, and track workers may work away from home for days at a time.

TRAINING

Most railroad workers are trained on the job by experienced employees. Training for some office and maintenance jobs is available in some high schools and vocational schools. Universities and technical schools offer courses in accounting, engineering, traffic management, transportation, and other subjects.

New employees in some occupations, especially those in operating service jobs such as locomotive engineer, start as extra board workers. They substitute for regular workers who are on vacation, ill, or absent for other reasons. They may also be called in when railroad traffic increases temporarily or seasonally.

Extra board workers with enough seniority move to regular assignments as they become available. The length of time on the extra board varies according to the number of available openings. In some cases it may take an employee a number of years to receive a regular assignment.

Beginners in shop trades usually are high school graduates with no previous experience. Shopworkers serve apprenticeships that last two to four years, depending on how much previous work experience the apprentice has.

Most applicants for railroad positions must pass physical examinations. Those interested in train crew jobs need excellent hearing and eyesight. Good eyesight is essential, and those who are color-blind are not hired for any jobs that involve interpreting railroad signals.

Railroad workers are promoted on the basis of seniority and ability. Job openings are posted on bulletin boards and workers may bid for those that interest them. The worker who is highest on the seniority list usually gets the job. However, to be promoted, workers may have to qualify by passing written, oral, and practical tests. Advancement in train and engine jobs is along established lines. All conductors, for example, are selected from qualified brake operators.

Besides determining advancement procedures, seniority also gives workers some choice of working conditions. A telegrapher, for instance, may have to work several years on a night shift at out-of-the-way locations before finally getting a day-shift assignment near home.

SOME TYPICAL RAILROAD JOBS

Conductor Conductors are in charge of train crews and are responsible for the safe and punctual delivery of freight and passengers. On freight trains, the conductor keeps records of each car's contents and its destination, and sees that cars are added or removed at proper points along the route. On a passenger train, the conductor collects tickets and fares and answers questions concerning timetables and schedules. At stops they ensure that all passengers getting off do so, and then signal the engineer to leave.

During runs, conductors regularly receive information from brake operators on the condition of the cars. If a problem develops, conductors arrange for either repairs or removal of the particular car to a siding. They keep in touch with the dispatcher and advise him of all developments, conditions along the route, and of problems. They do this through the use of two-way radio or by telephones along the track.

Yard conductors supervise the crews that assemble and disassemble trains. They also oversee the crews that move the cars within the railroad yards to facilitate loading and unloading freight. In those yards that have automatic classification systems, they may use electrical controls to operate the track switches that route the cars to the correct track.

Jobs as conductors are filled from the ranks of experienced brake operators who have passed tests covering signals, timetables, operating rules, and related subjects. Until permanent positions become available, new conductors are assigned to the extra board where they substitute for experienced conductors who are absent because of vacation, illness, or similar reasons, Seniority is almost always the main factor in determing promotion from brake operator to conductor and from extra board to a permanent position.

Most railroads maintain separate seniority lists for road service and yard service conductors; conductors usually remain in one type of service for their entire careers. Some railroads start conductors in the yards, then move them to freight service and so to passenger operations. Depending upon ability, some conductors advance to managerial positions such as trainmaster or yardmaster.

Yard conductors usually work a 40-hour week and receive premium pay for overtime. Road conductors are under a dual system of pay and are paid according to miles traveled or hours worked, whichever is greater.

Conductors often work nights, weekends, and holidays. Because of the distance traveled, they may also spend several nights away from home.

Brake Operators All passenger and most freight train crews include two road-brake operators—one in the locomotive with the engineer and another in the caboose with the conductor. Before departure, road-brake operators inspect the train to make sure that all couplers and airhoses are fastened, that handbrakes on all the cars are released, and that the airbrakes are functioning correctly. While the train is underway, they keep on the lookout for smoke, sparks, overheated axle bearings, and other faulty equipment. They may also make minor repairs to airhoses and couplers.

Road-brake operators throw switches to route freight trains onto industrial tracks, uncoupling cars that are to be delivered and coupling those that are to be removed. On passenger trains, they regulate car lighting, heat and air conditioning, and help the conductor collect tickets and assist passengers. They are also referred to as collectors on some passenger trains.

Yard-brake operators (also known as yard couplers or helpers) help assemble and disassemble trains in railroad yards.

Beginning brake operators make several trips with an experienced operator and conductor to become familiar with the job. They are then assigned to the extra board where they are given assignments to substitute for workers who are absent for reasons of illness or vacation. Usually they work a year or two before they learn the job thoroughly, and several more years before they have gained sufficient seniority to get a regular assignment.

Railroads prefer applicants who are high school graduates, or have the equivalent qualifications (GED). Good eyesight and hearing are essential and mechanical aptitude is helpful. Because of the nature of the job, which may entail climbing ladders, boarding moving trains, throwing switches, and operating handbrakes, good physical condition and stamina are necessary. In most cases applicants must pass a physical examination.

With sufficient seniority, brake operators advance to conductors. These jobs are always filled by promoting experienced brake operators who have qualified by passing written and oral tests on signals, brake systems, timetables, operating rules, and other subjects. Since promotion on all railroads is based upon seniority, it may take at least ten years to advance to conductor.

Locomotive Engineers Engineers operate locomotives in passenger, freight, and yard service. Road service engineers transport freight and passengers between stations, and yard engineers move cars within the yards to assemble or disassemble trains.

The engineer operates the throttle to start, stop, and accelerate the train. He also operates other controls such as light switches, and watches gauges and meters that measure fuel, electricity, and air pressure. He also watches for signals that indicate speed limits and track obstructions.

Before and after each run, the engineer checks the locomotive for mechanical problems. If a minor problem develops, the engineer may be able to fix it locally; otherwise the trouble is reported to the engine-shop supervisor.

Engineers are among the most skilled employees on the railroad. They must have a thorough knowledge of the signal systems, yards, and terminals along their route, and be constantly aware of the condition and makeup of the train.

Openings in engineer jobs are usually filled by training and promoting engineer helpers according to seniority rules.

Helpers ride in locomotives with engineers and assist them by inspecting locomotives, watching for signals and track obstructions, and monitoring gauges. New helpers receive on-the-job training lasting up to six weeks, during which time they learn their duties and the railroad rules and regulations. They are then assigned as engineer helpers on regular jobs. Railroads prefer applicants who have a high-school graduation diploma and who are at last twenty-one years of age. Applicants must also have good eyesight, color vision, and hearing. Good eye-hand coordination, manual dexterity, and mechanical aptitude are also necessary.

Helpers are placed in training programs for engineer jobs within one year following employment date. These programs, which last up to six months, include classroom and on-the-job training in locomotive operation. Helpers take qualifying tests covering locomotive equipment, airbrake systems, fuel economy, train handling techniques, and operating rules and regulations. They then become eligible for promotion to engineer.

As positions become available, qualified helpers who have the longest seniority are placed on the engineers extra board. Extra board engineers who do not have regular assignments substitute for regular engineers. It may take a number of years for an extra board engineer to receive a permanent assignment. The seniority rules will also determine an engineer's type of service. For example, the first regular assignment may be in yard work before moving on to road service.

Engineers must also take periodic physical examinations to determine fitness to operate locomotives. Those who fail to meet the physical standards are restricted to yard service, or are transferred to other jobs where the physical standards are lower.

Car Repairers The job includes rebuilding, maintaining, and inspecting passenger and freight cars, tank cars, and some sections of locomotives. Repairers visually examine cars, and periodically remove and inspect parts such as wheels, brake assemblies, and couplers. Some employees work in special yards rebuilding old or badly damaged cars. Railroads look for high school graduates who have had shop training in high school or in a vocational school. Automobile repair courses are helpful. Apprenticeship lasts three to four years, depending upon how much previous work experience and training the apprentice has.

Machinists They use metal cutting and forming tools to do the heavy work involved in servicing and overhauling locomotives and other equipment. Apprenticeship training is the most common way to enter the field.

Other shop trades There are several other types of positions that become available from time to time. These include electrical workers, sheet metal workers, boilermakers, blacksmiths, and several others.

Signal Installers They work in crews, usually consisting of five or more workers. They install new equipment and make major repairs. Much of their work is construction, and includes digging holes and ditches, hoisting poles, and mixing and pouring concrete to make foundations. They also assemble the control and communications devices, make the electrical connections, and perform the extensive testing that is required to assure that new signal systems are working properly.

Signal Maintainers They are assigned to a section of track and are responsible for keeping gate crossings, signals, and other control devices in good operating condition. They inspect and repair or replace wires, lights, and switches. Both signal installers and maintainers must have a thorough knowledge of electricity.

Railroads prefer high school graduates for both signal installers and maintainers. Courses in blueprint reading, electronics, and electricity provide a helpful background. Advancement can lead to signal inspector, technician, gang supervisor, and other supervisory positions.

Station Agents Station agents are the customer's contact with the railroad. They take orders from customers and arrange for railroad cars to transport their products. When goods are delivered, they notify the recipient, prepare the bill, and authorize the release of goods.

At passenger stations, agents supervise and coordinate the activities of workers who sell tickets and check baggage. At major stations and depots, the agent's job is supervisory, and he oversees other workers such as clerks, telegraphers, and others.

Station agents rise from the ranks of other railroad occupations. With sufficient seniority and ability, telephoners, telegraphers, tower operators, and clerks may eventually be promoted to agents in small stations and may advance to larger stations as they gain in seniority and experience.

Telegraphers, Telephoners and Tower Operators They control the movement of trains according to instructions given by train dispatchers. Tower operators work in towers located in yards or next to major junctions. They route train traffic by manipulating levers and other controls to activate signals and throw switches on the tracks.

Telephoners and telegraphers receive orders on train movements and cargo and pass this information on to train crews. They work at stations and may also assist station agents in taking orders and billing customers, or other similar clerical work.

Candidates for these positions should be high school graduates. It is usual for new employees to get on-the-job training, after which they are expected to pass an examination covering operating rules, train orders, and station operations, and must demonstrate their ability to use the necessary equipment before they can qualify. Applicants must have good hearing and eyesight, including normal color vision. They should also be responsible, alert, and capable of organizing thoughts and actions in emergency or pressure situations.

Track Workers Tracks workers construct, service, and repair railroad tracks and roadbeds. Many of these workers operate heavy machinery and equipment such as bulldozers and machines which lay rail. Others use power tools to drive and pull spikes, cut rails, tighten bolts and perform many other functions.

Most track workers learn their skills on the job, and the training takes about two years. Machine-operating jobs are assigned to workers by seniority.

Clerical positions All railroads have a complete range of office and clerical positions. These range from general clerks to the ticket agents who sell tickets to passengers at the station window. Most of the positions are similar to those found in other businesses and therefore are not mentioned in any depth here.

How to Apply Contact the nearest employment office. The Appendix contains a listing of the major railroads.

Chapter 6

STEAMSHIP AND CRUISE LINES

Seafaring employment offers a variety of interesting and rewarding careers as well as travel to many foreign lands.

The U.S. Merchant Marine consists primarily of private firms whose ships transport the Nation's exports and bring imports from many parts of the world. A small number of ships are operated by the Navy's Military Sealift Command (MSC) and are crewed by civilian personnel.

Nearly three-fifths of the ships in the merchant fleet are freighters. These include general cargo ships and special vessels such as container ships. About two-fifths of the ships are tankers that carry liquid products such as oil. Some ships are passenger-cargo carriers. Many ships operate on a regular schedule and go to specific ports; others sail to and from almost any port in the world.

Government subsidies ensure that the United States has a fleet of ships operating in regular or essential trade routes. The number of ships built, however, only slightly exceeds the number of older ships taken out of service. Therefore, the size of the U.S. Merchant fleet is not expected to grow significantly.

There are approximately 45,000 officer and non-officer jobs aboard U.S. merchant ships. The actual number of personnel employed at any one time varies depending upon trade conditions, international situations, and government policies. Apart from jobs on ocean-going ships, there are also many positions aboard Great Lakes vessels, river towboats, and various harbor craft. Cargo ships and tankers have crews of 13 to 65 persons, but this number could decline since new ships are equipped with labor-saving innovations such as automated engine rooms. Passenger ships may have crews of 300 or more.

It has been sad to see the decline in the number of U.S. passenger ships. Not too many years ago, passenger ships operated fast, convenient, service to major European ports. This service was maintained by the pride of the American Merchant Marine, the S.S. *United States.* American Export Lines operated the S.S. *Independence* and her sister ship, the S.S. *Constitution,* to Mediterranean ports. For years, Matson Lines ran luxury liners to Hawaii and the South Pacific, New Zealand, and Australia. Moore-McCormack Lines operated service and luxury cruises to South America, and American President Lines operated fast passenger service to and from the Orient. Rising labor costs made it impossible for American ships to compete with foreign ships, which usually have a much lower operating expense. Although there are a few passenger ships operating under the American flag, many vessels have been sold to foreign steamship lines, or are laid up.

Most of those employed ashore work in major cities, and most officers and sailors have their bases in these cities. The nation's largest port is New York. Other major Atlantic ports are Boston, Philadelphia, Baltimore, Norfolk, Charleston, Savannah, Tampa, and Jacksonville. Gulf ports that handle large volumes of cargo include New Orleans, Houston, and Galveston. Shipping on the West Coast is concentrated in the areas of San Francisco, Los Angeles, Seattle, and Portland. Major Great Lakes ports include Chicago, Detroit, Milwaukee, and Cleveland.

Years ago it was possible for the intrepid traveler to "work his way" to almost any point in the world that was visited by American merchant ships. He could sign on in a non-skilled position, leave the ship in some foreign port, then pick up a job on board another ship later. It is now impossible to "work passage" to foreign ports for personal travel. Conditions do not permit termination of a seaman's service in a foreign port.

SHIPBOARD DEPARTMENTS

The jobs on board ship are divided into three main departments:

Deck department Deck officers, or mates as they are called, direct the navigation of the ship and the maintenance of the deck and hull. They maintain the authorized speed and course, plot the vessel's position, post lookouts and record information in the log of the voyage. Sailors make up most of a merchant ship's crew. The ordinary and able seamen work under the direction of the deck officers.

Engine department Marine engineers operate and maintain the engines and other machinery aboard ship. The engineering staff consists of a variety of specialists with varying degrees of skill, from the entry level wiper to the refrigeration engineer.

Steward department Those employed in this department are responsible for the cooking and serving of food and the maintenance and upkeep of living quarters aboard ship. On passenger ships, the members of this department make up the bulk of the crew.

MERCHANT MARINE OFFICERS

EMPLOYMENT OUTLOOK

According to the U.S. Department of Labor, little change in the employment of ships' officers is anticipated through the mid-1980's because the number of merchant ships is not expected to increase significantly. However, some job openings will arise due to the need to replace experienced officers who retire, die, or take shoreside employment.

Employment opportunities will be best for those who graduate from maritime academies, particularly the U.S. Merchant Marine Academy at Kings Point, New York. Graduates who cannot find jobs in merchant ships may be able to locate employment in related fields. For example, trained officers are needed on oceanographic research vessels, Great Lakes vessels, and many others.

TRAINING AND EDUCATION

The fastest and surest way to becoming a well-trained deck or engineering officer is through an established training program. Such training is available at the U.S. Merchant Marine Academy at Kings Point, New York, and at five state merchant marine academies. About 550 students graduate each year from these schools, of which approximately one-half are trained as deck officers and one-half as marine engineers. Admission to the federal academy is through nomination by a member of congress, and entrance to the state academies is made through written application to the school. An applicant should be a high school graduate, a U.S. citizen, at least seventeen years of age, and not have passed his twenty-second birthday by July 1 of the year of admission. It is also necessary to be in excellent physical condition. Applicants should show an aptitude for mathematics and related subjects since deck officers have to make complex navigation and cargo calculations.

Most of the academies offer a four-year program in nautical science or marine engineering. Subjects of study include navigation, mathematics, electronics, propulsion systems, electrical engineering, languages, history, shipping management, plus practical experience at sea. Because of their thorough grounding, academy graduates are in the best position to move up to master and chief engineer ratings. Their education also helps qualify them for shoreside jobs of an administrative or executive nature.

After the graduate passes Coast Guard examinations, a license is issued for either third mate or third assistant engineer. In addition, graduates may receive commissions as ensigns in the U.S. Navy Reserve. Graduates of the U.S. Merchant Marine Academy have an obligation to serve a minimum of three years as officers in the merchant marine.

A number of trade unions in the maritime industry provide officer training. Most union programs are designed to upgrade experienced sailors to officer ratings, although some programs accept inexperienced young persons. One such program is that offered by the National Marine

Engineers' Beneficial Association (MEBA), which operates the Calhoon MEBA Engineering School in Baltimore, Maryland. This is open to high school graduates and consists of a three-year apprenticeship training program in preparation for a third assistant engineer's license. Trainees must agree to serve at least three years in the U.S. merchant marine.

Advancement for both deck and engineering officers is along well-defined lines, and depends upon seagoing experience, successful passage of a Coast Guard examination, and leadership qualities. Deck officers start off as third mates, and after a year's service are eligible to sit for a second mate examination. Officers in the engineering department commence their careers as third assistant engineers, and after one year of service can apply for a second assistant engineer's license. Captains, chief and second mates must be at least twenty-one years of age. The minimum age for third mates, third assistant engineers and radio operators is nineteen. It is also necessary to be a U.S. citizen, and to obtain a U.S. Public Health Service certificate attesting to vision, color perception, and general physical condition.

OFFICER RANKS

Captain The captain has complete authority and responsibility for the ship's operation, including discipline and order, and the safety of the crew, passengers and cargo. He is the shipowner's sole representative.

While in port, the captain may serve as the shipowner's agent in conferring with custom officials. Although not technically members of a specific department, captains are associated with the deck department from whose ranks they have been promoted.

Chief Officer Also known as the chief or first mate, is the captain's assistant in assigning duties to the deck crew and maintaining order and discipline. The chief mate also is responsible for planning and supervising the loading and unloading of cargo. He also assists the captain in taking the ship in and out of port.

Second Mate The second mate is the navigation officer. He sees that the ship is provided with the necessary navigation charts, and that all navigating equipment is maintained in proper condition.

Third Mate Third mates are the most junior-rated deck officers. They are responsible for the care and maintenance of the navigating bridge and chartroom. They also act as signal officer and are in charge of all signalling equipment. They assist in the supervision of cargo loading and unloading, and inspect lifesaving equipment to be certain that it is ready for use in an emergency.

Chief Engineer He supervises the engine department, and is responsible for the efficient operation of engines and other mechanical equipment throughout the ship. The chief engineer oversees the operation of the main powerplant and auxiliary equipment. He also keeps records of engine performance and fuel consumption.

First Assistant Engineer He supervises the engineroom personnel and directs operations such as starting, stopping, and controlling the speed of the main engines. The first assistant engineer also oversees and inspects the lubrication of engines, pumps, generators and other machinery. He also assists the chief engineer in undertaking all repairs that may be necessary.

Second Assistant Engineer He has charge of the boiler and associated equipment such as the water-feed system and pumps. The second assistant engineer also makes sure that proper steam pressure and oil and water temperatures are maintained. He also supervises the cleaning of the boilers.

Third Assistant Engineer Responsibilities include supervising the operation and maintenance of the lubrication system and other engineroom equipment. Some third assistant engineers are responsible for the electrical and refrigeration systems aboard some ships.

Radio Officer A ship maintains contact with the shore and with other ships at sea through its radio officer. Most cargo vessels employ one radio officer while a passenger ship may carry three to six radio officers. These officers send and receive messages by Morse code or by voice. They receive and record time signals, weather information, positions reports, and other information. On a passenger ship, a radio officer sends and receives cables and messages on behalf of the passengers, and arranges ship-to-shore telephone connections. Radio officers may also maintain depth recording equipment and electronic navigation equipment.

In order to obtain a Coast Guard license as a radio officer, applicants must have a first or second-class radiotelegraph operator's license issued by the Federal Communications Commission. For a license to serve as the sole radio officer on board a cargo ship, the Coast Guard requires six months of radio experience at sea.

Purser All passenger ships and some of the larger cargo vessels carry a purser. Passenger ships may have several assistant pursers on the staff. The purser, or an assistant, does the extensive paperwork that is required before a ship enters or leaves port. They prepare payrolls, and on passenger ships, perform many services such as cashing traveler's checks, selling foreign currency for the countries visited along the route, and selling shore tours and packages.

MERCHANT MARINE SAILORS

EMPLOYMENT OUTLOOK

According to the U. S. Department of Labor, the employment of non-officer seamen is expected to decline somewhat through the mid-1980's. The modern freighter is more automated than were its predecessors, and consequently, many new ships require smaller crews. However, some openings will arise each year because of the need to replace experienced sailors who retire, die, or leave the sea for other reasons. Competition for these jobs will be keen because the number of people seeking jobs is expected to exceed the number of available openings. There are few, if any, opportunities for the unskilled, and virtually none for the undedicated. It is not a career for those who want to run away to sea, or for those who want to travel and see the world.

TRAINING AND EDUCATION

Positions for entry-level ratings (no experience) are limited. Students and other persons seeking part-time or summer employment will find that unless they have special skills or seniority they will not be able to find a job. The best method of preparing for a career at sea is through a specialized training school.

There are a number of schools offering training for those without experience. The Seafarers' International Union operates the Harry Lundeberg School for Seamanship at Piney Point, Maryland. The purpose of the school is to train, guide, and encourage young people to seek a career of the sea, and to conduct training courses for experienced seamen so that they can achieve higher ratings. Candidates for the school should be be between the ages of sixteen and twenty-one; special waivers are available to young men with recent honorable service in the armed forces. Since ambition and a sincere desire to learn are considered more important than academic records, no high school or grammar school diploma is required, and no written examination is given. Applicants must be in good physical health. There are no tuition charges or fees of any type, and in addition to receiving a free education, each trainee receives $15 a week allotment for spending money.

The training course at the Lundeberg School lasts for 12 weeks. The trainee will acquire basic skills which will qualify him to serve as an entry-rated seaman in the deck, engine, or steward departments.

The National Maritime Union conducts a training and upgrading program, and a limited number of entry-rating trainees are accepted for each session. For more information on training programs, write to one of the unions or direct to the schools themselves. Addresses of unions are at the end of this chapter, and a listing of training schools will be found in the Appendix.

GETTING A JOB AS A SEAMAN

No person may be employed on a U. S. flag merchant vessel of 100 gross tons or more who has not first applied for, and been issued a Seaman's Certificate (merchant mariner's document) by the U. S. Coast Guard. Possession of this document does not guarantee a job, it only qualifies a person to be considered for a job when the supply of experienced seamen has been exhausted. Before the Coast Guard will accept applications for a certificate, the applicant must be referred by a recognized maritime training school, or he must have a letter of commitment from a shipping company or union addressed to the Coast Guard certifying that the applicant will be employed as a ship's crew member. Applicants must have reached the age of sixteen, and, if under eighteen years of age, must present a parent's or guardian's notarized consent. Applicants must also present a birth certificate, baptismal certificate, or other evidence of citizenship, and three passport-size photographs. Aliens must produce evidence of their nationality and acceptable evidence from the U. S. Immigration and Naturalization Service that the applicant has been lawfully admitted to the U. S. for permanent residence. There are Coast Guard Marine Inspection Officers throughout the U. S.

After the merchant mariner's document has been issued, it is necessary to register at the employment office (hiring hall) of one of the seaman's unions. Hiring halls are located in all major ports. Job seekers are given shipping cards when they register at the hiring hall. The shipping companies send job orders to the hiring hall, and those who have the most seniority get first preference on any job for which they are qualified. To be considered for a job, applicants must actually be present at the hall when jobs are announced. A new seaman is required to apply for membership in the union representing seamen on the vessel in which he is employed. Application must usually be made after serving 30 days.

ADVANCEMENT

Seamen advance in the deck and engine departments by serving a designated period in a rating, and by successfully completing a Coast Guard examination. For example, after serving for one year an ordinary seaman may apply to the Coast Guard for limited endorsement as able seaman. For full endorsement, the sailor must be at least nineteen years of age and pass an examination to test his knowledge of seamanship and his ability to carry out all of the duties required of able seamen. Able seamen who have supervisory ability and leadership qualities can advance to boatswain after years of service.

The unions offer excellent upgrading programs. The Harry Lundeberg School, which is operated by the Seafarers' International Union, has a number of upgrading courses for those who can qualify by having the necessary sea time and training. The school conducts upgrading programs in the deck, engine, and steward departments.

SEAMEN RATINGS

Boatswain Also known as the bosun, he is the highest ranking able seaman. As supervisor of the deck crew, the boatswain relays the deck officers' orders and ensures that these orders are carried out quickly and efficiently. The boatswain assists the chief mate in assigning work to crew members and directs general maintenance operations such as cleaning and polishing metalwork and painting.

Carpenter Some ships carry a carpenter who secures cargo hatches and ports, and braces cargo. The carpenter may also operate winches.

Able Seamen Able seamen make up about one-fifth of all sailors. They must have a thorough knowledge of all parts of the ship and be able to handle all gear and deck equipment. They act as quartermaster to steer the ship, usually taking two-hour turns at the wheel. They also act as lookouts, and report sightings to deck officers. They are also responsible for rigging, repairing, and stowing cargo-handling and other gear. They must be able to tie common knots and handle mooring lines when the ship is docking or departing.

Able seamen must be familiar with fire prevention and control methods. They must also participate in periodic lifeboat drills, and be able to handle all operations connected with launching lifeboats and liferafts.

Ordinary Seamen This is the entry level rating of the deck department. Ordinary seamen scrub decks, coil and splice ropes, paint, clean personnel quarters, and perform other general maintenance work. They may also relieve able seamen who steer the ship and act as lookouts.

Refrigeration Engineer This is a skilled position not found on every ship. He maintains proper temperatures in the refrigerator compartments for perishable cargos such as meat, fruit, and vegetables.

Electrician The ship's electrician repairs and maintains electrical equipment such as generators and motors. Electricians also test wiring, and remove and replace fuses and defective lights.

Firer-Watertender They check and regulate the amount of water in the boilers, inspect gauges, and regulate fuel flow to keep steam pressure constant. They also check the operation of evaporators and condensers, test water for salt content, clean oil burning equipment, and clean strainers used to filter dirt from oil.

Oiler Lubricates the mechanical equipment and makes regular rounds of ship machinery to check oil pressures and flow. Oilers also may help overhaul and repair machinery.

Wiper This is the entry level rating of the engine department. His basic job is to keep the engine room and machinery clean.

Chief Steward Supervises the preparation and serving of meals, and the upkeep of living quarters aboard ship. On a passenger ship, the chief steward supervises more staff than the head of any other department; he is in charge of all meal services, the cooking preparation and serving of all food to both the passengers and the crew. Since one of the major attractions of a cruise is the food served, the chief steward of a major cruise liner has an immense responsibility. He is usually assisted by assistant stewards.

Chief Cook Supervises the cooking and preparation of all meals. Is assisted by several assistant cooks on passenger ships and must be skilled at preparing a wide variety of gourmet meals. On freighters, the chief steward and chief cook may be combined into one position.

Utility Hand and Mess Attendant These are entry level jobs requiring little skill. Utility hands carry food supplies from the storeroom and iceboxes, prepare vegetables, wash cooking utensils, and scour galley equipment. Mess attendants set tables, serve meals, clean tables, wash dishes, and care for living quarters.

Due to the greater use of prepackaged foods and smaller crew sizes, many of the newer ships have reduced the number of workers in the steward's department.

Dining Room Steward This job is found on passenger and cruise vessels. He may be in charge of three or four tables in the dining room. Dining room stewards act as waiters and waitresses on board ship.

Cabin Steward On passenger ships the cabin steward is responsible for the cleaning of the passengers' cabin. Cabin stewards and stewardesses are assigned a number of cabins. They make up the beds in the morning, clean and tidy the cabin, replace beds with fresh linen, and in general are concerned for the comfort of the passengers during the voyage.

OTHER JOBS IN THE STEAMSHIP INDUSTRY

Because of the size and scope of the steamship industry, there are many jobs of both a general and skilled nature for those who want to make their careers in this field. Such jobs include secretary, typist, clerk, payroll clerk, and many more. More specialized jobs are billing clerks who type invoices that list items shipped and dates of shipment, manifest clerks who compile and type the ship's manifest, receipt and report clerks who prepare reports on labor and equipment costs for loading and unloading cargos. Most of the general clerical jobs, such as bookkeeper or secretary, usually require the completion of basic commercial courses in high school or business school.   Additional on-the-job training is necessary for specialized clerical occupations.

Administrative and executive postions are filled by college graduates who have degrees in business administration, travel and tourism, accounting, marketing, industrial relations or other specialized fields. A knowledge of the merchant marine is helpful.

Marine architects are licensed by the individual states. Requirements usually call for graduation from an accredited professional school followed by three years of practical experience in an architect's office.

Cruising is big business, and although most American cruise passengers are now carried by foreign-flag vessels, these companies do maintain sales offices in the U. S. Many of the cruise lines have offices located in certain key cities so that they may properly service travel agents and passengers in the area. While it is quite difficult to get a job on board a foreign-flag ship, there are many shoreside positions available. Such positions include reservationists to handle telephone reservations from travel agents and passengers; ticketing clerks; sales representatives to promote sales through travel agents, and many other general office positions.

On board passenger ships there are beauticians, barbers, hairdressers, social directors, entertainers, tour directors, sales persons and many others who are employed by the firms who perform these services on a concession basis. Check the Appendix for a list of both foreign and American cruise lines to whom you can write for more information on such jobs.

Registered nurses are employed aboard passenger vessels, but the number of available openings are extremely limited. Selection of nurse applicants for seagoing jobs is usually the responsibility of the Port Medical Director of each steamship company. Freighters that carry 12 passengers or less are not required to have medical personnel on board.

SOME USEFUL ADDRESSES

You will find the following unions and trade associations excellent sources for more detailed information on job opportunities, wage scales, qualifications, training and hiring procedures for the branch of the merchant marine that interests you. For shoregoing jobs, contact one or more of the American or foreign steamship lines listed in the Appendix. While many of the unions will be pleased to send you information on their training programs, you may wish to contact the academies and schools directly; they are listed in the Appendix also.

OFFICERS' UNIONS

International Organization of Masters, Mates and Pilots
39 Broadway
New York, NY 10006

National Marine Engineers' Beneficial Association
17 Battery Place
New York, NY 10004

RADIO OFFICERS' UNIONS

American Radio Association
207 Madison Avenue
New York, NY 10006

Radio Officers Union
225 West 34th Street
New York, NY 10001

SEAMENS' UNIONS

Seafarers' International Union of North America
675 Fourth Avenue
Brooklyn, NY 11232

National Maritime Union of America
36 Seventh Avenue
New York, NY 10011

Sailors' Union of the Pacific
450 Harrison Street
San Francisco, CA 94105

Marine Firemen, Oilers, Watertenders and Wipers Association
204 2nd Street
San Francisco, CA 94105

Marine Cooks and Stewards Union
350 Fremont Street
San Francisco, CA 94105

Atlantic, Gulf, Lakes and Inland Water District
675 Fourth Avenue
Brooklyn, NY 11232

Inland Boatmen's Union
675 Fourth Avenue
Brooklyn, NY 11232

OTHER TRADE ASSOCIATIONS

The Independent Tankers Association
53 Park Place
New York, NY 10007

The Great Lake Carriers Association
1205 Rockefeller Building
Cleveland, OH 44113

MILITARY SEALIFT COMMAND

The Military Sealift Command, Department of the Navy, operates numerous ships manned by civilian crews employed under Civil Service regulations. Experienced seamen are given preference for employment, and opportunities for inexperienced personnel are almost non-existent. MSC employment offices are located at the following ports:

Naval Supply Center
Oakland, CA 94625

58th Street and First Avenue
New York, NY 11250

Chapter 7

TOUR OPERATORS

The tour operator—also known as a wholesaler—plays a significant role in world tourism, and influences the development, growth and fiscal health of the travel industry. Thanks to him, travel has been made available to hundreds of thousands of people who otherwise could not have afforded it.

When a tour operator shops for hotel rooms, meals, transportation, and all of the other ingredients that go into a well-run tour, he buys on behalf of thousands of passengers, and takes advantage of preferential rates unavailable to the independent traveler. This savings of bulk-buying are passed on to the passenger, who can select from thousands of tours and itineraries, both domestic and overseas, at prices much lower than he would ordinarily have to pay.

Perhaps the best way to define the responsibilities of the tour operator is to say that he designs and operates tours and packages to world-wide destinations, and markets them through retail travel agencies and participating airlines.

The glossy brochure containing colorful photographs and attractive day-by-day itineraries is the end result of many hours and weeks of work. A tremendous amount of time and effort goes into the planning of even a simple package. Dozens of factors must be carefully considered and weighed before a tour program is finalized.

When planning a motorcoach tour, the distance between overnight stops must not only be within comfortable driving range, but the routing itself must be of scenic interest. Rest and meal stops have to be provided for along the way, and when a tour bus arrives at a restaurant, seating must be available, and the food prepared ready for serving. In Europe especially, allowance must be made for heavy traffic, congested roads, and possible delays at border-crossing stations at the height of the tourist season. Overnight stops must be made in cities where there are adequate hotel accommodations meeting specific standards, and space available to accommodate the tour group.

Castles, museums and other tourist attractions may be closed on certain days of the week, so the itinerary must be planned to work around these and other contingencies. The motorcoach itself must also be cleaned, maintained, and serviced if it is to operate efficiently, so stops must be made in cities that have adequate service facilities. When the passengers have a free - day without any organized activities, arrangements are made to service the equipment.

Depending upon the areas visited, other transportation and sightseeing vehicles have to be arranged for months in advance. Local trains, lake steamers, ferries, cable-cars, cog-wheel railways, river steamers, gondolas, jaunting carts, hydrofoils, and many others may be incorporated into the imaginative and well-planned tour. A quality tour will also include other specialities of the areas visited: theatre in London or Stratford, a luau in Hawaii, fondue dinner in Switzerland, a visit to the Tivoli Gardens in Copenhagen, opera or concert tickets in Italy and Austria. Caberet and night club programs and elegant dinners featuring specialities of the area are also frequently included. The list is endless— but all have to be booked months ahead of time.

Motorcoach equipment is not usually owned by the tour company itself, but is leased from companies specializing in bus operation. It is the responsibility of the leasing company to supply the equipment along with a competent driver to operate it. A tour bus driver is entrusted with the safety of thousands of passengers during the course of the touring season. In order to qualify for the job, he must have logged thousands of accident-free miles behind the wheel. He must also have an unblemished record of dependability and reliability; be thoroughly familiar with highways, interesting scenic routes, and with traffic patterns in major cities; have a cheerful personality, and be able to get along well with a group of people. A good driver is an indispensable asset, and his skills and attitude are essential to the success of any bus tour.

On an escorted tour, the tour conductor is responsible for the successful operation of the tour. A tour group may have to live with a tour escort for weeks at a time, so it isn't any wonder that a company will exercise great care in recruiting the men and women to lead its tours. The job requires far more than geographical knowledge or the ability to speak several languages. Tour conductors must have friendly personalities and the ability to live in close proximity with a group of people for weeks at a time. More information on a tour conductor's function will be found later in this chapter.

Tour operators range in size from major travel organizations such as American Express, which operates tours to many parts of the world, to small independents specializing in tours to one or two specific geographical areas or resort locations. One company may specialize only in ski programs or Hawaiian tours. Other operators may offer comprehensive programs to Mexico or Las Vegas. Some operators are skilled in tours to Israel or the South Pacific.

Large companies with diversified tour programs require staffing all the year round, while some of the smaller operators run seasonal tours, and so contract with many of the non-managerial employees to work for a set period during the busy months. The products of tour operators are generally sold through retail travel agents or the airlines; the employees are in contact with others in the travel industry rather than with the general public.

Those who work for tour operators are considered specialists, and so it is usually not necessary for them to possess the same amount of knowledge as the retail travel agent. A travel agent must be familiar with tour operators and travel requirements for all parts of the world; tour operators may specialize in one or two specific areas, and their staff need only be experts in Hawaii, Mexico, Europe or other areas covered by the company's tours.

Some of the larger companies may have different departments, each with its own specialists in one particular area, and so become unusually knowledgeable in a region or continent.

BENEFITS AND EARNINGS

The benefits enjoyed by tour operator staff are similar to those of the retail travel agent—discount air travel and reduced tours or other land arrangements. However, not all tour operators are members of both airline conferences or of a steamship conference. A company specializing in tours to Hawaii or other domestic areas may hold the Air Traffic Conference appointment, but not the appointment of the International Air Transport Association; therefore its employees could only receive reduced-rate travel over the routes of the domestic airlines.

Depending upon the company, the beginning salary is usually slightly higher than in a retail travel agency, and salary increases come more rapidly. Opportunities for advancement are also good. A reservationist can work up to a supervisory position either in reservations or on the operations desk. It is also possible for a motivated employee to advance to a sales or management position, or perhaps even to a tour guide.

TRAINING AND QUALIFICATIONS

As with most positions in the travel industry, it is necessary to have a high school diploma, or its equivalent. College training, while not essential, is most helpful; a degree with a travel and tourism major is an excellent credential for those who want to work in this field. Most tour operators prefer applicants who have two to five years of business experience. If you are still a student, you should concentrate on business courses, and an accurate typing speed of at least 45 words per minute. Good geographic knowledge is also a necessity, and a foreign language will also be helpful should you wish to become a tour guide. Graduation from a travel training school offering airline-type reservation procedures and training will be an asset, though such courses are not essential; the employer will expect you to complete his own training course.

Employers seek applicants who are mature and friendly. Much business is conducted on the telephone, so good telephone skills are essential. You must be able to work quickly and accurately without close supervision after completing the training program.

SOME TYPICAL POSITIONS

The following are some of the typical positions found in tour operator companies. Not all positions will be available with each company since much depends upon the size of the operator and the internal organization and personnel distribution.

Reservationist This position is similar to other reservation jobs in the travel industry. Reservationists handle telephone calls from travel agents, airlines, and others who wish to book the company's tours. They check the availability of tours and confirm the reservation over the telephone. If the tour requested is fully booked, the reservationist offers to place the passengers on the waiting list or suggests an alternative tour. Reservationists may also prepare and mail confirmations to travel agents. They must be thoroughly familiar with the tour programs of their company since they may be asked questions about hotels, meals, departure times, flight schedules, and other components of the tour. Applicants for this job must have a pleasant personality, a good telephone voice, initiative, a liking for people and the ability to work without close supervision.

Operations Clerk They are assigned to any number of behind-the-scenes functions. Some clerks may perform back-up services for reservationists by typing confirmations of tour bookings and mailing them to the travel agent along with tour information. Clerks who are assigned to the air desk prepare flight manifests (passenger lists) for each tour or block of reserved seats, issue tickets, and control all air reservations used in conjunction with the tours. The control unit is responsible for recording the names of each passenger booked on each tour, and preparing weekly, or daily, tour status data indicating which tours are sold out and which are still available for booking. This information is then passed to all reservation and sales staff who can advise the travel agent of the availability status of each tour. Some clerks prepare tour rooming and membership lists which are then supplied to airlines, hotels, tour escorts, bus contractors, and other suppliers with which the tour operator has contracted for services. Other clerks prepare the final tour documents which are presented to the passenger. These include a wallet with the day-by-day itinerary, baggage tags, mailing information, hotels used on the tour, air schedules, check-in time at the airport or other departure point, and other general travel information needed.

Reservation Supervisor Many tour operators employ a supervisor who is in charge of all of the reservation staff and procedures. The supervisor ensures that all reservation positions are manned; schedules lunch, coffee breaks, and vacations; and interviews, hires, and trains new reservationists. The supervisor may also personally handle group bookings or the reservations of special accounts such as large travel agencies which are major sources of business. The reservation supervisor must also handle complaints and be able to solve other booking or staff problems when they arise. It may take a number of years for a reservationist to achieve a supervisory position since the supervisor must be familiar with all procedures and possible problems. In addition to job and product knowledge, it is necessary for a supervisor to possess leadership qualities and have the ability to work with people under pressure.

Operations Supervisor He is responsible for all functions and procedures outlined for operations clerk. This is frequently an administrative position requiring in-depth knowledge of all systems and procedures. The supervisor must be able to work under pressure and be able to correctly judge the anticipated work flow so that all functions are performed within a specific time. Some months require overtime hours in order to get the necessary documentation completed in adequate time before the departure of a tour. The operations supervisor must also be able to solve problems quickly and efficiently, know how to go about obtaining alternative air reservations in the event of schedule delays or cancellations, and have a good working relationship with other suppliers with whom his company does business. If he works for a large company, there may be unit leaders who report directly to him; unit leaders may be in charge of one particular function, such as the air desk, and oversee other clerks. Good business skills are required to be considered for this position, and most tour operators conduct on-the-job training programs.

Sales Representative It is the responsibility of the sales representative to schedule personal calls on travel agents in order to induce the agent to book the company's tours. The job is similar to sales representative positions in other segments of the travel industry. The sales representative must understand the workings and problems of the retail travel agent and be fully conversant with the tour products of his company. Many sales representatives assist certain key travel agents by helping with a special sales promotion or by giving a talk and showing a film to the agent's group. Sales representatives may be promoted from within their company if they show aptitude for sales functions.

Tour Guide The success of any escorted tour depends largely upon how well the tour guide performs his job. There is an art to being a good tour director, and this art is something a person is born with. Tour guides are professionals who come from all walks of life. The personal characteristics they all must possess include intelligence, warmth, cheerfulness, and a love for people.

Those who conduct tours for the major European tour companies are nearly all European residents and may come from any one of the European countries. They must have a tremendous knowledge of Europe—its culture, history, and sights. They must not only speak perfect English but be fluent in two or three other languages. They must be familiar with customs, border-crossing procedures, hotels, restaurants, museums, railroads, and other modes of transportation. It is almost impossible for an American to find employment as a European tour guide since few Americans have the depth of knowledge necessary. Tour operators much prefer to hire qualified Europeans who have lived their lives in Europe.

It is the responsibility of the tour guide to ensure smooth operation of the tour once it has departed from home. He handles all border-crossing procedures, customs formalities, baggage, hotel check-in, transfers, sightseeing tours and transportation. He assists tour members with shopping expeditions and recommends local shops where unusual merchandise and bargains can be obtained. He arranges for additional sightseeing tours and side trips, theater parties, colorful or gourmet restaurant meals, and other special attractions of interest to tourists.

Above all, a tour guide must have the ability to handle groups of people with courtesy and diplomacy. When delays or problems develop, it is the tour guide who usually bears the brunt of the complaints, so he must know how to deal with difficult tour members. Many tour guides are so skilled at their jobs and are so popular that they have developed a following of clients who plan their vacations around the schedule of their favorite tour guide.

It is almost impossible to become a European tour guide, but some companies do hire well-traveled Americans for a limited number of tours. While some of the senior tour guides are permanent employees of the company, the majority of guides are hired for the season. This could be April through September for Europe, November through March or April for tours to South America and the Southern Hemisphere, and November through March for Ski tours. Many American tour companies operating bus or train tours within the United States or Canada hire tour guides. Applicants for these jobs must demonstrate maturity and responsibility, have good geographic knowledge of the areas to be visited, and be able to work well with people. School teachers and others in people-oriented professions make excellent tour guides, and since they are on vacation from their regular jobs during the peak summer travel period they are usually available to tour companies.

Training for tour guides may be lengthy; a professional hired to conduct foreign tours may accompany three or four tours as an assistant before he is assigned to his own group. Those hired for summer work only must also go through a comprehensive training program before being assigned to their own tours.

Tour conductors are usually paid by the day and may also receive tips from satisfied members of the tour group.

OTHER POSITIONS

Group Coordinators are responsible for the processing of group movements. They handle special-interest groups booked by travel agents. These include religious tours, gourmet tours, gardening tours, study tours, or convention and meeting programs for trade associations or corporations. Accountants handle all of the bookkeeping functions of the company. They send invoices to travel agents and make sure that payment is received by the deadline; they pay the hotels, restaurants, airlines, railroads, bus companies and other suppliers used to provide services; they handle the payroll. Administrative Assistants are usually trained secretaries who work for the sales manager or other executives. In addition to their secretarial functions, they coordinate special familiarization tours for travel agents and set up meeting schedules for their bosses. Costers obtain all rates, and if in foreign currency, convert them to U.S. dollars. They determine the individual cost of each component part of an itinerary so that management can establish the selling price of a tour. Writers draft the tour brochure and write sales copy designed to induce the reader to book the tour; they may also be involved in brochure layout, design, and production. Telex Operators operate telex equipment used for fast communication between a sales office and the home office, or a European or overseas office. In a large company there may also be key-punch and computer personnel if reservations are computerized.

Chapter 8

TRAVEL AGENCIES

In 1841 Mr. Thomas Cook of London arranged, for a fee, a rail tour on behalf of a group of travelers. He thus unwittingly created what we recognize today as the retail travel agent.

Unlike the personnel of airlines, railroads, hotels and motels, cruise lines, and tour operators, all of whom can be considered specialists, the travel agent is the jack-of-all-trades of the industry. Those who work in a travel agency must know something about almost everything related to travel—not only travel in the United States and Canada, but throughout the entire world. Although it is impossible to learn everything there is to know about every tourist destination, the travel agent must know where to find the information.

A professional travel consultant must be prepared to handle a vacation trip to Hawaii, reserve a car in New York, help a client choose the right cabin on a cruise liner, and plan an independent tour of Europe, all on the same day. It takes many years of intensive on-the-job training and experience to become a competent and knowledgeable travel consultant, who is equally at home in the South Pacific as he is in Florida.

A travel agent has strong obligations to the clients, who depend upon him for professional counsel on travel arrangements which often cost thousands of dollars. Should the agent be inefficient, or incompetent in the performance of his job, it will be the clients who suffer. A badly managed trip cannot be returned for exchange or credit in the same manner as a defective appliance or other tangible product. The travel agent does, therefore, bear a tremendous responsibility for a high standard of professional performance and ethics.

An "agent" is one who is entrusted with the business of another. He represents airlines, tour companies, hotels, cruise lines and many other travel suppliers from many parts of the world. A travel agent is recognized by a large section of the traveling public as a professional in his field, and the one to whom they should visit for competent travel planning.

By 1979 the number of retail travel outlets in the United States and Canada reached 17,000. This proliferation clearly indicates that the travel agent's share of the travel market is substantial, and that he plays a significant role in the development and promotion of world tourism. The travel agency field has enjoyed unprecedented growth during the last two decades, and according to all current indicators, the trend will continue in the years ahead, though perhaps at a somewhat slower pace. Expansion and growth have created an acute shortage of skilled, competent, staff; a good counselor with two or three years experience would not normally have any trouble finding employment.

The majority of travel agencies are small, family-owned businesses; some offices belong to major corporations such as Thomas Cooks or American Express. Owning and operating a travel agency is a good outlet for the independent businessman. Hundreds of new agencies are started each year by investors who are new to the field, or by experienced travel agents who have worked for someone else but have always yearned for the independence of an agency of their own.

LEGAL REQUIREMENTS FOR TRAVEL AGENCIES

Some years ago, the airlines and steamship companies formed their own consortiums known as conferences and established a set of rules and a strict code of ethics to which they agreed to adhere. Such conferences were considered necessary to protect the interests of the member company and the traveling public.

In the United States, all domestic airlines belong to the Air Traffic Conference (ATC). Foreign airlines and American flag airlines operating on international routes are members of the International Air Transport Association (IATA).

In addition to establishing regulations for themselves, the conferences incorporated rules and standards for those they appointed as authorized agents (the retail travel agent). Before an agency can gain accreditation, it must meet specific requirements in order to maintain a supply of tickets on the premises and to earn commissions on the sale of tickets. The three major criteria a travel agency must meet are:

(1) The agency must be located on suitable business premises. (This requirement is designed to preclude someone from setting up an agency in a home or apartment.)

(2) The agency must be bonded and must meet specific minimum financial standards.

(3) There must be at least one employee who has had a minimum of two year's full-time employment with an accredited agency. (The owner can meet this requirement and qualify the agency only if he has had two year's experience. Otherwise he must hire someone who can meet the legal requirements.)

The owner(s) of a new travel agency are required to complete lengthy application forms which are then filed along with certified financial statements and the bond. After the applications have been received and verified for basic requirements, arrangements are made for a representative to inspect the premises to ensure that all requirements are met. If everything is in order, the agency is appointed and is issued with a supply of tickets and the identification plate of each airline.

HOW A TRAVEL AGENCY IS COMPENSATED

The price of a ticket or other tour product is the same no matter where it is actually purchased. When a travel agency sells a ticket, it receives a commission from the airline or other supplier involved. The percentage of commission varies and may change. However, in 1979, the commission earned on a straight point-to-point air ticket was 7 percent of the fare on domestic and averaged 8 percent on international, depending upon the airline. Cruise and steamship lines commission was 10 percent; hotels and motels, 10 percent; railroads, 10 percent; and car rentals, 10 percent. The basic commission on package and group tours is generally 11 percent, but because of incentives offered by most tour companies, an aggressive travel agent can earn as much as 17 percent, based upon sales volume.

The travel agent, like others in service businesses, is at a serious disadvantage compared to those who sell tangible products. In the retail field, the vendor usually has a choice of selling his goods at the suggested list price or of offering them at a discount. If his merchandise is not selling, he can declare a sale and accept a lower margin of profit—he has several options open to him to get things moving again. The travel agent has no control over prices and must conform to a set commission structure established by his principals. Unless his suppliers (many of whom are caught in a profit-squeeze themselves) decide to boost commissions, there is little an agent can do to increase his earnings.

Due to the increase of travel agencies, the field is now intensely competitive. How well a client is treated when he contacts an agency for information and literature may determine whether he buys his travel arrangements there or elsewhere. A travel sales counselor must be knowledgeable, well trained, confident, sincere, and a good salesperson.

IS THIS THE RIGHT CAREER FOR YOU?

The nature of this career is so diversified and the responsibilities so exacting, that many people are unsuited to it. You should examine your motivations, and at the same time, take stock of your qualifications and business experience. Ask yourself why you really want to be a travel agent. Do you envisage such a job as fun, or as a possible escape from the boring job you now hold? Have you traveled extensively, and therefore consider yourself an expert? (It is one thing to have traveled, another to have the ability to impart your knowledge to others in a business context.) Do you expect to participate in world-wide travel at bargain-basement prices, or perhaps cram as many free familiarization trips as possible into your schedule?

You may be under the impression that meeting a variety of different people and talking about exotic and romantic destinations is a pleasant way of spending a workday.

If these are your primary reasons for entering the travel field, you should deliberate most carefully before involving yourself, especially if you happen to be an adult considering a career change. You should choose a career not only for what you can get out of it, but also for what you can contribute to your employer and the industry, for the opportunity to learn new skills, experience personal growth and achievement, and become a member of a respected profession.

You should have an outgoing personality without being overly aggressive. Good conversational ability is also a decided asset, because the easier you can communicate, the more successful you will be. You must be quick to learn new skills, and possess a retentive and inquisitive mind—a busy employer will not have the time to cover the same training material more than once. Precision in your work is absolutely essential, and frequent errors will result in dismissal; no agency can afford to employ inaccurate and careless staff.

You must possess the ability to work under pressure, and be able to get along with your employer, staff, and clients. You must be prepared to work long, hard hours during peak periods. You must also have good sales ability, because in time it will be your responsibility to convince prospective clients that not only is yours the agency to handle the business, but that *you* are the individual to do it.

EDUCATION

A high school diploma, or its equivalent, is the minimum standard expected, and most employers prefer at least some business experience or college training. If you are still in high school, you should concentrate on business courses.

Since travel agents deal with English-speaking travelers, it is not necessary to study a language. A language will be of little use to you unless the agency employing you is known as ethnic, (the clientele is composed of foreign-speaking travelers). There are few such agencies outside of the large metropolitan areas, and those that are in existence usually prefer to hire nationals of the countries whose immigrants they serve. In Canada, however, both English and French are official languages, and fluency in each is required by many employers.

Few travel agencies can afford to retain expensive secretarial help, so you should learn to type as quickly and as accurately as possible. Most travel consultants are completely autonomous and type their own letters, itineraries, reservation requests, invoices, etc. Strive for an accurate speed of at least 40 words per minute by the time you graduate from high school or from a typing course. Precision is absolutely essential; an itinerary or ticket containing a transposed flight time, incorrect figure, or other error will result in endless trouble and inconvenience for a client, as well as his loss of confidence in the agency and perhaps his loss as a client.

You will also have to be familiar with tariffs, compute fares, convert foreign currency into dollar equivalents, and prepare invoices; so try to include business math and accounting in your education. Your other studies should include sales techniques, English (learn how to spell correctly), grammar, communication skills, current events, and public speaking.

One subject that all too many high school graduates, and for that matter some adults, are deficient in is geography. Good geographical knowledge is an asset no matter where you might be employed in the travel industry, but is an absolute necessity for anyone working in a travel agency. If you don't know where places are, how can you expect to carry on an intelligent conversation with a prospective client? Many employers will quiz job applicants on basic geographical knowledge. If you don't have it, don't expect to get the job, even though you are well qualified in other areas.

If geography is a neglected part of your education, don't despair. Ascertain if there are evening courses in geography available in your vicinity. There are several different types of geography, so be certain that any courses you are considering will cover what it is you need to learn. Talk with the instructor before you sign up; let him know your career goals, and then decide if the program will conform to your needs.

If you are unable to find a suitable course of instruction, then you will have to resort to a self-study program. Geographical knowledge required by the travel industry is relatively easy to acquire, providing you know how to go about it.

Check the shelves of your local library for atlases and travel books. There are a number of good atlases on the market; before investing in your own copy familiarize yourself with several. Get to know the capital cities of as many foreign countries as possible. Study the major tourist resort areas both at home and overseas.

Collecting tour brochures is also an excellent method of acquiring knowledge. These can be obtained by writing to the airlines and tour companies which advertise in the travel sections of major newspapers; by contacting government or state tourist offices; and by visiting a local travel agent and asking for obsolete literature. Every travel agent is inundated with vast quantitites of literature which becomes obsolete as new rates take effect. Nevertheless, the geographical and travel data remain unchanged, so any brochures you can collect will be of tremendous help. Many travel agents are only too pleased to get rid of their outdated brochures.

Pan American publishes two inexpensive guides, each of which is packed with valuable information. Quite apart from being used by knowing travelers, these guides are so useful that most travel agencies include copies in their reference libraries for use by their employees. They are indispensable study tools for anyone studying geography, or for anyone who wants to learn more about foreign and domestic tourist areas. *Pan Am's World Guide,* $6.95, contains complete travel facts on more than 140 countries. It includes climate, currency, major tourist areas and attractions, restaurants, hotels and motels, local customs, etc. *Guide to the USA,* $5.95, — contains comprehensive travel facts on all 50 states. Order both from: Pan Am, Box 248, JFK Airport Station, Jamaica, New York 11430.

TRAVEL BENEFITS

Although the reduced-rate travel privileges available to travel agents are not quite so liberal as those of the airline industry, the overall benefits are excellent and in many ways are superior to those of airline employees. Most people think that a travel agent enjoys almost unlimited world-wide travel at bargain-basement rates, and can hop on a plane any time he wishes. Such belief is pure fantasy of course, and in actual fact the agent is somewhat restricted. There are also strict rules relating to reduced-rate transportation.

The rules are most specific, and clearly state who is and who is not eligible to participate in these privileges. An employee is considered qualified if he or she has been on continuous full-time salary, or on a salary plus commission basis, for a twelve-month period, and devotes at least thirty-five hours-per-week to the sale of air transportation and related services. The employee must not be engaged in any other gainful employment, and must also participate in the normal benefits of the agency (workman's compensation, health insurance, unemployment compensation, social security).

The regulations exclude absentee owners (even though they own the agency they are not entitled to travel passes since they are not working in the agency), accountants, bookkeepers, secretaries, outside sales persons employed on commission, and several others.

If an agent abuses the travel privileges by including unauthorized names on eligibility lists, he is subject to disciplinary action. Both the Air Traffic Conference and the International Air Transport Association impose penalties on those agencies whose applications and records contain false information; they can suspend reduced-rate privileges for one or more years and institute proceedings for suspension of agency appointments. Both of the conferences are embarking upon stricter enforcement procedures, including unannounced, on-premises inspections and careful review of all agency records.

An eligible employee can travel at 25 percent of the published fare. Airlines retain the right to refuse applications for discount travel during peak periods, or on a highly traveled route. In contrast to airline employees, who usually travel "space available," the travel agent is treated in much the same manner as a passenger paying full fare and travels with confirmed reservations. Discounts are not extended to a spouse or other dependents.

Cruise and steamship lines are more liberal when it comes to reduced rates. Travel agents travel at 25 percent of the minimum rate of the ship. (Each cabin carries a different rate, depending upon its size and location on the ship.) The spouse fares much better on board ship, as discounts are extended to husbands or wives, and even immediate dependents.

Travel agency discounts are also available from tour operators (wholesalers), though the actual percentage or reduction from the published tour price may vary from one company to another. The volume of business an agency generates for an operator may be an influencing factor in determining the degree of reduction. Hotels, car rental companies, and other suppliers also offer reduced rates. Hotels will grant complementary accommodations to a good agent if they are not fully booked and have adequate space available.

FAMILIARIZATION TRIPS

Participation in familiarization trips (fam trips, as they are known in the industry) is limited to full-time salaried staff. Bona fide travel agency personnel have a wide range of tours and cruises from which to choose when they go on vacation, and fam trips go almost everywhere in the world that is frequented by tourists. These specially planned programs are operated by tour companies in conjunction with the airlines and are available to qualified staff at prices well below those of regular tours.

Most of the programs are designed to appeal to the tastes and needs of the travel agent, and follow a basic pattern of frequent hotel inspections, special cocktail parties, gourmet dinners featuring epicurean specialities of the area, and sightseeing tours to points of interest.

There are also those fam trips which are by invitation only, with all expenses absorbed by the airlines, hotels, and perhaps, local city or government tourist boards—all of whom consider the cost an advertising expense and an investment in future tourism for the area. This type of tour is a means of introducing selected travel agents to a new airplane, cruise liner, or hotel. It may coincide with the opening of a new resort or other tourist facility.

Participation in almost any fam trip is an experience in itself. It can be so strenuous that members return to home base in a state of exhaustion, and take a day or two to recuperate before returning to work.

All fam trips should be considered an educational experience; a means of providing agency staff with first-hand exposure to destinations and services so that these employees will be more useful, knowledgeable, and productive. Such programs should not be viewed as junkets, though unfortunately, some may end up as such. They are on-the-job training sessions and are an essential part of an agent's training, development, and growth. A good agency manager will recognize the value of such trips, and see to it that each employee participates in at least one each year to an area not previously visited.

BENEFITS

Benefits vary widely among agencies; most agencies allow two week's vacation after completion of one year of service. Some agencies grant additional vacation with increased service; that is, three weeks vacation after five years of employment and one calendar month after ten years with the agency. Vacation time is usually restricted to off-peak months; staff are required to be in the office during the prime selling season and the busiest travel periods.

Although many larger agencies pay the cost of medical and hospitalization insurance (or at least contribute to a portion of the premiums), many smaller agencies cannot afford to do so (or, because of limited size, are unable to qualify for group plans.) Many agency owners consider it the employee's responsibility to arrange for insurance coverage.

Few independent agencies offer any type of retirement program, though pension plans do exist in some of the larger corporations.

SALARY

Salaries in the travel agency field are low compared to many other industries; they are also at the bottom of the salary scale within the travel industry itself. Trainee salaries vary depending on geographical location and size of the agency. In larger cities, the monthly starting salary is between $450 and $550. In rural areas or small communities and suburbs, these figures may be somewhat lower.

Increases in salary are commensurate with the acquisition of new skills and knowledge. Most permanent, full-time staff are employed on a straight salary basis, though some counselors may also be offered an incentive in the form of commission based upon either their sales volume or earnings produced. Some agencies also have profit-sharing programs in which all employees may participate.

Beware of trade-off schemes in which a travel agent offers to teach you the business if you agree to work in his office without financial compensation. Even if you are desperate for a training opening with a travel agency, avoid trade-offs—they are unprofessional and illegal, since they violate the Wage and Hour laws.

HOURS

The basic work week for the employees of an agency located in the central area of a major metropolis varies from thirty-five to forty hours, Monday through Friday. In the suburbs and in smaller communities, Saturday is also an important business day, and most agencies remain open until about noon. Agencies may also be available to their clients one or two evenings during the course of the week, if other businesses in the area remain open. Agencies located in shopping centers and malls have erratic hours because they usually conform to the hours of the entire complex. If office hours are irregular, agency staff take turns in staggering their work hours.

During peak travel periods, it is frequently necessary to work much longer than the basic number of hours; the employee is then entitled to compensation at the legal overtime rate.

CAREER POTENTIAL

The training and knowledge you acquire through working in a travel agency will be most beneficial in the development of your future career. As you gain confidence and experience you should be prepared to gradually accept greater responsibilities and involve yourself in more intricate functions of the agency.

If you expect to manage an agency, you must be prepared to handle all types of transactions and solve innumerable problems as they arise. You could be able to manage a small agency after five or six years experience, perhaps sooner if you are unusually energetic and capable of assimilating knowledge quickly. Of course, in addition to the technical knowledge required, you must possess management and leadership qualities.

Retail travel agency experience will also be helpful if you decide to move to another segment of the travel industry. All things being considered, experience with a good travel agency is in excellent credential.

SOME TRAVEL AGENCY POSITIONS

The following are condensed job descriptions detailing some of the responsibilities of agency staff. You should remember that it may take years for a new trainee to achieve proficiency in handling the job. Many agencies are too small to have any marked division between functions, and all staff must be prepared to handle all types of business. In a larger agency, there will usually be a clear differentiation between job functions; each staff member then operates as a specialist.

Commercial Counselor Companies large and small have executives and salespeople who travel frequently, and many agency managers actively solicit this business. Most trips are domestic (within the U.S. or Canada) in nature, but depending upon the company products and services, international travel may also be involved. The agency will also get business from other company employees, who tend to book their personal travel arrangements through the agency handling the corporate business. It is an ideal arrangement for both company and agency. A representative of the company contacts the counselor at the agency; the agent then makes all of the reservations for airlines, hotels, rental cars, etc. The tickets and confirmations are then sent to the client, and at the end of the month a consolidated billing is issued to cover the cost of all travel arrangements made through the agency during the month.

The travel requirements of some companies are so large that it is necessary to assign more than one counselor to handle the account. Other accounts are much smaller, so that one person is quite capable of handling the travel arrangements for three or four different companies, in addition to her individual clients. Many counselors who handle commercial business consider the position a stepping-stone to a more responsible job—though admittedly, in an agency specializing in corporate accounts, there may be little room for advancement or diversification.

Commercial counselors must have the following skills: complete familiarization with the route structures, fares, reservations and ticketing procedures for all domestic airlines; knowledge of international ticketing and fares is helpful; familiarity with the names of hotels and motels (especially in the vicinity of major airports) and reservations procedures; knowledge of airport facilities, railroad (Amtrak) services, limousine services, car rentals, and important domestic resort areas; good typing and telephone skills; the ability to work accurately and quickly without close supervision; a working knowledge of the Official Airline Guide and other reference material.

Domestic Counselor Those who specialize in domestic travel sales must have all the skills of the commercial counselor, and be thoroughly familiar with all aspects of travel within the United States and Canada, Hawaii, Alaska, the Caribbean, Mexico and Central America.

The position requires an in-depth knowledge of all tour programs and tour packages, hotels and resorts, and airlines serving these areas. It is also necessary to be familiar with the major cruise lines and various cruise liners. The domestic counselor must also be aware of climates, currency, health requirements, and similar items.

International Counselor Five years of intensive on-the-job training is the minimum time required to train a good international specialist, and many veteran agency owners would argue that five years of training is grossly inadequate to qualify for the title. Much, of course, depends upon the individual.

The tourist world is enormous, and even after years of experience a counselor will be familiar with only a portion of it. The international counselor is responsible for the sale and handling of all travel arrangements outside of the areas that are a domestic counselor's responsibilities. This could mean that in the course of just one day an individual would plan a tour to Scandinavia, a hunting or camera safari to Africa, a cruise to the Mediterranean, and an individually planned tour to Japan at the height of the Cherry Blossom season.

Other Positions Depending upon the size and type of the agency and the ideas and concepts of the manager or owner, there may be other positions in the organizational chart. These might include ticketing clerk (usually a trainee position), group sales consultant, accounting and file clerk, and several others.

COMMISSIONED SALESPERSON

Selling travel products as a part-time commissioned salesperson rather than as a permanent salaried employee is a good method of breaking into the travel industry for those who have spare time on their hands, or desire other than full-time employment. Many travel agency managers recognize the value of someone directing business to the agency, and are only too pleased to enlist the services of a commissioned sales representative, since it costs little, if anything, in terms of salary dollars until sales are generated and business is flowing into the agency. An agent has little to lose and everything to gain, since commissions paid are directly related to actual sales settled on the books. For a would-be travel agent, selling travel on a commission basis is an excellent introduction to the travel industry, and can be a stepping-stone to full-time salaried employment. It may also be helpful in determining whether or not a permanent career with a travel agency is a suitable occupation for you.

Working as a commissioned sales representative is an ideal enterprise for those who do not have to depend upon a steady income. Those who have been successful in the field include housewives who wish to return to the business world, retirees anxious to supplement pension and Social Security benefits, retired service officers, teachers and university professors, ministers, and many others.

AFFILIATING WITH A TRAVEL AGENCY

If you believe that you are likely to be successful, contact several agencies in your area to determine how amenable the managers would be in giving you a trial. Only consider an agency that has all of the essential conference appointments, has been established for a number of years, and enjoys a good reputation in the community. Many managers of new agencies will jump at the opportunity of finding someone who can bring in business at a critical period of growth; but not all new agencies survive, and if you involve yourself with a marginal or losing operation you may suffer embarrassment and the loss of clients. Even your good friends may forsake you if they receive unprofessional treatment, or if you involve them with a dubious operation. Take plenty of time to investigate an agency before you make the final decision.

Once you have chosen an agency, if you are to operate in a businesslike manner, you should insist upon a letter of agreement which will protect both you and your employer. Such an agreement need not be drawn up by an attorney, in fact the simpler the terminology the better, but it should clearly state: (1) Your rate of commission in each category of business. (2) What you can expect from the agency in terms of office space, use of the telephone, stationery, etc. (3) A clear definition of exactly what constitutes "new business." (4) How long the agreement will run. (5) What you will receive in terms of training and support from the agency.

All too often problems arise because there is no written agreement, or the two principals either forget or disregard what was contracted for between them. While a letter of agreement will not always preclude misunderstandings, it will serve to clarify the terms and conditions under which you are employed. Since it is illegal to perform services without remuneration, most agencies pay their commissioned staff a weekly draw against future commissions. Such compensation is only nominal and sufficient to comply with the Wage and Hour laws.

EXPERIENCE AND QUALIFICATIONS

The prime requirements are good salesmanship, a certain amount of free time, and a circle of friends who possess both the financial means and the time to travel (they will be the nucleus of your clientele). While actual travel agency exposure is certainly not a prerequisite, you should at least be reasonably familiar with basic air fares, geography, major travel products, and the prime resort destinations popular with travelers in your area. Take the time to study tour literature so you can carry on intelligent conversations with prospective clients. It will also be helpful if you have the ability to write simple air tickets. This basic knowledge can be acquired by attending a good trade school specializing in comprehensive travel agency techniques and procedures. While a classroom-type course is preferable, don't overlook a correspondence course should this be the only alternative available to you. Before you sign up, assure yourself that the course covers ticketing and other travel agency procedures. Once you get started with an agency there are any number of specialized tariff and ticketing courses offered by major airlines for agency personnel.

EARNING POTENTIAL

Though you cannot expect to earn the same income as a full-time travel consultant, your income can be substantial if you devote sufficient time to actively soliciting and promoting business.

The rate of compensation varies considerably from one agency or geographical location to another; nevertheless, there are industry standards you can use as guidelines in your negotiations with an agency manager. If all you are expected to do is to introduce your clients, after which a skilled consultant takes over, then you can expect to earn about 40 percent of the commission paid to the agency by the supplier. For example, if you sell a Grand Tour of Europe at a total cost of $1,200, and the agency earns 10 percent ($120), then your portion would amount to $48, with $72 accruing to the agency. On the other hand, if you have solid experience, a good following of clients, and possess the technical knowledge to handle all or most of the reservations, ticketing, and other detailed work yourself, then you could expect to earn 50 percent of the agency commission. Take note that these are only examples of industry policies, and that there are other arrangements which are also quite common.

You may also have to engage in one or two negotiating sessions. If you are inexperienced, yet give the appearance that you may be successful, you still have precious little with which to bargain. Until you have proven your sales ability, you may have to accept an earning schedule that is less desirable than you would have wished.

Housekeepers at this Holiday Inn check the cleanliness of their guests' rooms.

Eastern Airlines flight attendant trainees enjoy their classes in makeup application.

Locomotive engineers are among the most skilled employees on the railroad. (Santa Fe photo)

A mechanic ensures a trouble-free flight for this American Airlines DC-10.

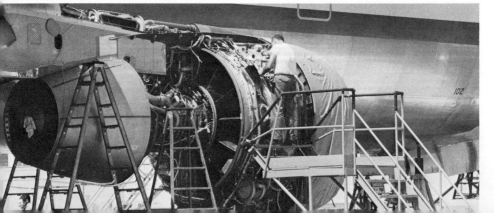

What, Saturday night again?!

Welcome aboard for cross-country guests of Greyhound Lines.

An air traffic controller monitors the air routes at a traffic control center.

Engineers monitor gauges in an engine room of a modern freighter. (NMU Pilot photo).

Emily Howell, the first female captain of a scheduled American airline. (Frontier Airlines photo).

"A little more to the right." On-the-job training at the Harry Lundeberg School of Seamanship.

It's back to school for these Air Canada flight attendant trainees.

Emergency evacuation procedures can be fun — in a practice run.

A Santa Fe foreman checks the day's work schedule.

"Serve from the left, clear from the right." Training restaurant personnel for Holiday Inns.

Car rental agents arrange transportation for busy travelers.

The captain, first officer and flight engineer perform the preflight check. (UAL photo).

Feeding millions of passengers starts in the flight kitchen. (UAL photo).

The switchman depends on his switchstand to keep cars routed properly in this Santa Fe yard.

A TWA ground hostess helps passengers with final preparations.

The chief chef of Delta Line's S.S. SANTA MAGDALENA displays his culinary artistry.

The yardmaster of this computer-controlled Santa Fe freight yard monitors operations from his desk.

Flight attendants are trained to give friendly, courteous service. (Delta Airlines photo).

"Hey, over here!" Ground operations personnel guide pilots to parking ramps. (Continental Airlines photo).

Reservationists book rooms around the world at a Holiday Inn reservation center.

Chapter 9

FOOD SERVICE

According to a survey conducted by the National Restaurant Association, the foodservice industry employs more than 8 million persons in restaurants of all types, fast food places, bars, hotels, factory and school cafeterias, hospitals, airline services, catering firms, etc. The foodservice industry is the Nation's largest employer after health services, and offers an enormous range of jobs, both full- and part-time, and for all ages.

The type of food and service a restaurant offers varies with its size and location, as well as with the type of customers it seeks to attract. Fast-food restaurants and cafeterias are characterized by rapid service and inexpensive meals. Steak houses, seafood restaurants, and pizzerias consider the quality of their speciality essential to attracting and keeping customers. On the other end of the scale, there are those restaurants that cater to those who desire to enjoy a leisurely meal in relaxed and elegant surroundings; their menus frequently include house specialities, unusual dishes, and an extensive wine cellar offering the customer a choice of a wide variety of domestic and imported wines. Somewhere between the extremes are ethnic restaurants specializing in the preparation of foods and culinary dishes of many foreign lands: Mexican, French, German, Japanese, Chinese, Italian, Greek, Indian, Scandinavian, Polish, Polynesian and others.

The reputation of a restaurant depends not only upon the quality of the food and how it is prepared, but also upon the standards of service rendered by its employees. A restaurant may have attractive decor, an excellent menu offering a variety of dishes, and well-prepared food; but if the waiters are slow or disinterested, or the food arrives cold at the table, then the best of restaurants can quickly lose its prestige and its customers. The men and women who come into personal contact with the customer—hostess, waiter, bus boy, wine waiter—make a significant contribution to a restaurant's reputation and success.

The food-service industry incorporates all establishments serving food. These include hospitals, schools and colleges, construction camps, retirement homes, institutions, catering establishments, mobile kitchens, employee cafeterias, executive dining rooms, vending operations, military feeding, airlines, steamships and railroads, and others.

EMPLOYMENT OUTLOOK

It is expected that employment in the food service industry will increase through the mid-1980's. In addition to the openings arising from normal anticipated employment growth, thousands of openings are expected each year just to cover replacements due to retirements, death, or departure from the industry for other reasons.

The majority of openings will be for waiters and kitchen helpers. These workers make up a large segment of all restaurant employees. Employment opportunities are also expected to be favorable for skilled cooks, assistant cooks, and salaried restaurant managers.

Population growth, rising personal incomes, and a greater amount of leisure time are expected to contribute to a growing demand for restaurant services. Increasing worker productivity, however, will prevent employment from growing as rapidly as the demands for restaurant services. Restaurants have become more efficient as fast-food service counters have become more popular, and as management has centralized the purchase of food supplies, introduced self-service, and used pre-cut meats and modern equipment. Many restaurants now use frozen entrees in individual portions, which require less time to prepare than do fresh foods.

PERSONAL CHARACTERISTICS

The National Restaurant Association states that: "The industry needs candidates who are friendly, energetic and who prefer to work as part of a group rather than alone. They must be able to receive strong personal gratification from service to people. They must take pride in getting along and satisfying people."

The NRA lists the following characteristics for those considering a career in food service:

(1) Good work habits, including punctuality and businesslike conduct, personal pride in dress and deportment.

(2) Willingness to work hard; ambition to learn; desire to invest time, thought, and energy in career advancement.

(3) The ability to adjust, to get along. A positive reaction to constructive criticism. The ability to take direction.

(4) Intelligence. The food-service industry offers a wide variety of jobs requiring different skills, different training, different levels of intelligence. Yet each makes a positive contribution to the success of the operation.

(5) Health and physical stamina. The responsibility of pleasing people and the demands of a kitchen call for good physical and mental resources. Hours are varied. Pressure is sometimes heavy.

YOUR EDUCATION AND TRAINING

The skills and experience needed vary from one occupation to another. Many jobs require no special training or experience, while others require a degree or actual work experience. The more training and education you have, the more likely you are to begin your career at a higher level of income and responsibility.

The following will give you an idea of the various types of training and available positions. This information is from NRA sources.

High school graduates For those who want to get started immediately upon graduation from high school, there are usually an adequate number of positions as waitresses, bus boys (and girls), kitchen helpers, dishwashers, counter and fountain workers. Newly hired employees are generally trained on the job. Kitchen workers, for example, may be taught to operate a lettuce shredder and shown how to make salads, take orders from customers, and serve food in a courteous and efficient manner. In smaller restaurants, the training is performed by the more experienced employees; in larger restaurants and chain operations there may be formal training programs.

As an individual gains experience and skills he can be promoted quickly to better paying jobs, and may advance to supervisory or management positions such as waiter-captain, hostess, dining room manager, maitre d'hotel and manager.

There are now many high schools offering food-service courses, either in conjunction with area vocational centers, or as part of occupational programs. These courses are designed to qualify those who have no intention of pursuing further education, or as an advance background of instruction in food preparation for those who desire to continue their education and whose goal is food-service supervision or management.

Vocational schools Although a diploma from a vocational school will not qualify someone to step into an immediate management position, such a course will help his progress greatly. Through this type of training, the student will be given a theoretical, and in many cases, a practical background, and an excellent preparatory base from which to begin a career.

Vocational courses provide special training for various types of food service positions. These are a combination of lectures and classroom discussions which are backed up by on-the-job training. Some of the trades taught in vocational courses are cook, assistant cook, vegetable cook, cold-meat cook, soup-and-sauce cook, roast-and-broil cook, fry cook, baker, pastry cook, and butcher.

Many courses also offer special work in menu planning, dining room service, food-service standards, restaurant accounting and restaurant public-relations.

Depending upon the program, these courses may last from three months to three years. Many public school systems are now offering courses in food services for those at the high-school level. There are also evening courses available.

Junior college training The junior college program is designed to prepare students for technical and administrative responsibilities in food service. Such colleges offer courses of study in food service leading to an associate degree and prepare graduates to perform effectively and quickly in supervisory and administrative capacities. Graduates qualify for beginning managerial and supervisory positions in restaurants and the food-service operations of clubs, hotels, colleges, department stores, industrial plants, institutions, hospitals, and schools.

The two-year program includes study in such areas as food preparation, menu planning, food purchasing and storage, equipment purchasing and layout, equipment operation, personnel management, job analysis, food standards and sanitation, diet therapy, catering, beverage control, food cost-accounting and record keeping. Also included are such general courses as psychology, economics, chemistry and nutrition. Classes, laboratory work, and practical experience combined with part-time work in food service are part of the program.

While many jobs exist for those who complete junior college training, many graduates decide to transfer credits to a four-year college for more advanced work.

Four-year college programs According to the National Institute for the Foodservice Industry, the demand for food-service management graduates of four-year colleges is great. One survey showed that the average four-year college graduate had a choice of about seven management level and management training job offers. The type of jobs offered to college graduates can be divided into eleven categories: multi-unit restaurants—20 percent; institutional feeding operations—15 percent; hospital food service and school lunch service—about 12.5 percent each. Other categories are hotel administration, industrial feeding, institutional sales and other positions with food manufacturing companies, club management, military service as commissioned officers in food service, family businesses, and inflight feeding.

The work and study programs offering a degree in restaurant, hotel, and institutional management are the best educational preparations for food-service administration. Graduates receive B.A. or B.S. degrees in restaurant administration, hotel administration, institutional management, dietetics, home economics or business administration. Graduate work is also available.

The undergraduate programs usually include preliminary and advanced courses in food preparation, specialized courses in restaurant accounting, catering, management, and sanitation. General courses such as economics, law, marketing, finance, and cost control are also part of the curriculum.

Students in food service are usually required to work three summers in restaurant or hotel jobs ranging from bus boy, food checker, and waiter to dining-room captain and assistant restaurant manager. Such summer employment frequently leads to a permanent position after graduation.

Food-service administration graduates are qualified for such positions as assistant manager, manager, food-production supervisor, purchasing agent, food cost-accountant, food-service director, director of recipe development, personnel director, sales manager, and banquet manager.

SOME TYPICAL FOOD SERVICE POSITIONS

Cooks and Chefs There were about 1,100,000 cooks and chefs employed in 1979. The reputation for serving fine food is an asset to any restaurant, and many chefs have earned fame for themselves and the restaurants where they are employed.

A cook's work depends partly on the size of the restaurant. Many smaller restaurants offer limited menus and the dishes are relatively easy to prepare. One cook usually prepares all of the food with the aid of a short order cook and perhaps one or two helpers.

Larger restaurants usually have more varied menus. In addition to the head cook, there may be several assistant cooks and many kitchen helpers. Each cook usually has a specific assignment which is reflected in his job title—pastry, fry, or sauce cook, for example.

In a hotel containing several restaurants and banquet rooms, the executive chef is responsible for the menus and preparation of all food. He is assisted by a head cook in each restaurant.

Most cooks acquire their skills on the job while employed as kitchen helpers. They gradually work up through the ranks until they have enough experience and ability to assume the senior position. However, it is becoming more common for training to begin in high school. Many of the larger hotels and restaurants also have their own training programs.

Inexperienced workers can qualify as assistants and fry cooks after several months of on the job training. Acquiring all of the skills needed as a head cook or chef in a fine restaurant may take years.

Those who have had courses in restaurant cooking will have an advantage when applying for jobs in larger restaurants and hotels, where hiring standards are usually high. Many vocational programs in both public and private high schools offer appropriate training to students. Other courses, ranging from a few months to two years or more, and open in some cases only to high school graduates, are given under the guidance of restaurant associations, hotel management groups, trade unions, and technical schools and colleges. The military is also a good source of training and experience in food-service work.

While curricula may vary widely, students usually spend most of their time learning to prepare food through actual practice in well-equipped kitchens. The students learn to bake, broil, and otherwise prepare food, and to use and care for kitchen equipment. They also may be taught to select and store food, plan menus, and buy food supplies in quantity. Hotel and restaurant sanitation and public health rules are also covered.

Cleanliness, the ability to work under pressure during busy periods, physical stamina, and a keen sense of smell and taste are among the most important qualifications needed for this career. A cook in a supervisory position must not only be able to organize and direct kitchen operations, he must also be a fine cook able to step in and solve problems at a moment's notice.

All cooks and chefs, in fact, anyone who works in food preparation, must be certified as being free of any communicable disease in order to be able to work. Most states require a health certificate.

Employment in this field is expected to increase faster than average for all occupations through the mid-1980's. In addition to employment growth, thousands of job openings will arise annually from the need to replace experienced workers who retire, die, or transfer to other occupations.

The demand for cooks and chefs will increase as the population grows and people spend more money on eating outside of the home. Smaller restaurants and other eating establishments having simple food preparation will provide the greatest number of entry-level positions for cooks, though beginners who have had vocational training may find jobs available in hotels and restaurants where foods are prepared more elaborately.

Waiters and Waitresses Waiters and waitresses take customers' orders, serve food and beverages, make out checks, and sometimes take payments. They may also have duties other than waiting on tables. In small restaurants, they may combine waiting on tables with counter service, preparing sandwiches, and working at the cash register. In larger restaurants, waiters and waitresses serve the food at a more leisurely pace and offer more personal attention to their customers.

About 1,300,000 waiters and waitresses were employed in 1979. More than half of them worked part-time. Some worked in hotels, colleges, and factories that have restaurant facilities. Jobs are located throughout the country, but are most plentiful in the larger cities and tourist areas. Many vacation resorts offer seasonal employment, and some waiters and waitresses alternate between summer and winter resorts.

Most employers prefer to hire applicants who have had at least two or three years of high school.

A neat appearance, an even disposition, and stamina are essential qualifications. Since they have to add up checks, they should also be good at arithmetic, and in some of the famous restaurants or those frequented by foreign guests, a second language is helpful.

Most waiters and waitresses are trained on the job by experienced employees, though some public and private schools offer training.

In many smaller establishments, opportunities for advancement are limited, and it may be necessary to transfer to a larger restaurant to gain an increase in earnings and better advancement possibilities. Promotion to cashier, hostess, maitre d'hotel, and headwaiter is possible.

Job openings are expected to be plentiful in the years ahead. Turnover is particularly high among part-time workers. For many employed in this field, tips are a major source of income and are larger than the hourly wages. Tips generally average between 10 and 20 percent of the check.

Bartenders More than 270,000 bartenders are employed in hotels, bars, taverns, private clubs, and restaurants. A growing number of bartenders are women. About one-third were women in 1979, compared to only one-tenth in 1960.

Cocktails are an important part of the restaurant business, and it takes time to learn how to properly mix and serve hundreds of different drinks and combinations. Many people have their own preferences for certain cocktail recipes, and bartenders are often asked to mix drinks to suit a customer's taste. In addition to serving mixed drinks, bartenders also serve wine, draft or bottled beer, and a wide variety of non-alcoholic beverages.

Bartenders are also responsible for ordering and maintaining adequate supplies of liquor, mixes, and other bar supplies.

In large restaurants or hotels, the bartender is usually assisted by a helper. Helpers keep the bar supplied with liquor, mixes, and ice. They stock refrigerators with wine and beer, connect kegs of beer to the taps, and keep the bar area clean. They may also wash glasses.

Most bartenders learn their trade on the job, or start off as helpers. Those who wish to become bartenders can get good experience by working as bartender helpers, dining room attendants, waiters or waitresses. Some private schools offer short courses in bartending that include instruction on state and local laws and regulations, cocktail recipes, attire and conduct.

Bartenders should have pleasant personalities because they deal with the public. They need physical stamina, since they stand most of the time. They may also have to lift heavy cases and kegs.

In most states, bartenders must be at least twenty-one years of age, but many employers prefer those who are twenty-five or older. Some states require bartenders to have health certificates indicating that they are free from any contagious disease. In some instances they must be bonded.

Small restaurants, neighborhood bars, and resorts usually offer a beginner the best opportunities for entry-level positions. After gaining experience, a bartender can move to a larger restaurant or cocktail lounge where the earnings may be higher and where there may be better opportunities for promotion. Advancement to head bartender, wine steward, or beverage manager is possible with larger organizations.

OTHER MANAGEMENT AND SPECIAL POSITIONS

Restaurant Manager Coordinates entire operation of restaurant for efficient, courteous food service. May deal with supervisory staff or in smaller organizations, work with kitchen and dining room personnel directly. Should be familiar with all jobs in restaurant.

Assistant Manager An understudy to manager. Usually assumes responsibility for overall operation and also has certain areas of specific responsibility. Takes over completely when manager is not present.

Food Production Manager Has charge of all food preparation. Must have knowledge of food preparation and appreciation of good food standards. Must be proficient in cost control. Supervises kitchen staff so he must know how to work with and direct people.

Chain Executive This position is found in large chain operations. It is largely administrative work and usually does not involve direct contact with food preparation and service. A thorough knowledge of food service is needed.

Personnel Director This position is found in large chain operations, large restaurants, and large hotels and motels. May be responsible for hiring and training employees, handling employee meetings, and promoting good employee relationships.

Menu Maker In large restaurants, one person may spend a considerable amount of time planning menus. Usually such a person must have a degree in dietetics or foods and nutrition. The job may also be handled by the food-production manager or chef.

Merchandising Supervisor This is a relatively new position found in some of the larger restaurants and chains. Requires skill in planning menu designs, seasonal displays, advertising, and creating new ideas to help attract customers.

Director of Recipe Development Some of the large restaurants and chain operations employ college-trained men and women to work in testing kitchens, creating new recipes to feature on menus. Requires creative ability and a thorough knowledge of food preparation.

Cashier Receives payment for meals, either from the customer or from the waiter or waitress. Must be accurate and fast in making change. May do some tabulating and record-keeping. May also handle customer complaints. Must be tactful and gracious.

Food Checker In cafeteria, itemizes and totals customers' orders. In restaurant dining room, may check food as it leaves the kitchen and tabulate each individual portion of food.

Pastry Chef and Baker Bakes cakes, cookies, pies and other pastry desserts. Bakes bread and rolls. Must plan so that fresh bread will be ready as needed. In some restaurants, skill in cake decoration is required.

Pantry Supervisor Supervises salad, sandwich, and beverage workers. Must know how to set up attractive food arrangements. Requisitions supplies as needed. May also oversee cleaning staff. This job may also be the responsibility of the chef or manager.

Foodservice Supervisor May have the title of dining-room supervisor, head waiter or waitress, or counter supervisor. May coordinate dining-room activities, train and supervise waiters, waitresses, and bus boys. Should have leadership qualities and the ability to handle people.

Purchasing Agent and Storeroom Supervisor May order, receive, inspect, and store all food and distribute it to different departments as requisitioned. Keeps a running inventory. Must keep posted on market prices. These jobs may also be the responsibility of the manager or chef.

Butcher Cuts, trims, and prepares meats to fill orders of cook. Must be expert at cutting carcasses. Stores meat. May also be poultry and fish butcher. This job may also be the responsibility of the meat cook.

OTHER POSITIONS

Beverage Worker Prepares hot beverages—usually coffee, tea, or hot chocolate. May assist in the pantry and help others in the kitchen during rush periods. Good beginner's job.

Bus Boy or Girl Clears tables and may reset with fresh linens and clean silver. Fills the water glasses and empties the ash trays. Helps keep the dining room clean. This is a good way to start learning the restaurant business.

Hostess Greets people when they enter the restaurant and escorts them to a table and presents the menus. Must be familiar with the duties of a waitress. Inspects the dining room for order and cleanliness. The job requires tact and a pleasant personality.

Kitchen Helper Assists the cooks and chefs by performing a variety of tasks under supervision. May do measuring, mixing, washing, and chopping vegetables and salad ingredients. This is an excellent starting position for someone who wants to learn the food preparation aspect of the business.

Dishwasher Operates special machines that clean silverware and dishes quickly and efficiently. Also has to scrub large pots and pans by hand. Additionally, cleans refrigerators, ovens, and other kitchen equipment. An ideal starting position for someone who is still in high school.

Sandwich Maker Makes sandwiches as orders come in. Prepares fillings and dressings. Must work quickly and carefully. Skills learned will help the person advance to a better position later.

Soda Fountain Worker Prepares the soft drinks and ice-cream dishes. In some places, may serve customers and prepare toast and sandwiches.

SOME USEFUL ADDRESSES

American Culinary Federation
P.O. Box 53
Hyde Park, New York 12538

The Educational Institute of the American Hotel & Motel Association
1407 South Harrison Road
East Lansing, Michigan 48823

National Institute for the Foodservice Industry
20 North Wacker Drive
Chicago, Illinois 60606

Council on Hotel, Restaurant and Institutional Education
11 Koger Executive Center
Norfolk, Virginia 23502

Chapter 10

HOTELS AND MOTELS

The occupation of innkeeper is an honorable one, and has been a respected profession ever since man became mobile and needed a place to rest and refresh himself when away from home. The first inns were built along trade and caravan routes and are mentioned in the Bible. As more and more of the world came under the influence of Rome, inns were needed to accommodate travelers traveling from one point to another within an Empire that stretched from Britain to Africa, and from Spain to Palestine. The monasteries were the hotels and inns of the Middle Ages, although guests did not pay for their accommodations. The guesthouse came under the direct supervision of the hosteller, whose responsibility it was to make sure that all travelers were made welcome, that the guest house itself was adequately furnished and kept clean, and that the food served was wholesome and properly cooked.

Today, in the United States, the hospitality industry is one of the largest in the nation and employs more than 900,000 men and women. The industry is growing each year, and as it expands the need for qualified employees increases proportionately. All current indicators point to the fact that the industry will offer excellent career opportunities in the years ahead.

Hotels range in size from those with only a few rooms and one person staffing the front desk, to establishments with more than 1,000 rooms and several hundred employees. The term "hotel" usually refers to a business that caters to business and convention travelers, or accommodates vacationers, if it is located in a major resort area. "Motel" or "motor hotel" means that the establishment caters to those traveling by car. They are nearly always accessible to motorists, and many are in close proximity to major highways. Some motels offer little more than basic services for those who want clean and comfortable accommodations for a one-night stay. Hotels and motels in resort areas often have recreational facilities such as golf courses, tennis courts, and swimming pools. Nearly all hotels and many motels offer a variety of conveniences for their guest. Motels usually have simple coffee shops, while hotels often have several restaurants and may offer live entertainment in one of them at night. Large hotels also may have newstands, barber and beauty shops, laundry and valet service, and theater and airline ticket counters. "Resorts" are usually in the luxury category and are often located some distance away from town. They are self-contained in that they offer their guests a variety of on-premises facilities. Apart from all of the services found in any good hotel, resorts offer such attractions as golf, swimming, sailing, tennis, horseback riding, hiking, scuba diving, and a host of other organized activities. Because of the variety of activities, the guests can enjoy a one- or two-week stay without ever leaving the premises.

HOTEL DEPARTMENTS

Front office When a guest enters the establishment, one of the first representatives he meets will be at the front desk. For this reason, employers exercise great care when hiring for front desk positions. Those who man the front desk register incoming guests, provide them with room keys, handle their mail, and check them out when they leave. Positions at the front desk include the front office manager, assistant manager, room clerk, reservation clerk, information clerk, telephone operator, and one or two others. This is about the best place to learn about the lodging industry and is considered an essential stepping stone to management positions

Service department Members of this department greet guests at the door, help them with their baggage, and after they have registered at the front desk, show them to their rooms. Positions include doorman, bellman, bell captain, elevator operator, lobby porter, checkroom attendant, and the supervisor of service. Many employees in this group are in close contact with guests and are in an excellent position to earn tips.

Accounting department This department is responsible for all of the fiscal operations of the hotel. The people who work here bill the guests, pay the wages of the employees, pay the bills for purchases made, and prepare accounting reports. In charge is usually the chief accountant or auditor. Assisting is an assistant auditor, night auditor, general cashier, restaurant and office cashiers, and perhaps a bookkeeper, and general clerks.

Food service According to the American Hotel and Motel Association, many of the best opportunities for advancement are in the food service and preparation departments.

The executive chef presides over all food preparation. He must be an expert in the culinary arts and have the ability to direct others. In a large hotel, or resort with several dining and banquet rooms, he will have an army of highly skilled people to help him. Such specialists would include a first assistant cook, a second cook, fry cook, vegetable cook, pastry chef, baker, butcher, pantry supervisor, and steward. Additionally, there may be a number of kitchen helpers whose job it is to assist the more experienced staff. There may also be a dietician supervising the balance of meals and checkers who inspect each dish before it is served to a guest.

After the food has been prepared, it is the responsibility of the food service department to see that it is served properly. In charge of this operation is the food and beverage director. Under him comes the catering manager, maitre d'hotel, headwaiter, bartender, waiters and waitresses, wine steward, busboys and busgirls. If there are several restaurants, each one has its own staff, and there may also be a special department to serve meals to guests in their rooms.

Many top chefs and maitres d'hotel learned their skills in Europe. Many American hotels now recognize the importance of highly skilled chefs who can command high salaries. The reputation of good food rests upon the skills of the chef, and any number of opportunities are open to those who have demonstrated above average skills in food preparation.

Housekeeping The executive housekeeper is in charge of all housekeeping functions. These include making up the rooms each day; changing linens and towels; cleaning, polishing floors and furniture; changing light bulbs, and inspecting and repairing furniture and curtains. She must also hire, train, and supervise the maids, housemen, seamstresses, linen room attendants, repairmen, carpenters, and others who work in this department. In larger hotels, interior decorating and re-upholstering may also be the responsibility of the executive housekeeper.

Other Departments The administration department includes the resident and general manager of the hotel. The sales manager may come under this department, or if the hotel is large enough, he may have his own department with one or two sales representatives to help him. The maintenance department is responsible for heating and air conditioning units, kitchen and laundry machinery, painting, and several other functions. This means that skilled plumbers, electricians, and other craftsmen must be employed. The valet department takes care of the cleaning, repair, and pressing of guest's clothes.

In many cases, job applicants must have a skilled trade or experience in a similar position before they are hired.

EMPLOYMENT OUTLOOK

According to the U.S. Department of Labor, employment in the hospitality industry is expected to grow through the mid-1980's. During this period many new hotels and motels are expected to be built to take advantage of interstate highway systems and resort locations.

Most of the anticipated employment growth will result from the need to staff new hotels and motels, but in addition to job openings resulting from expansion of the industry thousands of workers will be required each year to replace those who retire or leave the industry. Employment is expected to increase in both luxury and economy motels. Employment may decline, however, in older hotels or those unable to modernize; both are likely to experience low occupancy rates that may force them to reduce costs by eliminating some services and employees.

EDUCATION

High school graduates As a high school graduate, you could expect to be employed in one of a number of entry level positions. These would include bellman, houseman, maid, steward, linen room attendant, busboy or busgirl, waiter or waitress. In many cases, part-time employment can be arranged while you are still in school.

Promotion to a position of greater responsibility will depend on how well you perform your job, and whether or not you are willing to supplement on-the-job practical experience with vocational courses. If you expect to make any progress at all you will have to invest some time and perhaps a little money in additional training.

Junior college graduates Those who earn an associate degree in hotel and restaurant management will find a wide range of jobs open to them. The junior college programs are generally oriented to the technical or supervisory aspects of the job and will prepare students to perform effectively in supervisory and administrative capacities.

University graduates Those who graduate from a four-year degree course in hotel and restaurant administration are prepared for many positions in the hospitality field. They can expect to begin their careers as assistant managers in small hotels and motels, or in assistant managerial and supervisory positions in larger establishments. They may also start in the food and beverage department, or in sales. Several larger chains offer executive training programs to college graduates. The trainee spends a specific amount of time in several different departments so that he understands the workings of each.

Vocational schools The Educational Institute of the American Hotel and Motel Association is a non-profit establishment that is approved and supported by the industry. It offers extensive home-study courses and grants a diploma upon successful completion of ten required courses. Courses offered include introduction to hotel and motel management, front office procedures, hospitality industry accounting, sanitation, food and beverage purchasing, food production principles, food and beverage controls, and marketing of hospitality services.

Additional information, including tuition costs, can be obtained from the institute at 1407 S. Harrison, Michigan State University, East Lansing, Michigan 48823.

SOME TYPICAL HOTEL AND MOTEL POSITIONS

Hotel and motel managers Managers are responsible for the efficient and profitable operation of the hotel. They determine room rates; direct the operation of the kitchen, dining and banquet rooms; and manage the housekeeping, accounting and maintenance departments. They also have to solve any problems that may arise with guests and employees.

Those managers who run small hotels may do much of the front office and clerical work themselves, checking in guests, assigning rooms, and taking reservations.

The general manager of a large hotel or motel has assistants who are each responsible for running one particular facet of the hotel. Each assistant or supervisor reports to the general manager. For example, the front office manager is responsible for all staff and functions at the front office; the banquet manager oversees all special food services; the restaurant manager looks after the restaurants and bars; the executive housekeeper takes care of all housekeeping functions; the sales manager is responsible for advertising and marketing campaigns necessary to generate business for the hotel.

The quickest route to the manager's office is through college. Most employers believe that acquiring a degree in hotel and restaurant administration is the best education preparation.

A college program in hotel management usually includes courses in hotel administration, accounting, economics, food service management, maintenance, and engineering. Most colleges require that their undergraduate students work in hotels and restaurants during summer vacations.

Managers must possess initiative, self-discipline, and be able to organize work and direct others. They must be able to concentrate on details, deal with people, and solve problems.

Many large hotels, and hotel and motel chains, have special on-the-job management training programs for college graduates. Trainees rotate among various different departments to acquire a thorough knowledge of all operations. Promotion is earned, and advancement to responsible positions is governed by how well a person performs in his present job.

Salaries of hotel managers and assistants vary greatly depending upon the hotel and the responsibilities involved. University graduates can expect to start at an average salary of $10,000 to $14,000. Experienced managers may earn several times as much as beginners. In addition to salary, it is customary for many hotels to furnish managers and their families with lodging in the hotel, meals, parking facilities, laundry, and other services.

Employment outlook for managers is excellent, but applicants having college degrees in hotel administration will have an advantage in obtaining entry-level positions and later advancement.

Housekeepers and assistants All hotels and motels are concerned with the comfort of their guests. Housekeepers are responsible for keeping hotels and motels clean and attractive. It is their responsibility to hire, train, schedule and supervise cleaners, linen and laundry workers, maids, and others. They also maintain employee records and other supplies.

Housekeepers who work in small establishments may not only supervise the cleaning staff, but perform many housekeeping duties themselves. In larger hotels, motels, and resorts, their functions are primarily administrative.

In addition to supervising staff that may number in the hundreds, executive housekeepers prepare the budget for their departments and purchase supplies and furnishings. They work closely with the manager and report on the condition of the rooms, advising on those that need repair or other maintenance. Executive housekeepers are assisted by floor housekeepers who supervise the cleaning and maintenance on one or more floors of the hotel.

Most employers prefer applicants who have a high-school diploma. Several colleges and universities offer instruction in hotel administration that includes courses in housekeeping. Some junior colleges also include housekeeping functions in their hotel administration programs. Some courses are offered in summer and evening classes. Many schools have developed programs under the guidance of the National Executive Housekeepers Association. The American Hotel and Motel Association also offers courses for either classroom or home study. The most helpful courses are those covering housekeeping, personnel management, budget preparation, interior decorating, and the purchase, use and care of different types of fabrics.

Earnings depend upon experience in the field and the size of the establishment. Because hotels usually fill vacancies by promoting assistant housekeepers, newcomers to the field will find their best job opportunities to be in newly built hotels or motels.

Front office clerks The responsibilities of those who work at the front desk include greeting guests, handling room reservations, issuing keys and collecting payments. In the smaller hotels and motels, front office clerks may also work as bookkeepers, cashiers, or as telephone operators.

In larger establishments, clerks may be assigned to specific functions. Reservation clerks record written or telephoned reservations for rooms, type out registration forms, and notify room clerks of guest's anticipated arrival times. Room or desk clerks assign rooms and handle registration procedures. They may also answer questions about hotel services. Other clerks may be assigned to keep records of room assignments, or to work as cashiers or telephone operators.

A high school diploma is usually the minimum education standard considered by employers. Employers look for applicants who have clerical aptitude and a knowledge of basic accounting or bookkeeping. A typing speed of about 45 words per minute is also helpful and may be a requirement of many hotels. High school studies should include typing, a language, bookkeeping, and other subjects of a business nature. College training, while not essential for most entry level positions, is a decided asset for those who wish to advance into a managerial position.

Personal characteristics should include a friendly and courteous attitude and a desire to help people. A foreign language is also helpful for those who want to work in large hotels, or resorts that attract foreign guests.

Beginners usually start as mail, information, or key clerks. They receive on-the-job training. Most hotels prefer to promote from within, so a key or mail clerk may be promoted to a room clerk, then to assistant front-office manager, and even to front-office manager in time. Career opportunities can be improved by taking home-study courses in hotel management, such as those sponsored by the American Hotel and Motel Association.

Sales managers and sales representatives The sales manager is responsible for generating business for the hotel. In many large hotels, there is a complete sales force consisting of the sales manager and several sales representatives. They solicit business from travel agents, tour operators, bus companies, airlines, athletic teams, professional organizations, political organizations, clubs, business accounts, and organizations planning conventions and meetings. They also promote banquet facilities and the use of meeting rooms for lectures, business conferences, displays, and conventions.

They help customers plan their meetings and functions, arrange for meals and beverage services, act as liaison between customers and the various departments, and are often available during functions to ensure that everything runs smoothly and to overcome any problems that may develop.

They may also create and implement advertising and direct-mail sales promotions, write news and publicity releases, and participate in industry, community and civic programs.

A college degree in hotel administration, travel and tourism, or business and marketing is preferred by most employers. Preference will also be given to those management trainees who display an aptitude for sales. It is usually necessary to spend several years as a sales representative before becoming a sales manager. Some employers hire applicants who have had actual sales experience with an airline, car rental company, tour operator, or other travel-related organizations.

Employment outlook is good. The hotel business is competitive, and because it is, skilled sales staff will be needed to help generate sales. The hotel or motel must maintain as high an occupancy rate as possible if it is to operate profitably, and the sales staff is instrumental in keeping a hotel filled.

Reservationists Many hotel and motel chains have installed computerized reservation systems similar to those used by the airlines. If a guest wants to stay in a hotel or motel of a large company he dials a special number and his call is immediately routed to the reservation center. He relays his request to the reservationist who can usually confirm accommodations immediately for any hotel in the system. The guest is advised of the room rate and the type of room reserved, and is mailed a written confirmation the same day.

This job is heavy public contact, and applicants should possess a friendly personality with a good telephone voice. They must also enjoy working with people.

Employers prefer high school graduates who have taken business courses. A typing speed of about 45 words per minute is also necessary. Many employers prefer to hire applicants who have graduated from a trade or vocational airline-type school where the curriculum includes experience and instruction on a computer reservation system; such graduates will still be required to successfully complete the hotel's own training program, which may last from two to four weeks.

Bellhops and bell captains Bellhops carry baggage for hotel and motel guests and escort them to their rooms on arrival. They may also run errands for guests and may relieve elevator operators or switchboard operators.

Large hotels employ bell captains who supervise bellhops on the staff. They plan work assignments, record the hours each bellhop is on duty, and train new employees. Bell captains may also take care of any unusual requests guests may make, and handle complaints regarding their department.

Some of the larger hotels have large service departments and employ superintendents of service to supervise bell captains and bellhops, elevator operators, doorkeepers, and others.

While a high-school diploma is not essential for this type of work, it will improve the chances of promotion to a job as a desk or reservation clerk.

Because bellhops are in frequent contact with guests, they must be neat, tactful, and courteous. A knowledge of the local area is most helpful, since guests often ask about local tourist attractions, restaurants, and transportation services. They must also have stamina since they must carry baggage and stand for long periods.

Employment in this field is expected to grow slowly since the growing popularity of economy motels eliminates the need for bellhops. New workers will have better opportunities in motels and some of the smaller hotels since the large hotels prefer to hire experienced workers.

OPPORTUNITIES FOR EVERYONE

Because of the size and scope of the lodging industry, there is something for everyone who wants to work in this field.

Employment can be part-time or full-time, day or night, seasonal or year round, technical or non-technical, for men or women, for those of high-school age or adults. No matter what your skills and level of education, you will be almost certain to find an opening to fit your career goals and income needs. The industry provides excellent advancement possibilities for anyone who wants to get ahead. The industry also offers a degree of job security not found in many other fields. It also provides the satisfaction of doing a job and performing a service that is of benefit to others.

SOME USEFUL ADDRESSES

For career and training information write to:

The Educational Institute of the American Hotel and Motel Association
1407 S. Harrison Road
East Lansing, Michigan 48823

For additional information on hotel training opportunities and for a directory of schools and colleges offering courses in the field, write to:

Council on Hotel, Restaurant and Institutional Education
11 Koger Executive Center
Norfolk, Virginia 23502

For information on housekeeping opportunities, write to:

National Executive Housekeepers Association, Inc.
Professional Building
Gallipolis, Ohio 45631

Chapter 11

TRAVEL RELATED CAREERS

AMUSEMENT AND THEME PARKS

The original amusement parks in seventeenth-century England and France were known as pleasure gardens. One of the most famous was Vauxhall Gardens in London, where balloon ascensions, firework displays, and parachute drops were the chief attractions. Samuel Pepys, the famous English writer and diarist, was a regular visitor to Vauxhall Gardens in the 1600's. The park, which may have been the first to gain international fame, is described in Pepys' classic diary of 1662. Mozart, at the age of eight, in 1764, performed some of his own compositions on the harpsichord and organ before thousands of visitors at Ranelagh Gardens amusement park in London.

Some of the most famous amusement parks of the last century included Jone's Wood, which bordered New York's East River; Sealine Park at Coney Island; Ruggieri Gardens, Paris, and the Prater in Vienna—the site of the 1873 World's Fair.

Although rides and attractions have changed drastically over the years, some are as popular today as they were when they first appeared. Russian Mountains was the original name for the popular roller coaster. The Ferris Wheel traces its ancestry back to Europe and Asia; some of the first ones appeared in Russia, where they were known as Katcheli. The Tunnel-of-Love ride, an all-ages treat at amusement parks, originated as the Old Mill, and dates back to about 1902. The Merry-Go-Round developed from a horsemanship training device used by knights in the Middle Ages.

The amusement park structure, as it exists today, began around the turn of the century when traction companies, anxious to keep their trolly cars busy on weekends and holidays, established picnic groves at the end of the lines. Initially the idea was limited to transporting family groups, at the going rate of a nickel or dime one way, to a tree-shaded area that offered picnicking and recreational facilities.

Before long, the profitablity of selling fun, along with food and drink, asserted itself. The parks appealed to all age groups and the whole family could become involved. The more sedate could relax in the shade, while the younger generation concentrated on the exciting rides. Lovers were not excluded either. There were the dark rides, including the Tunnel of Love, that provided a few moments of darkness and the opportunity of a fleeting kiss.

Today the industry is bigger than ever, and growing. Parks and attractions now offer a variety of entertainment, recreation, education and family fun.

Career opportunities When one spends a day at a modern amusement or theme park it is sometimes hard to remember that behind all of the rides, the food services, and the excitement is a carefully skilled and highly trained staff who make everything work. An amusement park is a business, and as such it must operate under business principles. A large park has dozens of different departments each with its own management.

Executive positions would include Food Director; Ride Superintendent; Promotion Director; Entertainment Director; Director of Group Sales; Purchasing Agent; Manager of Public Relations; Operations Manager; Games Manager; Arcade Manager; Maintenance Director, and several others. Each supervises other specialists who have been trained in a specific field, or who are in the course of training and development.

Most employers prefer college graduates who have specific education and training. (e. g., food service background for a food service position; marketing training for a sales and marketing position etc.). However, amusement parks employ more than 150,000 seasonal employees annually. Many of these are college students who have a rapport with young people and are ideal family hosts. These people work as ride operators, game attendants, food service employees, souvenir and gift store clerks, guides and members of the clean-up brigade.

One of the best ways to break into the field is to work during the summer at an amusement park. The actual job performed is not too important; you will gain experience which will give you an edge over other applicants when the time comes to look for a full-time position.

CLUB MANAGEMENT

Private clubs have been in existence for many years in many forms. The ancient Greeks had their *hetaireias* and the Romans had their *sodalitas*. Individuals from both civilizations felt the need to join together for political, religious, and trade purposes. Julius Caesar felt that political clubs were dangerous and he forbade them.

The earliest London Club was formed in the early 1600's by Sir Walter Raleigh. The Maiden Taverne was the meeting place for the politicians, intellectuals, and literary geniuses of the day. William Shakespeare was a member of the Mermaid Club. At that time, "Clubbes" were actually nothing more than taverns where people took their meals by special invitation.

In America, the first country club was formed in 1882, and in 1888, a group of men joined together to form the first golf club. During the 1920's, there were 4,500 private clubs in the United States, though many of these were forced to close their doors during the depression. Today, there are more than 11,800 private clubs in operation. Of these clubs, about 8,500 are total facility clubs. These have a club house, and facilites for food and beverage service; in the case of country clubs, golf courses, and others of this type, there are complete recreational facilities as well as many planned programs for members.

Private clubs today include country, town, luncheon, athletic, women's, tennis, yacht, swimming, and others of similar character. Total membership at these clubs is some 7.5 million, but when families are included there are more than 19 million people using the clubs' facilities each year. There are also some 826,000 full and part-time employees at these clubs, with a total payroll of 3.2 billion dollars annually.

Career Opportunities A high school diploma is a prerequisite for almost any full-time entry level position. It will be necessary to supplement the basic education with on the job training and industry-related adult education courses. The courses offered by the Educational Institute of the American Hotel and Motel Association will be most helpful in gaining the skills necessary for employment in the private club field. However, a college degree in hotel and restaurant management is the best credential for those who desire to become club managers or assistant managers.

A club manager must be totally familiar with all aspects of club operation. These areas include: administration, food and beverage preparation, service and purchasing, maintenance and housekeeping, recreation, and personnel hiring and supervision. Many of the responsibilities are similar to those in the hotel and restaurant fields, but the manager of a private club must have a more personal relationship with the members, with whom he has the opportunity to form a stronger bond than managers do in other hospitality fields.

Salaries depend upon the size, type, and location of a club, and on experience and education. An assistant manager starts at about $12,000 to $20,000 annually, and a club manager at $18,000 to $45,000. Many clubs offer bonuses, housing, fringe benefits, good vacation time, meals, and many other advantages.

For more complete information on careers in club management write to: Club Managers Association of America, 7615 Winterberry Place, Washington, DC 20034.

CORPORATE TRAVEL DEPARTMENTS

Some large corporations engage in so much business travel that they prefer to employ their own staff to handle it rather than work through a travel agency. The staffs of these travel departments vary in size, from one employee to three or more.

Many corporations maintain a supply of air tickets and necessary reference materials such as schedules and tariffs. Some corporations generate more business for the airlines than do many travel agencies, and their offices are as professional and well equipped as those of travel agencies.

Corporate travel representatives handle business travel arrangements for company executives, salespeople, and other employees authorized to travel on company business. Using the appropriate manuals and tariffs, corporate travel representatives look up flights, call airlines, make the necessary reservations, and write air tickets. They also handle hotel and motel reservations, and arrange for car rentals and other services required by the traveler.

Although most corporate travel is domestic (within the U. S. and Canada), some corporations, by virtue of their products or services, may engage in foreign travel. Employees in these corporate travel departments must be cognizant of foreign fares and transportation, and international health and visa requirements for business travelers.

Most companies prefer to hire applicants who have experience with a travel agency or airline. In some cases, clerks and secretaries who are already working in the company, and have an aptitude for travel related functions, may be transferred and trained on the job.

Corporate travel representatives are not entitled to discount travel privileges. Still, many people prefer to work for large companies because of the good benefits, or because salaries are higher than those found in many travel agencies.

HOTEL REPRESENTATIVE COMPANIES

Many of these are private companies which specialize in providing marketing and reservation services for hotels located in other cities or countries. In some instances, a chain of foreign hotels may be large enough to warrant their own offices in the United States. However, the cost of maintaining a sales and marketing office abroad would be prohibitive for independent European hotels, so many contract with independent hotel representative companies to perform these services for them.

The usual entry level position is that of reservationist. The job is almost identical to that of any other hotel reservationist, and for a complete job description see the hotel section of this book.

Sales representative positions are available occasionally. Sales representatives call on travel agents and other travel industry organizations. They promote the hotels the company represents. Most employers prefer applicants who have sales representative experience with a tour operator or airline. Some hotel representative companies prefer to train their own sales staff, and look for qualified applicants from among their reservationists.

JOURNALISTIC OPPORTUNITIES

Breaking into the travel writing field is not an easy task by any means, yet a variety of opportunities do exist for those who have the required training and qualifications and are willing to take the time necessary to locate openings. In addition to a limited number of staff positions with newspapers and magazines, there are opportunities for freelance writers who have the ability and talent to write descriptive, authoritative copy on subjects and places that interest tourists.

NEWSPAPERS AND MAGAZINES

Most of the major newspapers include a travel section in their Sunday or weekend editions. Even many local or weekly newspapers have a page, or at least a column or two, devoted to travel topics. Both national and regional magazines feature regular travel articles, and nearly every airline has its own inflight publication which is placed on board its aircraft as reading material for the passengers. Many hotel chains publish magazines for their guests. There are a number of trade publications in the travel, foodservice, hotel and tourism fields, though most of these are so technical that only someone with specialized knowledge would be seriously considered as a job applicant, or commissioned to write articles.

The travel editor of a large city newspaper is a specialist and an authority on travel-related journalism. At large newspapers, there may also be one or two assistant travel editors, each of whom may travel on assignment to almost anywhere in the world. Travel editors are also responsible for buying articles submitted by freelance travel writers. A travel editor may receive many unsolicited articles each week, and he must be able to quickly select those that are possible for publication. A good travel editor need only read a few paragraphs of a manuscript to decide if it is an article worthy of consideration.

Accepted articles then require editing before they are suitable for publication. Travel editors also reply to authors' queries about prospective articles, and may even offer guidance to promising new writers.

Travel editors are deluged with press releases from airlines, cruise lines, tour operators, foreign and domestic tourist offices, hotels and many other organizations. But space in the travel section of a newspaper is limited, and travel editors must be highly selective in choosing their stories.

Other tasks include reading letters from readers and selecting some for publication, replying to readers' letters of comment or criticism, choosing photographs to complement written copy, and working on the layout and make-up of the travel pages.

Some newspapers do not have the budget to employ a full-time travel editor, so some editors may also double as the automotive editor or the food editor.

Almost any position in the professional journalistic field requires a degree in journalism. Many of those assigned to the travel section of newspapers or magazines began their careers in training programs, or as reporters or copy editors.

FREELANCE WRITING

There are opportunites for freelance writers to derive at least some income from their literary accomplishments. However, the average freelance writer must supplement his income with other, steadier work, and not regard his writing as a means of total support.

It is often an arduous task for any nonfiction writer to get his articles accepted for publication. The freelance travel writer is no exception, and he is likely to receive one rejection after another before he finally sells an article. Travel and magazine editors prefer articles from established, recognized authors rather than from unknowns. Despite this policy, which makes it difficult for a new writer to break into the field, the door is not completely closed to someone of talent and persistence.

First, be certain you are thoroughly familiar with your subject; this may require hours of research, frequent travel, and thorough investigation and inspection of the area or subject. There is nothing worse, however, than for a travel editor to receive letters from readers citing inaccuracies in an article authored by one of his freelance writers.

It is not always necessary to have earned a degree in journalism in order to write interesting and readable articles. However, you will be more likely to write acceptably if you complete a course in nonfiction journalism. Many community and junior colleges offer adult extension courses in journalism, creative writing, and related subjects. While no amount of education will make good writers out of people who cannot write, a specialized course may help develop the writing abilities of those who have the aptitude. Alternatively, read all the books you can on English composition and grammar, punctuation, usage, structure, and nonfiction writing.

You may also want to subscribe to writers' magazines. There are two publications of particular interest to writers: *Writer's Digest,* 22 E. 12th Street, Cincinnati, OH 45210; and *The Writer,* 88 Arlington Street, Boston, MA 02116. Both of these magazines also offer a selection of practical books to help writers improve their writing skills.

If you expect to see your articles in print they must conform to a standard style and format. Study the travel pages of as many newspapers and magazines as you can find; they are indicators of the type and length of articles travel editors accept from freelance writers. Your writing should conform to what you see in print.

Your manuscript must also be prepared in a conventional manner; if your writing is to be taken seriously it must look professional. For information on the correct method of manuscript preparation, obtain a copy of *Preparing the Manuscript* by Udia G. Olsen; this is published by *The Writer, Inc.,* 8 Arlington Street, Boston, MA 02116. Your library also has books on the subject.

Once you have prepared your manuscript, it should be checked for style, content, grammar and typographical errors. It is better to have someone else proofread the manuscript. (No author should do his own proofreading.)

It is often advisable to first query editors before you submit the manuscript. Doing so may save you hours of work writing something that no editor is likely to buy. A query need be nothing more than an outline of an article that you intend to write. Be sure to enclose a stamped, addressed, return envelope with your query.

If you are unfamiliar with a particular magazine, you can ask for a sample copy which may cost you about $1. Many magazines will also send, upon request, a copy of their guidelines for writers.

What to write about? The list is endless. Travel writing offers almost unlimited subject matter for those who have a fertile imagination. Careful scrutiny of the travel pages of various magazines and newspapers will reveal the variety of subjects covered by freelance travel writers; use them as examples of what is being accepted for publication. A list of travel-related magazines will be found in the Appendix.

PERSONNEL WORK

Personnel departments exist in airlines, hotels, railroads, car rental companies, and many other travel organizations. These companies sometimes have openings for those who are trained for, or have experience in personnel work.

Personnel workers interview, select, and recommend applicants to fill job openings. They handle wage and salary administration, training and career development, and employee benefits. Some personnel workers specialize in labor relations. They help company officials prepare for collective bargaining sessions, participate in contract negotiations with the union, and handle other labor-relations matters.

In a large company, the personnel staff may include recruiters, interviewers, counselors, job analysts, education and training specialists, labor-relations specialists, and technical and clerical workers.

Many employers prefer to fill beginning positions in personnel and labor relations with college graduates who have the potential to advance into management jobs. Some employers look for graduates who have majored in personnel administration or industrial and labor relations. Others prefer college graduates with a general business background.

While many personnel workers have a college degree, some people enter the field at the clerical level and advance to professional positions on the basis of experience. Because so many personnel jobs require specialized knowledge of a particular industry, most people tend to remain in their own field. For example, airline personnel workers may change jobs, but they normally remain in the airline industry.

Opportunities for personnel work exist not only at the home office of a company, but at many field locations too.

PUBLIC RELATIONS JOBS

Public relations departments are found at almost all major travel industry organizations. The department is headed by a public relations director who is aided by a staff trained in public relations work.

Public relations workers assemble and publicize information on the activities of their employees. Such data for an airline might include news of the introduction of a new aircraft, new rates, fares or schedules, new routes, statistical information on corporate earnings or number of passenger miles flown, and other important newsworthy developments.

After preparing the information, the public relations staff contact people in the news media who might be interested in publishing the material. Many television and radio commercials, special reports, newspaper items and magazine articles start at the public relations department. The job also may entail writing speeches and setting up speaking engagements for company executives. Public relations staff also may show slides to schools and colleges, plan conventions, engage in community projects and perhaps even manage charitable fund-raising campaigns. Some public relations staff may be assigned to write and produce promotional films, training films, and slide presentations, and write and design tour brochures and other promotional literature.

A college education combined with experience in advertising or journalism is the best preparation for public relations work. Although most beginners have a college degree in journalism, English, or public relations, some travel industry employers prefer a background in the transportation or hospitality fields.

RECREATION

Jobs in the recreation field focus on dealing with people, in natural as well as man-made environments. Employment can be found in local, county, state, and federal agencies; voluntary youth-service organizations; public and private institutions; and colleges and universities.

Jobs include therapeutic recreation specialists; program specialists in dance, dramatics, fine arts, and sports; camp counselors and outdoor recreationists; wilderness leaders; and senior-citizens program directors.

In the area of management of parks and natural resources, jobs include grounds and facilities maintenance; park rangers; outdoor recreation specialists ; landscape architects; foresters; soil, range and wildlife conservationists; park managers; and supervisors and administrators.

The National Recreation and Parks Association suggests that those who are interested in exploring this career further should seek part-time summer and   after-school employment in recreation programming or with parks and natural resource centers. You can also volunteer at local park and recreation departments, YMCA's, churches, nursing homes, or camps. Conversations with local park and recreation professionals will give you more information about this career.

Industrial recreation covers a wide range of activities. Many large corporations recognize the need for balanced leisure programs for their employees, and these companies maintain employee recreation clubs which are supervised by specialists trained in leisure programs.

Activities of employee recreation clubs include domestic and foreign tour programs; bridge and chess clubs; contact sports; educational programs; gardening; winter sports; physical fitness programs; ballroom dancing; flying and boating; bowling; golf; choral singing, and many others.

The manager of recreation services is responsible for the employee recreation activities. Depending upon the size of the company, and the diversity of activities, he may have full-time activity specialists to assist him with the development, implementation, and operation of programs.

More than 85,000 recreation workers are employed on a full-time year-around basis. Additionally, over 100,000 recreation workers are employed for the summer months only.

Formal training in a college recreation curriculum is becoming increasingly more important for those seeking a career in this field. A high school education is usually the minimum requirement for full-time employment; however, these positions have limited potential for advancement. An associate degree in recreation from a community or junior college usually is preferred as a minimum requirement for both year-round and seasonal employment.

Those with college training generally start at a higher salary and have better advancement opportunities. Activity specialists must have specialized training in a particular field, such as art, music, drama or athletics.

Two-year associate degree programs in parks and recreation are offered at more than 200 junior colleges. Additionally, four-year baccalaureate degrees in this field are available at about 200 universities. There are also about 90 graduate programs leading to a masters or doctoral degree. The typical program of recreation study includes courses in communications, natural sciences, the humanities, philosophy, sociology, psychology, drama, and music. Courses in recreation per se include program planning and organization, group leadership, health and safety procedures, outdoor sports, dance, arts and crafts. Field work involving recreation leadership experience is also required.

Those interested in industrial or other types of commercial recreation may find it more appropriate to take courses in business administration or travel and tourism. Students interested in therapeutic recreation should take courses in psychology, health education, and sociology.

Activity planning frequently calls for creativity and resourcefulness. In addition, the recreation worker must be in good health, and have a great deal of physical stamina.

According to the U. S. Department of Labor, employment in the recreation field is expected to grow. An increase in recreation areas will accompany the creation of many new parks, playgrounds and national forests. The best opportunities for full-time employment will go to those who have four-year and graduate degrees, and related work experience prior to graduation. However, since more students are studying in the recreation field, competition for jobs is expected to be keen.

More information on careers in recreation can be obtained by writing to one or more of the following associations:

National Recreation and Parks Association
1601 Kent Street
Arlington, VA 22209

National Industrial Recreation Association
20 North Wacker Drive
Chicago, IL 60606

American Camping Association
Bradford Woods
Martinsville, IN 46151

TOURIST OFFICES

FOREIGN TOURIST OFFICES

The governments of many foreign countries maintain tourist offices in the United States. These offices are responsible for promoting trade and tourism to their respective countries by distributing travel literature and conducting advertising campaigns. Most foreign tourist offices are located in New York City, but some of the countries with large tourism budgets have established branch offices in other major cities such as Chicago, Los Angeles, and San Francisco.

The staff of some foreign tourist offices include the director or general manager, a public relations director, travel-trade representatives, information clerks and secretaries. A large office may also have a promotions director and a sales manager. When the operating budget is limited, or in branch office locations, the staff may only consist of the area or regional manager and a secretary or two.

The director or general manager is almost always a national of the country represented. He is a career executive and may even hold civil-service status in his government. While many branch offices are also managed by foreign nationals, there are several instances where Americans hold the senior position. If there is a public relations director, he is usually American, and there are even some foreign tourist offices where the entire staff is American.

Although many foreign tourist offices now retain an independent advertising agency to handle their advertising and public relations functions, there are those offices that prefer to handle these responsibilities themselves. In these cases one of the most important jobs is that of the public relations director. His responsibilities are comprehensive and varied and include writing press releases and distributing them to selected news media; conducting press conferences; writing the copy for tourist brochures for distribution to the American market; conducting lectures and film promotions; supervising receptions, dinners and other social events, and managing the advertising program. The job requires years of training, preparation, and experience. A degree in journalism, business administration, travel and tourism, or public relations is almost a necessity. Education which is supplemented with experience in the public relations department of an airline, hotel corporation, or other major travel industry organization operating at the international level will be helpful. Fluency in two or three languages is usually necessary, and comprehensive knowledge of the customs, economics, culture, and travel attractions of the particular country is essential. If a candidate has actually lived or studied in the country, such credentials are prime assets.

Sales representatives are responsible for promoting tourism through travel agencies, tour operators, airlines, and other travel related organizations. They call on travel agents; man information booths at trade and travel shows; see that the travel agents in their area are supplied with current literature; conduct talks and film shows; and perform a variety of other public-relations-oriented functions. Many such positions are open to Americans, though most employers prefer to hire those who have experience with a travel agency, tour operator, or airline, since such applicants will already have a good knowledge of the travel industry.

Information clerks work in the office. They distribute literature on the country they represent and answer inquiries from people who request information about the particular country or area.

There are few entry level positions for Americans at foreign tourist offices, though openings do occur from time to time for typists, secretaries, and office clerks. Fluency in the language of the country is usually required, but not always essential.

STATE AND CITY TOURIST OFFICES

Most states and many major cities with convention facilities or tourist attractions maintain travel and convention promotion departments whose job it is to promote tourism to their respective areas.

The travel and tourism department is not always separate, but frequently is a division within the Department of Commerce, or similar agency.

State and city tourist offices function in much the same way as foreign tourist offices. Their staff prepare and distribute tourist literature; work closely with hotels, convention facilities, and the local chamber of commerce; assist local tour operators and bus companies, and help them create tourist packages and tours; disseminate information and statistical data on conventions; solicit organizations and associations for convention and meeting business; supervise and coordinating conventions.

Opportunities sometimes exist for sales representatives, information clerks, typists and secretaries, and several other positions.

APPENDIX

This quick-reference directory will be helpful to anyone about to embark on a serious job hunt, and for those who seek more information on professional training programs and higher-education opportunities.

With the exception of educational establishments, which are listed by state, the listings are alphabetical by category. Only the head, or main office of a company is listed here. However, many of the companies and organizations maintain sales, reservation or personnel offices in other parts of the U.S.; your local telephone directory will reveal which companies are located in your area. In most cases, offices of major companies will be confined to the larger cities, but if a particular carrier serves your area, you should be able to at least pick up an employment-application form and ascertain what entry-level job opportunities are likely to occur.

Every effort has been made to include accurate information, but the publisher will appreciate learning of any errors or omissions so that future editions can be corrected.

In the case of amusement and theme parks, only the major attractions are included. The criterion used for "major" is 10 or more major rides, but this yardstick may not be the standard used by the industry itself to distinguish between major and minor "Theme" or amusement parks. (We are restricted by space.) The International Association of Amusement Parks and Attractions, (listed in the Appendix), may be able to furnish a more complete listing.

There are few travel agency chains in operation these days, but those with nation-wide locations include American Express, Ask Mr. Foster, and Thomas Cook. The head office of each of these companies is listed, but since in most cases each office manager is autonomous and responsible for hiring and training his own staff, your best approach would be to apply at your nearest office. The motor clubs are often overlooked by those seeking a travel agency career. This is unfortunate because most motor clubs operate like any other full-service travel agency and offer a complete range of professional world-wide travel services, in addition to providing benefits to their motoring members. Many city or state motor clubs are unusually large by virtue of their branch offices and generate a substantial volume of business annually.

The private trade schools offer a variety of training programs, and the only way to determine whether or not a school meets your needs and budget is to study its brochure. It should be clearly understood that the inclusion of a private travel training school in this listing does not constitute an endorsement of either the school or its curriculum by the

139

author or the publisher. Similarly, exclusion of a school does not infer in any way that its courses or policies are questionable. If a school does not appear here it is probably because the information requested by the author did not arrive by the deadline, or that the school is unknown to the author. It should also be noted that there are many travel agency technique courses conducted in high school and community college classrooms which cannot be listed here.

Not all colleges and junior colleges listed under Hotel and Restaurant Administration offer courses in both fields. For example, some colleges have courses in Hotel Administration while others specialize in the restaurant or food service field. A thorough study and comparison of the catalogs of the various colleges will be helpful in selecting the right school.

AIRLINES

Domestic airlines

AIR CALIFORNIA 3636 Birch St., Newport Beach, CA 92660
AIR FLORIDA 3900 N.W. 79th Avenue, Miami, FL 33156
ALASKA AIRLINES, INC. Seattle-Tacoma International Airport, Seattle, WA 98158
ALLEGHENY AIRLINES, INC. National Airport, Washington, DC 20001
ALOHA AIRLINES, INC. P. O. Box 30028, Honolulu, HI 96820
AMERICAN AIRLINES, INC. 633 Third Avenue, New York, NY 10017
BRANIFF INTERNATIONAL AIRWAYS P. O. Box 35001, Dallas, TX 75235
CONTINENTAL AIRLINES, INC. International Airport, Los Angeles, CA 90009
DELTA AIRLINES, INC. Atlanta Airport, Atlanta, GA 30320
EASTERN AIRLINES, INC. International Airport, Miami, FL 33148
FRONTIER AIRLINES, INC. 8250 Smith Road, Denver, CO 80207
HAWAIIAN AIRLINES, INC. P. O. Box 30008, Honolulu, HI 96820
HUGHES AIRWEST International Airport, San Francisco, CA 94128
NATIONAL AIRLINES, INC. P. O. Box 592055, AMF, Miami, FL 33159
NEW YORK AIRWAYS, INC. P. O. Box 426, La Guardia Airport Station, Flushing, NY 11371
NORTH CENTRAL AIRLINES, INC. 7500 Northliner Road, Minneapolis, MN 55450
NORTHWEST ORIENT AIRLINES, INC. International Airport, Minneapolis, MN 55111
OZARK AIRLINES, INC. Lambert Field, St. Louis, MO 63145
PACIFIC SOUTHWEST AIRLINES 3225 North Harbor Drive, San Diego, CA 92112
PAN AMERICAN WORLD AIRWAYS Pan Am Building, 200 Park Avenue, New York, NY 10017
PIEDMONT AIRLINES, INC. Smith-Reynolds Airport, Winston-Salem, NC 27102
PRINAIR International Airport, Isla Verde, PR 00913
SOUTHERN AIRWAYS, LTD. Atlanta Airport, Atlanta, GA 30320
SOUTHWEST AIRLINES, INC. 1820 Regal Row, Dallas, TX 75235
TEXAS INTERNATIONAL AIRLINES, INC. P. O. Box 12788, Houston, TX 77017

TRANS WORLD AIRLINES, INC. 605 Third Avenue, New York, NY 10016
UNITED AIRLINES P. O. Box 66100, Chicago, IL 60666
WESTERN AIRLINES, INC. P. O. Box 92005, Airport Station, Los Angeles, CA
  90009
WIEN AIR ALASKA, INC. 4100 International Airport, Anchorage, AK 99502

Supplemental airlines

CAPITOL INTERNATIONAL AIRWAYS, INC. Smyrna Airport, Smyrna, TN
  37167
MODERN AIR, INC. International Airport, Miami, FL 33148
OVERSEAS NATIONAL AIRWAYS, INC. 147-39 175th Street, Jamaica, NY
  11430
TRANS INTERNATIONAL AIRLINES, INC. P.O. Box 2504, Oakland, CA
  94614
WORLD AIRWAYS Oakland International Airport, Oakland, CA 94614

Cargo airlines (Some operate passenger charters)

AIRLIFT INTERNATIONAL, INC. P.O. Box 1447, Travis AFB, CA 94535
FLYING TIGER LINE 7401 World Way West, Los Angeles, CA 90009
SEABOARD WORLD AIRLINES, INC. JFK International Airport, Jamaica, NY
  11430

Foreign flag airlines with U.S. offices

AER LINGUS 122 E. 42nd Street, New York, NY 10017
AEROCONDOR AIRLINES 301 S. E. 2nd Street, Miami, FL 33131
AEROFLOT-SOVIET AIRLINES 545 Fifth Avenue, New York, NY 10017
AEROLINEAS ARGENTINAS 9 Rockefeller Plaza, New York, NY 10020
AEROMEXICO 8400 N.W. 52nd Street, Miami, FL 33166
AEROPERU 1st Federal Building, Miami, FL 33131
AIR AFRIQUE 683 Fifth Avenue, New York, NY 10022
AIR CANADA 600 Madison Avenue, New York, NY 10022
AIR FRANCE 1350 Avenue of the Americas, New York, NY 10019
AIR INDIA 345 Park Avenue, New York, NY 10022
AIR JAMAICA 19 E. 49th Street, New York, NY 10017
AIR NEW ZEALAND 510 West 6th Street, Los Angeles, CA 90014
AIR PANAMA INTERNATIONAL 304 N.E. First Street, Miami, FL 33132
AIR SIAM 6733 S. Sepulveda Blvd., Los Angeles, CA 90045
ALIA—THE ROYAL JORDANIAN AIRLINE 535 Fifth Avenue, New York, NY
  10017
ALM ANTILLEAN AIRLINES 97-77 Queens Blvd., Rego Park, NY 11374
ALITALIA 666 Fifth Avenue, New York, NY 10019
ANSETT AIRLINES OF AUSTRALIA 510 West 6th Street, Los Angeles, CA
  90014
ARIANA AFGHAN AIRLINES 535 Fifth Avenue, New York, NY 10017
AVENSA AIRLINES One Rockefeller Plaza, New York, NY 10020
AVIANCA AIRLINES 6 West 49th Street, New York, NY 10020
AVIATECA P.O. Box 592496 Miami Int'l. Airport, FL 33159
BRITISH AIRWAYS 245 Park Avenue, New York, NY 10017
BRITISH CALEDONIAN AIRWAYS 415 Madison Avenue, New York, NY 10017
BRITISH WEST INDIAN AIRWAYS 610 Fifth Avenue, New York, NY 10020
CATHAY PACIFIC AIRWAYS 291 Geary Street, San Francisco, CA 94102
CHINA AIRLINES 391 Sutter Street, San Francisco, CA 94108
CP AIR 233 N. Michigan Avenue, Chicago, IL 60601

CZECHOSLOVAK AIRLINES 545 Fifth Avenue, New York, NY 10017
EAST AFRICAN AIRWAYS 600 Fifth Avenue, New York, NY 10020
ECUATORIAL de AVIACION P.O. Box 52-2970, Miami, FL 33152
EGYPTAIR 720 Fifth Avenue, New York, NY 10019
EL AL ISRAEL AIRLINES 850 Third Avenue, New York, NY 10022
ETHOPIAN AIRLINES 405 Lexington Avenue, New York, NY 10017
FINNAIR 10 E. 40th Street, New York, NY 10016
GULF AIR 245 Park Avenue, New York, NY 10017
IBERIA AIR LINES OF SPAIN 97-77 Queens Blvd., Rego Park, NY 11374
ICELANDIC AIRLINES 630 Fifth Avenue, New York, NY 10020
IRAN AIR 345 Park Avenue, New York, NY 10022
JAPAN AIRLINES CO. 655 Fifth Avenue, New York, NY 10022
KLM ROYAL DUTCH AIRLINES 437 Madison Avenue, New York, NY 10022
KOREAN AIR LINES 1813 Wilshire Blvd., Los Angeles, CA 90057
KUWAIT AIRWAYS 30 Rockefeller Plaza, New York, NY 10020
LACSA AIRLINES 200 S.E. First Street, Miami, FL 33131
LAN-CHILE AIRLINES 630 First Avenue, New York, NY 10020
LANICA AIRLINES P.O. Box 52306, Miami, FL 33152
LOT—POLISH AIRLINES 500 Fifth Avenue, New York, NY 10036
LUFTHANSA GERMAN AIRLINES 1640 Hempstead Turnpike, East Meadow,
    L.I., NY 11554
MALAYASIAN AIRLINES SYSTEM 510 W. 6th Street, Los Angeles, CA 90014
MALEV HUNGARIAN AIRLINES 630 Fifth Avenue, New York, NY 10020
MEXICANA AIRLINES 851 Burlway Road, Burlingame, CA 94010
MIDDLE EAST AIRLINES 680 Fifth Avenue, New York, NY 10019
NIGERIA AIRWAYS 30 Rockefeller Plaza, New York, NY 10020
OLYMPIC AIRWAYS 647 Fifth Avenue, New York, NY 10022
PAKISTAN INTERNATIONAL AIRLINES 545 Fifth Avenue, New York, NY
    10017
PHILIPPINE AIR LINES 212 Stockton Street, San Francisco, CA 94108
QANTAS AIRWAYS 1211 Avenue of the Americas, New York, NY 10036
ROYAL AIR MAROC 680 Fifth Avenue, New York, NY 10019
SABENA BELGIAN WORLD AIRLINES 125 Community Drive, Great Neck,
    NY 11201
SAUDI ARABIAN AIRLINES 747 Third Avenue, New York, NY 10017
SCANDINAVIAN AIRLINES SYSTEM 138-02 Queens Blvd., Jamaica, NY 11435
SINGAPORE AIRLINES 510 West 6th Street, Los Angeles, CA 90014
SOUTH AFRICAN AIRWAYS 605 Fifth Avenue, New York, NY 10017
SPANTAX 500 Fifth Avenue, New York, NY 10036
SWISSAIR 608 Fifth Avenue, New York, NY 10020
TACA INTERNATIONAL AIRLINES P.O. Box 20047, AMF, New Orleans, LA
    70141
TAN AIRLINES P.O. Box 222, Miami International Airport, Miami, FL 33148
TAP—PORTUGUESE AIRLINES 1140 Avenue of the Americas, New York, NY
    10036
TAROM ROMANIAN AIRLINES 200 E. 38th Street, New York, NY 10016
THAI AIRWAYS INTERNATIONAL 51 Kearny Street, San Francisco, CA
    94108
UTA FRENCH AIRLINES 9841 Airport Blvd., Los Angeles, CA 90045
VARIG—BRAZILIAN AIRLINES 622 Third Avenue, New York, NY 10017
VIASA 1401 Brickell Avenue, Miami, FL 33131
YUGOSLAV AIRLINES—JAT 630 Fifth Avenue, New York, NY 10020
ZAMBIA AIRWAYS 1 Rockefeller Plaza, New York, NY 10020

AMUSEMENT AND THEME PARKS

ADVENTURELAND 21 West Lake Street, Addison, IL 60101
ADVENTURELAND 2245 Broad Hollow Road, E. Farmingdale, NY 11735
ADVENTURELAND I-80 at Hwy. 65, Des Moines, IA 50316
ASTROLAND 1000 Surf Avenue, Brooklyn, NY 11224
ASTROWORLD USA 9001 Kirby Drive, Houston, TX 77001
BEECH BEND PARK Beech Bend Road, Bowling Green, KY 42101
BELL'S AMUSEMENT PARK P. O. Box 4752, Tulsa, OK 74104
BELMONT AMUSEMENT PARK 3000 Mission Blvd., San Diego, CA 92109
BERTRAND ISLAND PARK P. O. Box 395, Mt. Arlington, NJ 07856
BOB-LO AMUSEMENT PARK Michigan & Hwy. 18, Detroit, MI 48226
BOSTON VENTURES, INC. Route No. 128, Wakefield, MA 01880
BUCKEYE LAKE PARK Box 116, Buckeye Lake, OH 43008
BUSCH GARDENS 2800 S. Ninth Street, St. Louis, MO 63118
BUSCH GARDENS—LOS ANGELES 16000 Roscoe Blvd., Van Nuys, CA 91406
BUSCH GARDENS—TAMPA 3000 Busch Blvd., Tampa, FL 33612
BUSCH GARDENS—WILLIAMSBURG 51 Kingsmill Road, Williamsburg, VA 23185
BUSHKILL PARK AMUSEMENT CO. 2125 Bushkill Park Dr., Easton, PA 18042
CAMDEN PARK RECREATION CENTER P. O. Box 1794, Huntington WV 25718
CANOBIE LAKE PARK N. Policy Street, Salem, NH 03079
CAROWINDS P. O. Box 15514, Charlotte, NC 28210
CASINO, PIER AND POOL Grant and Boardwalk, Seaside Heights, NJ 08751
CEDAR POINT, INC. P. O. Box 759, Sandusky, OH 44870
CHILHOWEE PARK Magnolia Avenue, Knoxville, TN 37914
CHIPPEWA LAKE County Road 19, Chippewa Lake, OH 44125
CLEMENTON LAKE PARK 144 Berlin Road, Clementon, NJ 08021
COLONIAL WILLIAMSBURG P. O. Box C, Williamsburg, VA 23185
CONNEAUT LAKE PARK Conneaut Lake, PA 16316
CRESCENT PARK Bullock's Point Avenue, Riverside, RI 02915
CRYSTAL BEACH AMUSEMENT PARK P. O. Box 640, Buffalo, NY 14203
DANDILION PARK P. O. Box 52, Muskego, WI 53150
DEAN AND FLYNN AMUSEMENTS Ocean Front, Salisbury Beach, MA 01950
DICKENSON COUNTY AMUSEMENT CO. Box 438, Arnold Park, IA 51331
DISNEYLAND 1313 Harbor Blvd, Anaheim, CA 92803
DOGPATCH U.S.A., INC. Dogpatch, AR 72648
DORNEY PARK 3830 Dorney Park Road, Allentown, PA 18104
DUTCH WONDERLAND 2249 Lincoln Hwy. East, Lancaster, PA 17602
EAGLE PARK Rt. 1, Cache, OK 73527
EDGEWATER PARK 23500 W. 7 Mile Road, Detroit, MI 48219
ENCHANTED FOREST AMUSEMENT PARK U.S. 20 at Indiana 49, Chesterton, IN 46304
FAIRYLAND PARK 7501 Prospect Avenue, Kansas City, MO 63132
E. K. FERNANDEZ SHOWS, INC. 91-246 Oihana Street, Ewa Beach, HI 96706
FRONTIER CITY, USA 11601 N.E. Expressway, Oklahoma City, OK 73111
FRONTIERLAND Cherokee, NC 28719
FRONTIER VILLAGE 4885 Monterey Road, San Jose, CA 95111
FUN PIER Box 232, Wildwood, NJ 08260
FUNTOWN AMUSEMENT PARK 1711 East 95th Street, Chicago, IL 60617
FUNTOWN USA 1806 A Boardwalk, Seaside Park, NJ 08752
GASLIGHT VILLAGE Route 9, Lake George, NY 12845
GOLDRUSH JUNCTION P. O. Box 128, Pigeon Forge, TN 37864
GRAND STRAND AMUSEMENT PARK 408 S, Ocean Blvd., Myrtle Beach, SC 29577

GWYNN OAK PARK 6000 Gwynn Oak Avenue, Baltimore, MD 21207
HOLIDAY HILL 9741 Natural Bridge Road, St. Louis, MO 63134
HUNT'S PIER Wildwood, NJ 08260
IDELWILD PARK Box C, Ligonier PA 15658
THE IDORA PARK Rt. 62, Canfield Rd., Youngstown OH 44511
INDIANA BEACH 306 Indiana Beach Road, Montecello, IN 47960
INDIAN NATIONS PARK P. O. Box 1002, Jenks, OK 74037
JOYLAND AMUSEMENT CO. 2801 South Hillside, Wichita, KS 67216
JOYLAND PARK 27th and California Ave., Topeka, KS 67205
KENNYWOOD PARK CORP. 4800 Kennywood Blvd., West Mifflin, PA 15122
KINGS ISLAND P. O. Box 400, Kings Mills, OH 45034
KNOEBEL'S GROVES Rt. 487, Elysburg, PA 17824
KNOTT'S BERRY FARM 8039 Beach Blvd., Buena Park, CA 90620
LAGOON 464 South Main Street, Salt Lake City, UT 84101
LAKELAND 3970 Canada Rd., Memphis, TN 38128
LAKEMONT PARK 118 6th Street, Altoona, PA 16602
LAKE QUASSAPAUG AMUSEMENT PARK Rt. 64, Middleburg, CT 06762
LAKESIDE AMUSEMENT PARK 1526 East Main Street, Salem, VA 24153
LAKE VIEW AMUSEMENT PARK Rt. 16, Mendon, MA 01756
LAKEVIEW AMUSEMENT PARK 947 Walnut Street, Royersford, PA 19468
LEGEND CITY 120 West Washington Street, Tempe, AZ 85281
LeSOURDSVILLE LAKE 5757 Hamilton Middletown Rd., Middletown, OH 45043
LINCOLN PARK AMUSEMENT CO. State Road, North Dartmouth, MA 02747
MAGIC MOUNTAIN 26101 Magic Mountain Parkway, Valencia CA 91355
MARRIOTT'S GREAT AMERICA Box 1976, Gurnee, IL 60031
MARRIOTT'S GREAT AMERICA P. O. Box 393, Santa Clara, CA 95052
MARSHALL HALL PARK CORP. Rt. 1, Box 156, Bryans Road, MD 20616
MILLION DOLLAR PIER Arkansas and Boardwalk, Atlantic City, NJ 08401
MIRACLE STRIP AMUSEMENT PARK P. O. Box 2000, Panama City, FL 32401
MOREY'S PIER 25th and Boardwalk, Wildwood, NJ 08260
MOUNTAIN PARK P. O. Box 29, Holyoke, MA 01040
MOXAHALA PARK Moxahala Park Road, South Zanesville, OH 43701
MYRTLE BEACH PAVILION P. O. Box 2095, Myrtle Beach, SC 29577
NOBLE PARK FUNLAND, INC. 2600 N. 10th Street, Paducah, KY 42001
OAK'S AMUSEMENT PARK Portland, OR 97202
OCEAN VIEW AMUSEMENT PARK 223 East Main Street, Norfolk, VA 23503
OLD CHICAGO Interstate 55 and Route 53, Bolingbrook, IL 60439
OLYMPIC PARK 1300 Scottsville Rd., Rochester, NY 14624
OPRYLAND USA P. O. Box 2138, Nashville, TN 37214
PALACE PLAYLAND 1 Old Orchard Street, Old Orchard Beach, ME 04064
PARAGON PARK 175 Nantasket Avenue, Hull, MA 02045
PASSPORT TO FUN WORLD P. O. Box 54, Daytona Beach, FL 32018
PEONY PARK 81st and Cass Street, Omaha, NB 68114
PETTICOAT JUNCTION P. O. Box 9110, Panama City, FL 32401
PLAYLAND Rye, NY 10580
PLAYLAND AMUSEMENT PARK 2222 North Alamo, San Antonio, TX 78215
PLAYLAND AMUSEMENT PARK 65th Street, Ocean City, MD 21842
PLAYLAND PARK, INC. 2135 Magsillon Road, Akron, OH 44312
POINT PLEASANT PAVILLION, INC. Arnold Ave. and Boardwalk, Point
    Pleasant, NJ 08742
PONTCHARTRAIN BEACH Elysian Field Ave. and Lakeshore Dr., New
    Orleans, LA 70122
REVERE BEACH 151-161 Boulevard, Boston, MA 02151
RIVER GLEN PARK 230 South Western Pkwy., Louisville, KY 40212
RIVERSIDE PARK Main Street, Agawam, MA 01001

RIVERVIEW AMUSEMENT PARK Hwys. 12 and 23, Wisconsin Dells, WI 53965
RIVERVIEW PARK 8th and Corning, Des Moines IA 50313
ROCKAWAY'S PLAYLAND 185 Beach, Rockaway Beach, NY 14624
ROCKY POINT PARK Warwick, RI 02889
RON AND JUDY'S AMUSEMENT CO. Wisconsin Dells, WI 53965
ROSELAND PARK Lake Shore Drive, Canandaigua, NY 14424
SEA BREEZE PARK 4600 Culver Rd., Rochester, NY 14622
SEMINOLAND AMUSEMENT PARK 5995 State Rt. 7, Ft. Lauderdale, FL 33314
SHAHEEN'S FUN-O-RAMA PARK 26 F. Ocean Front, Salisbury Beach, MA
    01950
SIX FLAGS OVER GEORGIA P. O. Box 43187, Atlanta, GA 30336
SIX FLAGS OVER MID-AMERICA P. O. Box 666, Eureka, MO 63025
SIX FLAGS OVER TEXAS Arlington, TX 76010
SPORTLAND PIER 23rd and Boardwalk, Wildwood, NJ 08260
SPRINGLAKE AMUSEMENT PARK 1800 Springlake Drive, Oklahoma City,
    OK 73111
STEEPLECHASE AMUSEMENT PARK 1600 Surf Avenue, Brooklyn, NY 11224
STORYTOWN USA P. O. Box 511, Lake George, NY 12845
SUBURBAN PARK Rt. 92, Manlius, NY 13104
TRIMPER RIDES AND AMUSEMENTS Boardwalk at Division, Ocean City, MD
    21842
UNCLE CLIFF'S FAMILYLAND, USA 5301 San Mateo N.E., Albuquerque, NM
    87109
VALLEY PARK, INC. 10700 Lyndale Ave. South, Bloomington, MN 55426
WALDAMEER PARK, INC. Rt. 832 N., Erie, PA 16505
WALT DISNEY WORLD P. O. Box 40, Lake Buena Vista, FL 32830
WESTERN PLAYLAND P. O. Box 148, El Paso, TX 79942
WEST POINT PARK, INC. Park Rd., West Point, PA 19486
WEST VIEW PARK CO. Rt. 19 N, Pittsburgh, PA 15229
WHALOM PARK AMUSEMENT CO. Rt. 13, Lunenburg, MA 01462
WILDWOOD MARINE PIER AND PLAYLAND Wildwood, NJ 08260
WILLIAMS GROVE PARK 1 Park Avenue, Mechanicsburg, PA 17055
WILLOW GROVE PARK Willow Grove, PA 19090
WONDERLAND AMUSEMENT CENTER Amarillo, TX 79106
WONDERLAND PIER 6th and Boardwalk, Ocean City, NJ 08226
WORLDS OF FUN 4545 Worlds of Fun Avenue, Kansas City, MO 64161

BUS COMPANIES

AMERICAN SIGHTSEEING INTERNATIONAL 420 Lexington Avenue, New
    York, NY 10017
CONTINENTAL TRAILWAYS 1500 Jackson Street, Dallas, TX 75201
GRAY LINES SIGHTSEEING COMPANIES ASSOCIATED 7 West 51st Street,
    New York, NY 10019
GREYHOUND LINES, INC. Greyhound Tower, Phoenix, AZ 85077

CAR RENTAL COMPANIES

AJAX RENT-A-CAR 8818 West Olympic Blvd., Beverly Hills, CA 90211
AMERICAN INTERNATIONAL RENT-A-CAR 9864 Monroe Drive, Dallas, TX
    75220
AVIS RENT-A-CAR SYSTEM 900 Old Country Road, Garden City, NY 11530
BUDGET RENT-A-CAR 35 East Wacker Drive, Chicago, IL 60601
DOLLAR RENT-A-CAR SYSTEMS 5307 West Century Blvd., Los Angeles, CA
    90045

ECONO-CAR INTERNATIONAL 300 Sevilla, Coral Gables, FL 33134
GREYHOUND RENT-A-CAR 2875 N.E. LeJune Road, Miami, FL 33159
HERTZ CORPORATION 60 Madison Avenue, New York, NY 10021
NATIONAL RENT-A-CAR SYSTEM 5501 Green Valley Dr., Minneapolis, MN
    55437
PAYLESS CAR RENTAL P. O. Box 8211, Spokane, WA 99203
SEARS RENT-A-CAR 35 East Wacker Drive, Chicago, IL 60601
THRIFTY RENT-A-CAR SYSTEM 2422 N. Sheridan Road, Tulsa, OK 74151

HOTEL AND MOTEL SYSTEMS

ADMIRAL BENBOW INNS P. O. Box 2608, Mobile, AL 36625
AIRWAY HOTELS, INC. 4230 Genesee Street, Buffalo, NY 14225
ALAMO PLAZA HOTEL COURTS 1830 Sylvan Drive, Dallas, TX 75208
ALLEN FIELD ENTERPRISES 5711 Austin Street, Houston, TX 77004
ALLIED PROPERTIES 340 Mason Street, San Francisco, CA 94102
AMBASSADOR INNS OF AMERICA 8121 East Florence Avenue, Downey, CA
    90220
AMERICANA HOTELS 605 Third Avenue, New York, NY 10016
AMERICAN HOST INNS 3131 Mobile Highway, Montgomery, AL 36108
AMERICAN LIBERTY HOTELS CORP. 4100 1st National Bank Building,
    Dallas, TX 75202
AMERICAN MOTOR INNS, INC. 1917 Franklin Road, Roanoke, VA 24007
AMERICAN UNITED INNS 1213 East Dublin-Granville Road, Columbus, OH
    43229
AMERICA-WEST CORPORATION 4507 Brooklyn Avenue, N.E., Seattle, WA
    98105
ARISTOCRAT INNS OF AMERICA 23rd and the Lake, Chicago, IL 60616
ASSOCIATED FEDERAL HOTELS, INC. 1520 Mercantile Securities Building,
    Dallas, TX 75201
ASSOCIATED RESORT HOTELS 3425 Collins Avenue, Miami Beach, FL 33139
ASTROWORLD HOTEL CORP. P. O. Box 1555, Houston, TX 77001
ATLANTIC COAST HOTELS Warner Hotel, Harrisburg, PA 17101
ATLAS HOTELS, INC. 500 Hotel Circle, San Diego, CA 92138
AVERY VERMONT INNS Tavern Motor Inn, Montpelier, VT 05602
BANKERS SECURITIES CORP. Bellevue Stratford Hotel, Philadelphia, PA
    19102
BEST EASTERN MOTELS P. O. Box 6088, Hollywood, FL 33021
BEST WESTERN, INC. 2910 Sky Harbor Blvd., Phoenix, AZ 85034
BLANKSTEIN HOTELS 720 North 3rd Street, Milwaukee, WI 53203
BOND HOTELS 300 4th Street North, St. Petersburgh, FL 33731
BONER HOTELS COMPANY 2654 South Ames Way, Lakewood, CO 80227
BOSS HOTELS 1000 Walnut Street, Des Moines, IA 50309
BRECKENRIDGE HOTELS CORP. 2816 Breckenridge Industrial Court, St.
    Louis, MO 63144
BROWN HOTELS 1535 Collins Avenue, Miami Beach, FL 33139
BRITISH TRANSPORT HOTELS 1270 Avenue of the Americas, New York, NY
    10020
CALIFORNIA INNKEEPERS 1900 Alameda de las Pulgas, San Mateo, CA 94403
CALIFORNIA THEME RESORTS 696 South Coast Highway, Laguna Beach, CA
    92651
CARAVAN MOTOR HOTELS 2601 Jacksboro Highway, Fort Worth, TX 76114
CARTER HOTELS OPERATING CORP. 250 West 43rd Street, New York, NY
    10036
CENTURY HOTEL MANAGEMENT CO. 850 Moraga Dr., Los Angeles, CA
    90049

CINERAMA HAWAII HOTELS 2169 Kalia Road, Honolulu, HI 96815
CLAYTON HOUSE MOTELS 1098 South Milwaukee Avenue, Wheeling, IL 60090
COLONEL SANDERS INNS, INC. 1441 Gardiner Lane, Louisville, KY 40213
COLONIAL MOTOR HOTEL CORP. Audubon Road, Wakefield, MA 01880
COLONY HOTELS, INC. 16055 Ventura Blvd., Encino, CA 91416
CONSOLIDATED HOTELS 6945 North Clark Street, Chicago, IL 60626
CONSOLIDATED HOTELS OF CALIFORNIA 1301 Wilshire Blvd., Los Angeles, CA 90017
CONTINENTAL HOTEL SYSTEM 122 North Central Avenue, Glendale, CA 91203
CONTINENTAL HOTELS, INC. 7300 World Way West, Los Angeles, CA 90009
CONTINENTAL SERVICES CORP. 2951 South Bayshore Drive, Miami, FL 33133
CROWN INNS OF AMERICA, 115 East Morehead Street, Charlotte, NC 28202
CUNARD HOTELS AND RESORTS 555 Fifth Avenue, New York, NY 10017
DAVENPORT HOTEL MANAGEMENT 1017 Grove, Maitland, FL 32751
DAVIS BROS. MOTOR LODGES 3833 First National Bank Building, Atlanta, GA 30303
DAYS INNS OF AMERICA, INC. 2751 Buford Highway, N.E., Atlanta, GA 30324
DEL WEBB HOTELS INTERNATIONAL P. O. Box 14066, Las Vegas, NV 89114
DILLON HOTELS COMPANY 1118 South 72nd Street, Omaha, NB 68124
DISTINGUISHED RESORTS OF WISCONSIN 100 West Michigan, Kalamazoo, MI 49006
DORAL HOTELS CORPORATION 600 Madison Avenue, New York, NY 10022
DOUBLETREE INC. 2345 University Drive, Phoenix, AZ 85034
THE DOWNTOWNER/ROWNTOWNER SYSTEM INC. P. O. Box 161356, Memphis, TN 28116
DOYLE HOTELS AND MOTELS 137 North Main Street, Rice Lake, WI 54868
DREIER HOTEL COMPANY 227 West 45th Street, New York, NY 10036
DUNFEY FAMILY—HOTELS & MOTOR INNS Hampton, NH 03842
DUTCH INNS OF AMERICA, INC. 299 Alhambra, Coral Gables, FL 33134
ECONO-TRAVEL MOTOR HOTELS 3 Koger Executive Center, Norfolk, VA 23502
EXECUTIVE HOUSE, INC. 71 East Wacker Drive, Chicago, IL 60601
FABULOUS INNS OF AMERICA 2485 Hotel Circle Place, San Diego, CA 92110
FAIRMONT HOTEL COMPANY San Francisco, CA 94106
FELS HOTELS OF KANSAS CITY 3835 Main Street, Kansas City, MO 64111
FENWAY MOTOR HOTELS 475 Commonwealth Avenue, Boston, MA 02215
FLAGLER SYSTEM, INC. 45 Cocoanut Row, Palm Beach, FL 33480
FLORIDA RETIREMENT COMMUNITY HOTELS, INC. 130 S. Massachussets Ave., Lakeland, FL 33801
FRED HARVEY, INC. 111 South Hill Drive, Brisbane, CA 94005
FRIENDSHIP INNS INTERNATIONAL 739 South 4th West Street, Salt Lake City, UT 84101
GAC PROPERTIES, INC. 7880 Biscayne Blvd., Miami, FL 33138
GAL-TEX HOTEL CORPORATION P. O. Box 59, Galveston, TX 77550
GILL HOTELS P. O. Box 21277, Fort Lauderdale, FL 33316
GLACIER NATIONAL PARK HOTELS East Glacier Park, MT 59434
GOLD COAST HOTELS 616 North Rush Street, Chicago, IL 60611
GOLDEN EAGLE INNS, INC. 1028 South Blvd., Charlotte, NC 28203
GOLDEN TULIP WORLD-WIDE HOTELS 609 Fifth Avenue, New York, NY 10019
GOTHAM HOTELS 405 Lexington Avenue, New York, NY 10017
GRAND METROPOLITAN HOTELS 119 West 57th Street, New York, NY 10019

GRAND TETON LODGE COMPANY P. O. Box 250, Moran, WY 83013
GRENOBLE HOTELS, INC. 400 Payne Shoemaker Building, Harrisburg, PA 17101
HANDLERY HOTELS 351 Geary Street, San Francisco, CA 94102
HAWAIIAN PACIFIC RESORTS 1150 South King Street, Honolulu, HI 96814
HERITAGE HOTELS MANAGEMENT CORP. 14 East 28th Street, New York, NY 10016
HERITAGE INTERNATIONAL HOTELS 7000 Beach Blvd., Buena Park, CA 90620
HERSHEY ESTATES Hershey, PA 17033
HICKEL HOTELS P. O. Box 2280, Anchorage, AK 99501
HILTON HOTELS CORPORATION 720 South Michigan Avenue, Chicago, IL 60605
HILTON INTERNATIONAL CO. 301 Park Avenue, New York, NY 10022
HOLIDAY INNS, INC. 3742 Lamar Avenue, Memphis, TN 38118
HOSPITALITY MOTOR INNS, INC. 2100 Terminal Tower, Cleveland, OH 44113
HOST INTERNATIONAL HOTELS Tampa Airport, Tampa, FL 33607
HOST ENTERPRISES, INC. 2300 Lincoln Highway East, Lancaster, PA 17602
HOTEL CORPORATION OF THE PACIFIC 2299 Kuhio Avenue, Honolulu, HI 96815
HOTEL MANAGEMENT CORP. OF AMERICA P. O. Box 3521, Washington, DC 20007
HOUSTON INTERNATIONAL HOTELS, INC. P. O. Box 1379, Houston, TX 77001
HOWARD JOHNSON'S MOTOR LODGES 222 Forbes Road, Braintree, MA 02184
HUGHES RESORT HOTELS 3421 Las Vegas Blvd. South, Las Vegas, NV 89109
HYATT CORPORATION 1338 Bayshore Highway, Burlingame, CA 94010
IMPERIAL '400' NATIONAL, INC. 375 Sylvan Avenue, Englewood Cliffs, NJ 07632
IMPERIAL HOUSE MOTELS, INC. 90 Compark Road, Dayton, OH 45459
INTER-CONTINENTAL HOTELS Pan Am Building, New York, NY 10017
INTER-ISLAND RESORTS, LTD. P. O. Box 8539, Honolulu, HI 96815
INTERNATIONAL AIRPORT HOTEL SYSTEM, INC, 6225 W. Century Blvd., Los Angeles, CA 90045
INTERNATIONAL HOTELS, INC. 2800 Fisher Bldg., Detroit, MI 48202
INTERNATIONAL ROADRUNNER MOTOR INNS, INC. 2625 Louisiana, Houston, TX 77006
IN TOWN MOTOR HOTEL MANAGEMENT CO. 7711 Woodmont Avenue, Bethesda, MD 20014
ISLAND HOLIDAYS RESORTS 2222 Kalakaua Avenue, Honolulu, HI 96815
JACK TAR HOTELS Reserve Life Building, Dallas, TX 75202
THE KAHLER CORPORATION 2nd Avenue & Center Street S.W., Rochester, MN 55901
KNOTT HOTELS CORPORATION 840 Madison Avenue, New York, NY 10021
KRODELL AND KRODELL HOTELS 921 South Grand Avenue, Los Angeles, CA 90015
LEAMINGTON HOTELS 10th Street & 3rd Avenue South, Minneapolis, MN 55404
LEE HOTEL CORPORATION 16152 Beach Blvd., Huntington Beach, CA 92647
LEEDS HOTELS 110 South Dearborn, Chicago, IL 60603
LEX HOTELS, INC. 745 Fifth Avenue, New York, NY 10022
LOEWS HOTELS 666 Fifth Avenue, New York, NY 10019
LUCAYAN HOTEL CORP. 3200 West Market Street, Akron, OH 44313
L Q MOTOR INNS, INC. Century Building, San Antonio, TX 78216

MANAGEMENT RESOURCES, INC. 2639 North Monroe, Tallahasse, FL 32303
MARKS INNS OF AMERICA 4498 Washington Road, East Point, GA 30344
MARRIOTT HOTELS, INC. 5161 River Road, Washington, DC 20016
MASTER HOSTS INNS P. O. Box 2509, Daytona Beach, FL 32015
MELIA HOTELS 580 Fifth Avenue, New York, NY 10036
METROAMERICA HOTELS CORP. 225 North Wabash, Chicago, IL 60601
METRO INNS MANAGEMENT COMPANY 6060 North Central Expressway, Dallas, TX 75206
ERNEST E. MICHAELSON-MOTELS 476 North Parkview Avenue, Columbus, OH 43209
MIDLAND HOTELS COMPANY 800 National Building, Minneapolis, MN 55402
MILNER HOTELS AND INNS 1526 Center Street, Detroit, MI 48226
MOTEL 6, INC. 1888 Century Park East, Los Angeles, CA 90067
NATIONAL INNS LTD. P. O. Box 1138, Atlantic City, NJ 08404
ORVIN INNS P. O. Box 482, Charleston, SC 29402
OUTRIGGER HOTELS 2335 Kalakaua Avenue, Honolulu, HI 96815
PACIFIC HOST INC. P. O. Box 781, Encino, CA 91316
PACIFIC WESTERN HOTELS CORP. 825 Sutter Street, San Francisco, CA 94109
PACKARD HOTEL COMPANY Curtis Hotel, Mount Vernon, OH 43050
PARADISE ISLAND LIMITED 915 N.E. 125th Street, North Miami, FL 33161
PARADISE RESORTS P. O. Box 6725, Surfside Stn., Miami Beach, FL 33154
PARK LANE PROPERTIES CO. 550 Geary Street, San Francisco, CA 94102
PARKWAY INNS, INC. 610 Empire Building, Des Moines, IA 50309
PARRISH HOTELS, INC. P.O. Box 268, Grand Bend, KS 67530
PICK HOTELS CORPORATION 532 South Michigan Avenue, Chicago, IL 60605
PLAYBOY CLUBS-HOTELS 919 North Michigan Avenue, Chicago, IL 60611
PRINCESS HOTELS INTERNATIONAL 1345 Avenue of the Americas, New York, NY 10019
PROM MOTOR HOTELS 6th & Main Streets, Kansas City, MO 64105
QUALITY INNS 10750 Columbia Pike, Silver Springs, MD 20901
RADISSON HOTEL CORPORATION 12805 State Highway 55, Minneapolis, MN 55441
RAMADA INNS INC. P. O. Box 590, Phoenix, AZ 85001
RANK HOTELS (SALES) LTD. 444 Madison Avenue, New York, NY 10022
REALTY HOTELS, INC. Biltmore Hotel, 43rd St. & Madison Ave., New York, NY 10017
RED CARPET INNS OF AMERICA, INC. P. O. Box 2510, Daytona Beach, FL 32015
RICH HOTELS 3831 North Fremont Street, Chicago, IL 60613
RICHMOND HOTELS, INC. 2501 West Broad Street, Richmond, VA 23220
THE RINN CORPORATION P. O. Box 80368, San Diego, CA 92138
ROCKRESORTS, INC. 30 Rockefeller Plaza, New York, NY 10020
RODEWAY INNS OF AMERICA P. O. Box 34736, Dallas, TX 75234
ROGER SMITH HOTELS CORP. 276 Park Avenue South, New York, NY 10010
ROMNEY INTERNATIONAL HOTELS, INC. P. O. Box 7098, Phoenix, AZ 85011
ROYAL INNS OF AMERICA, INC. 4855 North Harbor Drive, San Diego, CA 92106
SADDLEBACK INNS OF THE AMERICAS 1660 E 1st Street, Santa Ana, CA 92701
SAUSMAN MOTOR INNS 1510 Boardwalk, Ocean City, NJ 08226
SCHINE HOTELS, INC. 919 Third Avenue, New York, NY 10022
SCOTTISH INNS OF AMERICA, INC. 125 North Kentucky Street, Kingston, TN 37763
SHERATON HOTELS AND MOTOR INNS 470 Atlantic Avenue, Boston, MA 02210

SONESTA INTERNATIONAL HOTELS CORP. 390 Commonwealth Avenue, Boston, MA 02215
SOUTHWEST HOTELS, INC. P. O. Box 389, Little Rock, AR 72203
SPENCER-TAYLOR HOTELS 100 East 42nd Street, New York, NY 10017
SQUIRE INNS 666 Squire Place, N.E., Atlanta, GA 30324
STOUFFER HOTELS 1375 Euclid Avenue, Cleveland, OH 44115
SUPERIOR MOTELS, Inc. 1747 Van Buren Street, Hollywood, FL 33020
SWISS CHALET, INC. P. O. Box 12038, Santurce, PR 00914
THUNDERBIRD MOTOR INNS 1115 Esther Street, Vancouver, WA 98660
TOM SAWYER MOTOR INNS 3142 Third Avenue North, St. Petersburg, FL 33713
TOWNE HOTELS 105 West Michigan Street, Milwaukee, WI 53203
TOWNSEND PROPERTIES, INC. 1701 Northside Dr., N.W., Atlanta, GA 30318
TRAVELODGE INTERNATIONAL, INC. 250 Travelodge Drive, El Cajon, CA 92040
TREADWAY INNS AND RESORTS 140 Market Street, Paterson, NJ 07505
TRUST HOUSES FORTE LTD. 1290 Avenue of the Americas, New York, NY 10019
TWA SERVICES, INC. P. O. Box 400, Cedar City, UT 84720
TYLER MOTELS OF NEW MEXICO 525 Tyler Road, N.W., Albuquerque, NM 87107
UNITED HOTELS COMPANY 246 Madison Avenue, Detroit, MI 48226
UNITED INNS, INC 5100 Poplar Avenue, Memphis, TN 38137
UPTOWNER INNS, INC. 1415 4th Avenue, Huntington, WV 25701
VAGABOND MOTOR HOTELS, INC. 1810 State Street, San Diego, CA 92101
VANCE HOTELS AND MOTOR INNS Tower Building, Seattle, WA 98101
VANCE HUCKINS HOTELS 225 Powell Street, San Francisco, CA 94102
VOYAGER INNS 8115 Market Street, Youngstown, OH 44512
WAIKIKI HOTELS 226 Lewers Street, Honolulu, HI 96815
WAYFARER INNS, INC. Beekman Arms Hotel, Rhinebeck, NY 12572
WESTERN GUARANTY CORP. 2600 Auburn Blvd., Sacramento, CA 95821
WESTERN INTERNATIONAL HOTELS Olympic Hotel, Seattle, WA 98111
WM CAPITAL AND MANAGEMENT CORP. 60 East 42nd Street, New York, NY 10017
WRATHER HOTELS, INC. Disneyland Hotel, Anaheim, CA 92802
YELLOWSTONE PARK COMPANY Yellowstone National Park, WY 82190
YORK ENTERPRISES, INC. 3706-A Nolensville Road, Nashville, TN 37211
YOSEMITE NATIONAL PARK HOTELS Yosemite National Park, CA 95389
YOUR HOST, INC. 170 South Parkview Avenue, Columbus, OH 43209

HOTEL REPRESENTATIVES/RESERVATION SERVICES

ALEXANDER ASSOCIATES 2607 Nostrand Avenue, Brooklyn, NY 11210
ADVENTURE ASSOCIATES 5925 Maple, Dallas, TX 75235
AMBASSADOR SERVICE HOTELS OF SWITZERLAND 500 Fifth Avenue, New York, NY 10036
AMERICAN-INTERNATIONAL HOTEL REPRESENTATIVES 500 Fifth Avenue, New York, NY 10036
AMTOUR CORP. 421 Powell Street, San Francisco, CA 94102
BAHAMAS HOTEL RESERVATIONS SERVICE 255 Alhambra, Coral Gables, FL 33143
BEST WESTERN, INC. 2910 Sky Harbor Blvd., Phoenix, AZ 85034
BRITISH AIRWAYS ASSOCIATE HOTELS 245 Park Avenue, New York, NY 10017
BTH HOTELS P.O. Box 48, Rego Park, NY 11374
CAESAR HOTELS OF ITALY 7733 Forsyth Blvd., St. Louis, MO 63105

CASH ASSOCIATES 6405 North Sheridan Road, Chicago, IL 60626
CIGA HOTELS, INC. 745 Fifth Avenue, New York, NY 10022
CREATIVE LEISURE CORP. 1280 Columbus Avenue, San Francisco, CA 94133
DAVID GREEN ASSOCIATES Commodore Hotel, Park Avenue, New York, NY 10017
DAVID B MITCHELL & COMPANY 217 East 49th Street, New York, NY 10017
DESTINATION FRANCE 521 Fifth Avenue, New York, NY 10017
DESTINATION MARKETING 5250 West Century Blvd., Los Angeles, CA 90045
DOWNTOWNER/ROWNTOWNER SYSTEM P. O. Box 161356, Memphis, TN 38116
ERNEST J. NEWMAN 380 Madison Avenue, New York, NY 10017
EUROTEL BOOKING OFFICE 608 Fifth Avenue, New York, NY 10020
ESCALANTE AND NADELL 118-21 Queens Blvd., Forest Hills, NY 11375
FAR EAST EXPRESS 617 South Olive Street, Los Angeles, CA 90014
FRANTEL HOTELS 521 Fifth Avenue, New York NY 10017
FRED HARVEY 111 South Hill Drive, Brisbane, CA 94005
HARBINGER HOTEL REPRESENTATIVES, INC. 226 East 54th Street, New York, NY 10022
HARRY JARVINEN & ASSOCIATES, INC. 1717 North Highland Avenue, Los Angeles, CA 90028
HAWAII HOTEL MARKETING, INC. 1717 North Highland Avenue, Los Angeles, CA 90028
HILTON RESERVATION SERVICE 415 Seventh Avenue, New York, NY 10001
HOLIDAY INNS, INC. 3742 Lamar Avenue, Memphis, TN 38118
HOTEL REPRESENTATIVE, INC. 770 Lexington Avenue, New York, NY 10021
HOTEL RESERVATIONS UNLIMITED 10776 Wilshire Blvd., Los Angeles, CA 90024
HOTEL RESERVATIONS BY IVERS 2026 Chestnut Street, Philadelphia, PA 19103
HOTELS UNLIMITED, 230 Park Avenue, New York, NY 10022
HOWARD JOHNSON'S MOTOR LODGES 222 Forbes Road, Braintree, MA 02184
HSI RESERVATIONS, 3030 Dundy Drive, Los Angeles, CA 90066
HYATT HOTELS WORLDWIDE RESERVATIONS CENTER 3425 North 90th Street, Omaha, NB 68134
INDEPENDENT RESERVATION SYSTEM 2 Penn Plaza, New York, NY 10001
INTER-CONTINENTAL RESERVATION SERVICE Pan Am Building, New York, NY 10017
JACK HUGEN INTERNATIONAL 929 Sunrise Lane, Fort Lauderdale, FL 33304
JANE CONDON CORP. 211 East 43rd Street, New York, NY 10017
JAPAN HOTEL RESERVATIONS CENTER 45 Rockefeller Plaza, New York, NY 10020
JOHN PARKER & ASSOCIATES, INC. 324 Vance Building, Seattle, WA 98101
JOHN A TETLEY CO., INC. 3075 Wilshire Blvd., Los Angeles, CA 90010
KATHLEEN R WOLFF & ASSOCIATES Bank of America Center, San Francisco, CA 94104
LEONARD HICKS 8101 Biscayne Blvd., Miami, FL 33138
LEX RESERVATION SERVICE 745 Fifth Avenue, New York, NY 10022
LOEW'S RESERVATIONS, INC. 666 Fifth Avenue, New York, NY 10019
MARKETING COORDINATORS INTERNATIONAL 1001 Connecticut Ave., N.W., Washington DC 20036
MARTHA LEE SENNEFF 3930 Dosh Road, Des Moines, IA 50310
MELIA HOTELS 580 Fifth Avenue, New York, NY 10036
MEXICO HOTEL & TRAVEL RESERVATIONS 248 S. Robertson Blvd., Beverly Hills, CA 90211

M & M RESERVATIONS 15300 Ventura Blvd. Sherman Oaks, CA 91403
I OLIVER ENGEBRETSON, INC. 919 3rd Avenue, New York, NY 10022
OROZCO INTERNATIONAL, INC. 551 Fifth Avenue, New York, NY 10017
OUTRIGGER HOTEL RESERVATIONS SERVICE 2335 Kalakaua Avenue, Honolulu, HI 96815
PENTA HOTELS 575 Madison Avenue, New York, NY 10022
PRINCESS HOTELS INTERNATIONAL P. O. Box 592258 AMF, Miami, FL 33159
QUALITY INNS 10750 Columbia Pike, Silver Springs, MD 20901
RALPH LOCK RESERVATIONS 315 East 72nd Street, New York, NY 10021
RAMADA INNS 3838 East Van Buren Street, Phoenix, AZ 85008
RAY MORROW ASSOCIATES 51 East 42nd Street, New York, NY 10017
RESORT REPRESENTATION SERVICE, INC. 30 Rockefeller Plaza, New York, NY 10020
ROBERT REID ASSOCIATES 1270 Avenue of the Americas, New York, NY 10020
ROBERT F. WARNER 711 Third Avenue, New York, NY 10020
RODEWAY INNS OF AMERICA 2880 LBJ Freeway, Dallas, TX 75234
ROYAL INNS OF AMERICA, INC. P. O. Box 80938, San Diego, CA 92138
SCANWORLD HOTEL AND TRAVEL MARKETING 12444 Ventura Blvd., Studio City, CA 91604
SCOTT CALDER 295 Madison Avenue, New York, NY 10017
SHERATON RESERVATION SERVICE 470 Atlantic Avenue, Boston, MA 02210
SOFITEL 250 West 57th Street, New York, NY 10019
STEIGENBERGER RESERVATION SERVICE 40 East 49th Street, New York, NY 10017
TERRI POLLACK INTERNATIONAL, INC. 500 Fifth Avenue, New York, NY 10036
THUNDERBIRD AND RED LION MOTOR INNS 1115 Esther Street, Vancouver, WA 98660
TOUREX CO. OF AMERICA, INC. 29 Broadway, New York, NY 10006
TRANSPORTATION CONSULTANTS INTERNATIONAL 6290 Sunset Blvd., Hollywood, CA 90028
TRAVELODGE INTERNATIONAL, INC. 250 Travelodge Drive, El Cajon, CA 92040
TRAVEL MARKETING REPRESENTATIVES 509 Madison Avenue, New York, NY 10022
TRAVEL MARKETING 323 Geary Street, San Francisco, CA 94102
TRUST HOUSES FORTE 810 Seventh Avenue, New York, NY 10019
UTELL INTERNATIONAL 119 West 57th Street, New York, NY 10019
WESTERN INTERNATIONAL RESERVATION SERVICE 411 Senaca Street, Seattle, WA 98111
WHITNEY, INC. HOTEL REPRESENTATIVES 250 Ward Avenue, Honolulu, HI 96814
WILLIAM R TOBIAS & ASSOCIATES 1005 Market Street, San Francisco, CA 94103
WOLFE INTERNATIONAL 500 Fifth Avenue, New York, NY 10036
WORLD-WIDE RESERVATIONS 2690 Dove Street, San Diego, CA 91203

MAGAZINES

Trade and professional publications

AIRFARE INTERLINE MAGAZINE 9800 South Sepulveda Blvd., Los Angeles, CA 90045

AIR LINE PILOT 1625 Massachusetts Ave., N.W., Washington, DC 20036
AIR TRANSPORT WORLD 1155 15th Street, N.W. Washington, DC 20005
AMUSEMENT BUSINESS 1719 West End Avenue, Nashville, TN 37203
ASTA TRAVEL NEWS 488 Madison Avenue, New York, NY 10022
BUSINESS AND COMMERCIAL AVIATION One Park Avenue, New York, NY 10016
CLUB AND FOOD SERVICE P. O. Box 788, Lynbrook, NY 11563
COMMERCIAL FOODSERVICE ILLUSTRATED 2177 Ocean Street, Marchfield, MA 02050
COOKING FOR PROFIT 1202 South Park Street, Madison, WI 53715
DESTINATION AMERICA 205 East 42nd Street, New York, NY 10017
DISCOVER AMERICA PUBLICATIONS 605 Fifth Avenue, New York, NY 10017
EXECUTIVE HOUSEKEEPER 401 N. Broad Street, Philadelphia, PA 19108
FOOD EXECUTIVE 508 IBM Building, Fort Wayne, IN 46805
FOOD SERVICE MARKETING P. O. Box 1648, Madison, WI 53701
GENERAL AVIATION BUSINESS P. O. Box 1094, Snyder, TX 79549
GROUP TRAVEL 60 East 42nd Street, New York, NY 10017
HOSPITALITY MAGAZINE 614 Superior Avenue, W., Cleveland, OH 44113
HOTEL AND MOTEL MANAGEMENT 845 Chicago Avenue, Evanston, IL 60202
INSTITUTIONS/VOLUME FEEDING MANAGEMENT 5 South Wabash Ave., Chicago, IL 60603
INTERLINE REPORTER 2 West 46th Street, New York, NY 10036
JET CARGO NEWS 5314 Bingle Road, Houston, TX 77018
LODGING AND FOOD-SERVICE NEWS 131 Clarendon Street, Boston, MA 02116
MEETINGS AND CONVENTIONS MAGAZINE One Park Avenue, New York, NY 10016
MILE HIGH 200 Park Avenue, New York, NY 10017
MOTEL/MOTOR INN JOURNAL P. O. Box 769, Temple, TX 76501
NATION'S RESTAURANT NEWS Two Park Avenue, New York, NY 10016
PACIFIC TRAVEL NEWS 274 Brannan Street, San Francisco, CA 94107
PIZZA AND PASTA 23 North Washington, Ypsilanti, MI 48197
RECREATION MANAGEMENT 20 North Wacker Drive, Chicago, IL 60606
RESORT MANAGEMENT P. O. Box 4169, Memphis, TN 38104
RESTAURANT BUSINESS 633 Third Avenue, New York, NY 10017
TRAVEL/AGE EAST 888 Seventh Avenue , New York, NY 10011
TRAVEL/AGE MIDAMERICA 2416 Prudential Plaza, Chicago, IL 60601
TRAVEL/AGE WEST 582 Market Street, San Francisco, CA 94104
THE TRAVEL AGENT 2 West 46th Street, New York, NY 10036
TRAVEL INDUSTRY NEWS One Park Avenue, New York, NY 10016
TRAVEL INDUSTRY PERSONNEL DIRECTORY 2 West 46th Street, New York, NY 10036
TRAVEL NORTH AMERICA One Park Avenue, New York, NY 10016
TRAVELSCENE MAGAZINE 888 Seventh Avenue, New York, NY 10011
TRAVEL MANAGEMENT DAILY 888 Seventh Avenue, New York, NY 10019
TRAVEL TRADE 605 Fifth Avenue, New York, NY 10017
TRAVEL WEEKLY One Park Avenue, New York, NY 10016

Inflight, hotel, and credit card company publications

AIR CALIFORNIA MAGAZINE P. O. Box 21, Corona del Mar, CA 92625
ALOFT (National Airlines) 2701 South Bayshore Drive, Miami, FL 33133
AMERICAN WAY 633 Third Avenue, New York, NY 10017
CARTE BLANCHE MAGAZINE 3460 Wilshire Blvd., Los Angeles, CA 90010

CLIPPER MAGAZINE (Pan American) 5900 Wilshire Blvd., Los Angeles, CA 90036
CONTINENTAL TRAILWAYS MAGAZINE 1500 Jackson Street, Dallas, TX 75201
FLIGHTIME (Allegheny, Ozark, Continental) 5900 Wilshire Blvd., Los Angeles, CA 90036
FRONTIER NEWS 8250 Smith Road, Denver, CO 80207
GO GREYHOUND Greyhound Tower, Phoenix, AZ 85077
HOLIDAY INN COMPANION 5900 Wilshire Blvd., Los Angeles, CA 90036
HOOFBEAT (Best Western Motels) 2910 Sky Harbor Blvd., Phoenix, AZ 85034
INSIDER INTERNATIONAL (Travelodge) P. O. Box 308, El Cajon, CA 92022
JET BIRD NEWS (Hawaiian) P. O. Box 9008, Honolulu, HI 96820
LATELY (Sheraton) 15383 N.W. Seventh Avenue, Miami, FL 33169
MAINLINER (United) 5900 Wilshire Blvd., Los Angeles, CA 90036
LATITUDE/20 (Hawaiian) 1649 Kapiolani Blvd., Honolulu, HI 96814
LIVELY WORLD (Marriott) 747 Third Avenue, New York, NY 10017
NORTHLINER (North Central) 1999 Shepard Rd., St. Paul, MN 55116
NORTWEST EXPERIENCE 7020 125th Street S.E., Renton, WA 98055
PASSAGES (Northwest Orient) 747 Third Avenue, New York, NY 10017
PASTIMES 4 West 58th Street, New York, NY 10019
PSA MAGAZINE 5900 Wilshire Blvd., Los Angeles, CA 90036
REFLECTIONS (Ramada Inns) 5900 Wilshire Blvd., Los Angeles, CA 90036
THE REPORTER (Quality Inns) 10750 Columbia Pike, Silver Springs, MD 20901
REVIEW (Eastern) 5900 Wilshire Blvd., Los Angeles, CA 90036
SIGNATURE (Diners Club) 260 Madison Avenue, New York, NY 10016
SKY (Delta) 5900 Wilshire Blvd., Los Angeles, CA 90036
SUNDANCER (Hughes Airwest) 5900 Wilshire Blvd., Los Angeles, CA 90036
TALKING TOTEM (Alaska Airlines) Seattle-Tacoma Int'l Airport, Seattle, WA 98158
TRAVEL AND LEISURE (American Express) 61 West 51st Street, New York, NY 10019
TWA AMBASSADOR 1999 Shepard Rd., St. Paul, MN 55116
WESTERN'S WORLD 141 El Camino, Beverly Hills, CA 90212

Consumer and other travel related publications

ADVENTURE ROAD (Amoco Motor Club) P.O. Box 4778, Chicago, IL 60680
AERO MAGAZINE P.O. Box 1184, Ramona, CA 92065
AIR FACTS MAGAZINE 110 East 42nd Street, New York, NY 10017
AIR PROGRESS 8490 Sunset Blvd., Los Angeles, CA 90069
THE AOPA PILOT 7315 Wisconsin Ave., Bethesda, MD 20014
ARIZONA HIGHWAYS 2039 West Lewis Avenue, Phoenix, AZ 85009
AVIATION MONTHLY 306 Dartmouth St., Boston, MA 02116
AVIATION QUARTERLY P.O. Box 7070, Arlington, VA 22207
AVIATION TRAVEL 6045 Wilson Blvd., Arlington, VA 22205
BON APPETIT MAGAZINE 4700 Belleview, Kansas City, MO 64112
CHEVRON USA, P. O. Box 6227, San Jose, CA 95150
CONTINENTAL MAGAZINE (Ford) The American Road, Dearborn, MI 48121
DISCOVERY Allstate Plaza, Northbrook, IL 60062
FORD TIMES The American Road, Dearborn, MI 48121
FRIENDS MAGAZINE (Chevrolet) 30400 Van Dyke, Warren, MI 48093
GOURMET 777 Third Avenue, New York, NY 10017
HOLIDAY 1100 Waterway Blvd., Indianapolis, IN 46202
NATIONAL GEOGRAPHIC MAGAZINE 17th and M Streets, N.W., Washington, DC 20036
ODYSSEY (Gulf Travel Club) 300 S. Wacker Drive, Chicago, IL 60606

PLANE AND PILOT P. O. Box 1136, Santa Monica, CA 90406
PRIVATE PILOT 2377 S. El Camino Real, San Clemente, CA 92672
ROTOR AND WINGS News Plaza, Peoria, IL 61601
SKI MAGAZINE 235 East 45th Street, New York, NY 10017
SUNSET MAGAZINE Middlefield and Willow Road, Menlo Park, CA 94025
TRAVEL MAGAZINE, INC. 51 Atlantic Ave., Floral Park, NY 11001
VISTA/USA (Exxon Travel Club) 850 Third Avenue, New York, NY 10022

RAILROADS

AMTRAK 955 L'Enfant Plaza North, S.W., Washington, DC 20024
AUTO-TRAIN CORPORATION 1801 K Street, N.W., Washington, DC 20006
BANGOR AND AROOSTOOK RAILROAD Route 2, Box 14, Bangor, ME 04410
BESSEMER AND LAKE ERIE RAILROAD P.O. Box 536, Pittsburgh, PA 15230
BOSTON AND MAIN CORP. 150 Causeway Street, Boston, MA 02114
BURLINGTON NORTHERN 176 East 5th Street, St. Paul, MN 55101
CHESSIE SYSTEM 2 North Charles Street, Baltimore, MD 21201
CHICAGO & ILLINOIS MIDLAND RAILWAY CO. P.O. Box 139, Springfield, IL 62705
CHICAGO & NORTH WESTERN TRANSPORTATION CO. 400 West Madison Street, Chicago, IL 60606
CHICAGO, MILWAUKEE, ST. PAUL AND PACIFIC RAILROAD 516 West Jackson Blvd., Chicago, IL 60606
CHICAGO, ROCK ISLAND AND PACIFIC RAILROAD LaSalle Street Station, Chicago, IL 60605
CLINCHFIELD RAILROAD 229 Nolichucky Avenue, Erwin, TN 37650
CONSOLIDATED RAIL CORPORATION (CONRAIL) 6 Penn Center Plaza, Philadelphia, PA 19104
DELEWARE AND HUDSON RAILWAY 40 Beaver Street, Albany, NY 12207
DENVER AND RIO GRANDE WESTERN RAILROAD P.O. Box 5482, Denver, CO 80217
DETROIT AND TOLEDO SHORE LINE RAILROAD 131 West Lafayette Avenue, Detroit, MI 48226
DETROIT, TOLEDO AND IRONTON RAILROAD One Parklane Blvd., Dearborn, MI 48126
DULUTH, MISSABE AND IRON RANGE RAILWAY 227 West 1st Street, Duluth, MN 55802
ELGIN, JOLIET & EASTERN RAILWAY P.O. Box 880, Joliet, IL 60434
THE FAMILY LINES SYSTEM 500 Water Street, Jacksonville, FL 32202
FLORIDA COAST RAILWAY One Malaga Street, St. Augustine, FL 32084
GEORGIA RAILROAD 1590 Marietta Blvd., N.W., Atlanta, GA 30318
GRAND TRUNK LINES 131 West Lafayette Blvd., Detroit, MI 48226
ILLINOIS CENTRAL GULF RAILROAD 233 North Michigan Avenue, Chicago, IL 60601
ILLINOIS TERMINAL RAILROAD P.O. Box 7282, St. Louis, MO 63177
KANSAS CITY SOUTHERN RAILWAY 114 West 11th Street, Kansas City, MO 64105
LONG ISLAND RAILROAD Jamaica Station Building, Jamaica, NY 11435
LOUISVILLE AND NASHVILLE RAILROAD P.O. Box 1198, Louisville, KY 40201
MAINE CENTRAL RAILROAD 242 St. John Street, Portland, ME 04102
MISSOURI-KANSAS-TEXAS RAILROAD 701 Commerce Street, Dallas, TX 75202
MISSOURI PACIFIC RAILROAD 210 North 13th Street, St. Louis, MO 63103
NORFOLK AND WESTERN RAILWAY 8 North Jefferson Street, Roanoke, VA 24042

NORTHWESTERN PACIFIC RAILROAD One Market Plaza, San Francisco, CA 94105
PITTSBURGH AND LAKE ERIE RAILROAD P. & L. E. Terminal Bldg., Pittsburgh, PA 15219
RICHMOND, FREDERICKSBURG AND POTOMAC RAILROAD CO. P.O. Box 11281, Richmond, VA 23230
ST. LOUIS-SAN FRANCISCO RAILWAY 906 Olive Street, St. Louis, MO. 63101
ST. LOUIS SOUTHWESTERN RAILWAY CO. One Market Plaza, San Francisco, CA 94105
SANTA FE RAILWAY 80 East Jackson Blvd., Chicago, IL 60604
SEABOARD COAST LINE RAILROAD 500 Water Street, Jacksonville, FL 32202
SOO LINE RAILROAD P.O. Box 530, Minneapolis, MN 55440
SOUTHERN PACIFIC TRANSPORTATION CO. One Market Plaza, San Francisco, CA 94105
SOUTHERN RAILWAY SYSTEM P.O. Box 1808, Washington, DC 20013
TEXAS MEXICAN RAILWAY P.O. Box 419, Laredo, TX 78040
TOLEDO, PEORIA & WESTERN RAILROAD 2000 East Washington Street, East Peoria, IL 61611
UNION PACIFIC RAILROAD 1416 Dodge Street, Omaha, NB 68179
WESTERN PACIFIC RAILROAD 526 Mission Street, San Francisco, CA 94105

PASSENGER STEAMSHIP AND CRUISE LINES

American flag passenger and cruise lines

AMERICAN CRUISE LINES, INC. Steamship Landing, Haddam CT 06438
DELTA QUEEN STEAMBOAT CO. 511 Main Street, Cincinnati, OH 45202
DELTA LINE One Market Plaza, San Francisco, CA 94106

Foreign flag passenger and cruise lines

BERGEN LINE 505 Fifth Avenue, New York, NY 10017
CARNIVAL CRUISE LINES, INC. 820 Biscayne Blvd., Miami, FL 33132
CARRAS CRUISES One Maritime Plaza, San Francisco, CA 94111
CHANDRIS, INC. 666 Fifth Avenue, New York, NY 10019
COMMODORE CRUISE LINE, LTD., 1015 North America Way, Miami, FL 33132
COSTA LINE 733 Third Avenue, New York, NY 10017
CUNARD LINE, LTD. 555 Fifth Avenue, New York, NY 10020
EASTERN STEAMSHIP LINES 1220 Biscayne Blvd., Miami, FL 33101
EPIROTIKI LINES, INC. 608 Fifth Avenue, New York, NY 10020
HELLENIC MEDITERRANEAN LINES 200 Park Avenue, New York, NY 10017
HOLLAND AMERICA CRUISES 2 Pennsylvania Plaza, New York, NY 10001
HOME LINES One World Trade Center, New York, NY 10048
ITALIAN LINE CRUISES INTERNATIONAL 366 Madison Avenue, New York, NY 10017
KARAGEORGIS LINES CRUISES 1350 Avenue of the Americas, New York, NY 10019
K LINES-HELLENIC CRUISES 645 Fifth Avenue, New York, NY 10022
LAURO LINE CRUISES, INC. One Biscayne Tower, Miami, FL 33131
LINDBLAD TRAVEL, INC. 133 East 55th Street, New York, NY 10022
MARCH SHIPPING PASSENGER SERVICES One World Trade Center, New York, NY 10048
NORWEGIAN AMERICA LINE 29 Broadway, New York, NY 10006
NORWEGIAN CARIBBEAN LINES 100 Biscayne Blvd., Miami, FL 33132
PACQUET CRUISES, INC. 1370 Avenue of the Americas, New York, NY 10019

PRINCESS CRUISES 2020 Avenue of the Stars, Century City, CA 90067
ROYAL CARIBBEAN CRUISE LINE, INC. 903 South America Way, Miami, FL 33132
ROYAL CRUISE LINE One Maritime Plaza, San Francisco, CA 94111
ROYAL VIKING LINE One Embarcadero Center, San Francisco, CA 94111
SITMAR CRUISES 10100 Santa Monica Blvd., Century City, CA 90067
SUN LINE CRUISES 1 Rockefeller Plaza, New York, NY 10020
WINDJAMMER CRUISES P.O. Box 120, Miami Beach, FL 33139

TOURIST OFFICES

Government tourist offices and other travel promotion agencies

ALPINE TOURIST COMMISSION 60 East 42nd Street, New York, NY 10017
ANTIGUA TOURIST BOARD 610 Fifth Avenue, New York, NY 10020
ARAB INFORMATION CENTER 747 Third Avenue, New York, NY 10017
ARUBA INFORMATION CENTER 576 Fifth Avenue, New York, NY 10036
AUSTRALIAN TOURIST COMMISSION 1270 Avenue of the Americas, New York, NY 10020
AUSTRIAN NATIONAL TOURIST OFFICE 545 Fifth Avenue, New York, NY 10017
BAHAMAS TOURIST OFFICE 30 Rockefeller Plaza, New York, NY 10020
BARBADOS TOURIST BOARD 800 Second Avenue, New York, NY 10017
BELGIAN NATIONAL TOURIST OFFICE 745 Fifth Avenue, New York, NY 10022
BERMUDA DEPARTMENT OF TOURISM 630 Fifth Avenue, New York, NY 10020
BONAIRE INFORMATION CENTER 685 Fifth Avenue, New York, NY 10022
BRITISH TOURIST AUTHORITY 680 Fifth Avenue, New York, NY 10019
BRITISH VIRGIN ISLANDS 515 Madison Avenue, New York, NY 10022
BULGARIA TOURIST OFFICE (BALKANTOURIST) 50 East 42nd Street, New York, NY 10017
CANADIAN GOVERNMENT OFFICE OF TOURISM 1251 Ave. of the Americas, New York, NY 10020
CARIBBEAN TOURISM ASSOCIATION 20 East 46th Street, New York, NY 10017
CAYMAN ISLANDS DEPARTMENT OF TOURISM 250 Catalonia Ave., Coral Gables, FL 33134
CEYLON TOURIST BOARD 609 Fifth Avenue, New York, NY 10017
CHINA TOURISM BUREAU (TAIWAN) 210 Post Street, San Francisco, CA 94108
COLUMBIAN GOVERNMENT TOURIST OFFICE 140 East 57th Street, New York, NY 10022
CURACAO TOURIST BOARD 604 Fifth Avenue, New York, NY 10020
CYPRUS TOURIST OFFICE 13 E. 40th Street, New York, NY 10016
CZECHOSLOVAK TRAVEL BUREAU (CEDOK) 10 E. 40th Street, New York, NY 10016
DANISH NATIONAL TOURIST OFFICE 75 Rockefeller Plaza, New York, NY 10019
DANUBE COUNTRIES PROMOTION GROUP 380 Madison Ave., New York, NY 10017
DOMINICAN REPUBLIC TOURIST OFFICE 64 West 50th Street, New York, NY 10020
DOMINICAN TOURIST INFORMATION CENTER 485 Madison Avenue, New York, NY 10022

EAST ASIA TRAVEL ASSOCIATION 45 Rockefeller Plaza, New York, NY 10020
EASTERN CARIBBEAN TOURIST ASSOCIATION 220 E. 42nd Street, New York, NY 10017
EGYPTIAN GOVERNMENT TOURIST OFFICE 630 Fifth Avenue, New York, NY 10020
EUROPEAN TRAVEL COMMISSION 576 Fifth Avenue, New York, NY 10036
FINNISH NATIONAL TOURIST OFFICE 75 Rockefeller Plaza, New York, NY 10019
FRENCH GOVERNMENT TOURIST OFFICE 610 Fifth Avenue, New York, NY 10020
FRENCH WEST INDIES TOURIST OFFICE 610 Fifth Avenue, New York, NY 10020
GERMAN NATIONAL TOURIST OFFICE 630 Fifth Avenue, New York, NY 10020
GHANA TOURIST OFFICE 445 Park Avenue, New York, NY 10022
GREEK NATIONAL TOURIST ORGANIZATION 645 Fifth Avenue, New York, NY 10022
GRENADA TOURIST INFORMATION OFFICE 866 Second Avenue, New York, NY 10017
HAITI GOVERNMENT TOURIST BUREAU 30 Rockefeller Plaza, New York, NY 10020
HONG KONG TOURIST ASSOCIATION 160 Sansome Street, San Francisco, CA 94104
INDIAN GOVERNMENT TOURIST OFFICE 30 Rockefeller Plaza, New York, NY 10020
IRANIAN INFORMATION AND TOURIST CENTER 10 W. 49th Street, New York, NY 10020
IRISH TOURIST BOARD 590 Fifth Avenue, New York, NY 10036
ISRAEL GOVERNMENT TOURIST OFFICE 488 Madison Avenue, New York, NY 10022
ITALIAN GOVERNMENT TRAVEL OFFICE 630 Fifth Avenue, New York, NY 10020
JAMAICA TOURIST BOARD 866 Second Avenue, New York, NY 10017
JAPAN NATIONAL TOURIST ORGANIZATION 45 Rockefeller Plaza, New York, NY 10020
JORDAN TOURIST INFORMATION CENTER 535 Fifth Avenue, New York, NY 10017
KENYA TOURIST OFFICE 60 E. 56th Street, New York, NY 10022
KOREA NATIONAL TOURISM CORP. 460 Park Avenue, New York, NY 10022
LEBANON TOURIST AND INFORMATION OFFICE 405 Park Ave., New York, NY 10022
LUXEMBOURG TOURIST INFORMATION OFFICE One Dag Hammarskjold Plaza, New York, NY 10017
MALAYSIAN TOURIST INFORMATION CENTER 600 Montgomery Street, San Francisco, CA 94111
MEXICAN GOVERNMENT TOURIST DEPT. 630 Fifth Avenue, New York, NY 10022
MEXICAN NATIONAL TOURIST COUNCIL 405 Park Avenue, New York, NY 10022
MONACO GOVERNMENT TOURIST BUREAU 20 E. 49th Street, New York, NY 10017
MOROCCAN NATIONAL TOURIST OFFICE 521 Fifth Avenue, New York, NY 10017
NETHERLANDS NATIONAL TOURIST OFFICE 576 Fifth Avenue, New York, NY 10036

NEW ZEALAND GOVERNMENT TOURIST OFFICE One Maritime Plaza, San Francisco, CA 94111

NORWEGIAN NATIONAL TOURIST OFFICE 75 Rockefeller Plaza, New York, NY 10019

PACIFIC AREA TRAVEL ASSOCIATION 228 Grant Street, San Francisco, CA 94108

PANAMA GOVERNMENT TOURIST BUREAU 630 Fifth Avenue, New York, NY 10020

PHILIPPINES MINISTRY OF TOURISM 556 Fifth Avenue, New York, NY 10036

POLISH TRAVEL BUREAU (ORBIS) 500 Fifth Avenue, New York, NY 10036

PORTUGUESE NATIONAL TOURIST OFFICE 548 Fifth Avenue, New York, NY 10036

ROMANIAN NATIONAL TOURIST OFFICE 573 Third Avenue, New York, NY 10016

SCANDINAVIAN NATIONAL TOURIST OFFICE 75 Rockefeller Plaza, New York, NY 10019

SINGAPORE TOURIST PROMOTION BOARD 251 Post Street, San Francisco, CA 94108

SOUTH AFRICAN TOURIST CORP. 610 Fifth Avenue, New York, NY 10020

SPANISH NATIONAL TOURIST OFFICE 665 Fifth Avenue, New York, NY 10022

ST. KITTS-NEVIS-ANGUILLA TOURIST BOARD 20 E. 46th Street, New York, NY 10017

ST. LUCIA TOURIST BOARD 220 E. 42nd Street, New York, NY 10017

ST. MAARTEN, SABA & ST. EUSTATIUS INFORMATION OFFICE 4 W. 58th St., New York, NY 10019

ST. VINCENT AND THE GRENADINES TOURIST BOARD 220 E. 42nd Street, New York, NY 10017

SURINAM TOURIST BUREAU One Rockefeller Plaza, New York, NY 10020

SWEDISH NATIONAL TOURIST OFFICE 75 Rockefeller Plaza, New York, NY 10019

SWISS NATIONAL TOURIST OFFICE 608 Fifth Avenue, New York, NY 10020

THAILAND TOURIST ORGANIZATION 510 West 6th Street, Los Angeles, CA 90014

TRINIDAD AND TOBAGO TOURIST BOARD 400 Madison Ave., New York, NY 10017

TUNISIAN NATIONAL TOURIST OFFICE 630 Fifth Avenue, New York, NY 10020

TURKISH TOURISM AND INFORMATION OFFICE 821 U.N. Plaza, New York, NY 10017

U.S.S.R. (INTOURIST) 630 Fifth Avenue, New York, NY 10020

VENEZUELAN GOVERNMENT TOURIST BUREAU 450 Park Avenue, New York, NY 10022

YUGOSLAV NATIONAL TOURIST OFFICE 630 Fifth Avenue, New York, NY 10021

ZAMBIA NATIONAL TOURIST BUREAU 150 East 58th Street, New York, NY 10022

State and local tourism bureaus

ALABAMA: Bureau of Publicity and information, State Hwy. Bldg., Montgomery, AL 36130

ALASKA: Division of Tourism, Pouch E, Juneau, AK 99811

AMERICAN SAMOA: Office of Tourism, P.O. Box 1147, Pago Pago, American Samoa 96799

ARIZONA: Office of Tourism, 1700 W. Washington, Phoenix, AZ 85007

ARKANSAS: Dept. of Parks and Tourism, State Capitol Bldg., Little Rock, AR 72201

BALTIMORE: Convention and Visitors Bureau, 22 Light Street, Baltimore, MD 21202

S. CALIFORNIA: Visitors Council, 705 W. 7th Street, Los Angeles, CA 90017

CHICAGO: Convention and Tourism Bureau, 332 S. Michigan Ave., Chicago, IL 60604

COLORADO: State Div. of Commerce and Devel. 1313 Sherman St., Denver, CO 80203

CONN: Dept. of Commerce, Div. of Tourism, 210 Washington St., Hartford, CT 06106

D.C.: Washington Area Convention and Visitors Bur., 1129 20th St. N.W., Washington, DC 20036

DELAWARE: State Visitors Service, 630 State College Rd., Dover, DE 19901

FLORIDA: Dept. of Commerce, Div. of Tourism, 107 W. Gaines St., Tallahasee FL 32304

GEORGIA: Bur. of Industry and Trade, Tourist Div., Box 38097, Atlanta, GA 30334

GUAM: Visitors Bureau, P.O. Box 3520, Agana, Guam 96910

HAWAII: Visitors Bureau, 2270 Kalakaua Ave., Honolulu, HI 96815

IDAHO: Div. of Tourism & Industrial Devel., State Capitol Bldg., Boise, ID 83720

ILLINOIS: Office of Tourism, Dep. of Business & Econ. Devel., 205 W. Wacker Dr., Chicago, IL 60606

INDIANA: Dept. of Commerce, Tourist Div., 336, State House, Indianapolis, IN 46204

IOWA: Development Comm., 250 Jewett Bldg., Des Moines, IA 50309

KANSAS: Dept. of Econ. Devel., 503 Kansas Avenue, Topeka, KS 66603

KENTUCKY: Dept. of Public Info. Advt. & Tvl. Promotion, Capitol Annex, Frankfort, KY 40601

LAS VEGAS: Convention & Visitors Authority, Box 14006, Las Vegas, NV 89114

LOUISIANA: Tourist Devel. Comm., Box 44291, Baton Rouge, LA 70804

MAINE: State Devel. Office, State House, Augusta, ME 04333

MARYLAND: Div. of Tourist Development, 1748 Forest Drive, Annapolis, MD 21401

MASS: Dept. of Comm. & Dev, Div. of Tourism, 100 Cambridge St., Boston, MA 02202

MICHIGAN: Travel Bur., Dep of Comm., 300 S. Capitol Ave., Lansing, MI 48913

MINNESOTA: Dept. of Econ. Dev., 480 Cedar St., St. Paul, MN 55101

MISS: Travel Dept., Agricultural & Industrial Board, Box 849, Jackson, MS 39205

MISSOURI: Div. of Tourism, Box 1055, Jefferson City, MO 65101

MONTANA: Travel Promotion Unit, Dep. of Highways, Helena, MT 59061

NEBRASKA: Dep. of Economic Devel. Div. of Tourism, Box 94666, Lincoln, NB 68509

NEVADA: Dep. of Economic Devel., Capitol Complex, Carson City, NV 89710

NEW HAMPSHIRE: Div. of Economic Devel., Box 856, Concord, NH 03301

NEW JERSEY: Office of Tourism & Promotion, Box 400, Trenton, NJ 08625

NEW MEXICO: Dep. of Development, 113 Washington Ave., Santa Fe, NM 87503

NEW YORK CITY: Convention & Visitors Bur., 90 E. 42nd Street, New York, NY 10017

NEW YORK STATE: Dep. of Commerce, 99 Washington Ave., Albany, NY 12245

NORTH CAROLINA: Dep. of Natural & Econ. Resources, Box 27687, Raleigh, NC 27611

NORTH DAKOTA: Highway Dep., Capitol Grounds, Bismarck, ND 58501
OHIO: Dep. of Economic & Comm. Devel., 30 East Broad St., Columbus, OH 43215
OKLAHOMA: Tourism Promotion Div., 500 Will Rogers Bldg., Oklahoma City, OK 73105
OREGON: State Hwy., Div., Travel Info. Section, 101 St. Hwy. Bldg., Salem, OR 97310
PENNSYLVANIA: Dep. of Comm., Travel Devel. Bur. 432 S. Office Bldg., Harrisburg, PA 17120
PHILADELPHIA: Convention & Visitors Bur., 1525 John F. Kennedy Blvd., Philadelphia, PA 19102
PUERTO RICO: Tourism Devel. Co., G.P.O. Box "BN" San Juan, P.R. 00936
REDWOOD EMPIRE ASSOC. 476 Post St., San Francisco, CA 94102
RHODE ISLAND: Dep. of Econ. Devel., 1 Weybosset Hill, Providence, RI 02903
SAN FRANCISCO: Convention & Visitors Bur., 1390 Market St., San Francisco, CA 94102
SOUTH CAROLINA: Dep. of Parks, Rec. & Tourism, 1205 Pendleton St., Columbia, SC 29201
SOUTH DAKOTA: Div. of Tourism, Joe Foss Bldg., Pierre, SD 57501
TENNESSEE: Dep. of Tourist Devel., 505 Fesslers Lane, Nashville, TN 37210
TEXAS: Tourist Dev. Agency, Box 12008 Capitol Station, Austin, TX 78711
U. S. TRAVEL SERVICE: U. S. Dep. of Commerce, Washington, DC 20230
U.S. VIRGIN ISLANDS: Box 1692, Charlotte Amalie, St. Thomas, U.S.V.I. 00801
UTAH: Travel Council, Council Hall, Salt Lake City, UT 84114
VERMONT: Agency of Dev. & Comm. Affairs, 61 Elm St., Montpelier, VT 05602
VIRGINIA: State Travel Service, 6 N. Sixth St., Richmond, VA 23219
WASHINGTON: Dep. of Commerce & Econ. Devel., General Admin. Bldg., Olympia, WA 98504
WELCOME WEST: 220 Montgomery Street, San Francisco, CA 94104
WEST VIRGINIA: Dep. of Comm. Tvl. Devel. Div., 1900 Washington St., Charleston, WV 25305
WISCONSIN: Dep. of Bus. Devel., Div. of Tourism, 123 W. Washington, Madison, WI 53702
WYOMING: Travel Commission, I-25 at Etchepare Circle, Cheyenne, WY 82002

TOUR OPERATORS; LARGE TRAVEL AGENCIES; FOREIGN TOUR AND RAIL COMPANIES

AAA WORLD-WIDE TRAVEL 8111 Gatehouse Rd., Falls Church, VA 22042
ABBOTT TOURS, INC. 2609 Canal Street, New Orleans, LA 70119
ADVENTURE HOLIDAYS INTERNATIONAL 337 Merrick Rd., Lynbrook, NY 11563
ADVENTURE TOURS 3653 Offut Road, Randallstown, MD 21132
ALEXANDER CHARTERS 2607 Nostrand Avenue, Brooklyn, NY 11210
ALOHA HAWAII TRAVEL 1600 Kapiolani Blvd., Honolulu, HI 96814
AMERICAN EXPRESS COMPANY American Express Plaza, New York, NY 10004
AMERICAN GRAND CIRCLE, 555 Madison Avenue, New York, NY 10022
AMERICAN SIGHTSEEING INTERNATIONAL 420 Lexington Avenue, New York, NY 10017
AMERICAN TRAVEL ABROAD, INC. 250 West 57th Street, New York, NY 10019
AMEROPA TRAVEL INC. 26 Court Street, Brooklyn, NY 11242
ASENSIO TOURS 501 Fifth Avenue, New York, NY 10017
ASK MR. FOSTER 16055 Ventura Blvd., Encino, CA 91316
ASTI TOURS 21 East 40th Street, New York, NY 10016
A.T.E.S.A. 500 Fifth Avenue, New York, NY 10036

ATLAS INTERNATIONAL TOURS 580 Fifth Avenue, New York, NY 10036
ATPAC TOURS 3 E. 54th Street, New York, NY 10022
AUTO EUROPE 1270 Second Avenue, New York, NY 10021
BACHELOR PARTY TOURS, INC. 444 Madison Avenue, New York, NY 10022
BAHAMA ISLAND TOURS 255 Alhambra Circle, Coral Gables, FL 33134
BAMACO HOUSE 58-33 College Pt. Blvd., New York, NY 11355
BENNETT TOURS, INC. 270 Madison Avenue, New York, NY 10016
BETANZOS OK TOURS 323 Geary Street, San Francisco, CA
    94102
BOOK-COUZENS TRAVEL SERVICE 1 Northland Plaza, Southfield, MI 48075
BREAKAWAY TRAVEL, INC. 1938 Williamsbridge Road, Bronx, NY 10461
BRENDAN TOURS 510 West Sixth Street, Los Angeles, CA 90001
BRITRAIL INTERNATIONAL INC. 270 Madison Avenue, New York, NY 10016
BROWNELL TOURS P. O. Box 2087, Birmingham, AL 35201
BRUWAL TOURS, LTD. 212-29 Jamaica Ave., Queens Village, NY 11428
CALIFORNIA PARLOR CAR TOURS Jack Tar Hotel, San Francisco, CA 94101
CARAVAN TOURS, INC. 401 North Michigan Avenue, Chicago, IL 60611
CARIBBEAN HOLIDAYS 711 Third Avenue, New York, NY 10017
CARTAN TRAVEL BUREAU One Crossroads of Commerce, Rolling Meadows,
    IL 60008
CASSER TOURS 46 W. 43rd Street, New York, NY 10036
CAVELCADE TOURS, INC. 254 West 31st Street, New York, NY 10001
CHARTER TRAVEL CORP. 180 N. LaSalle Street, Chicago, IL 60601
C.I.E. TOURS 178 Forbes Road, Braintree, MA 02184
CIT TRAVEL SERVICE, INC. 500 Fifth Avenue, New York, NY 10036
CLARA LAUGHLIN TRAVEL SERVICES, INC. 655 Madison Avenue, New
    York, NY 10021
CLUB MEDITERRANEE 40 West 57th Street, New York, NY 10019
COLUMBIA TOURS, Inc. 535 Fifth Avenue, New York, NY 10017
COMPASS TOURS, INC. 70 West 40th Street, New York, NY 10018
CONTINENTAL EXPRESS 144 Beverly Drive, Beverly Hills, CA 90212
CONTINENTAL TRAILWAYS TOURS, INC. 1512 Commerce Street, Dallas, TX
    75201
THOMAS COOK 587 Fifth Avenue, New York, NY 10017
CREATIVE WORLD TRAVEL 1 Market Plaza, San Francisco, CA 94105
CROWN PETERS WHOLESALE TOUR OPERATORS 555 Fifth Avenue, New
    York, NY 10017
DAPHNA TOURS, INC. 444 Madison Avenue, New York, NY 10022
DAVID TRAVELS, INC. 1175 N.E. 125th Street, N. Miami, FL 33161
DEL WEBB WORLD TRAVEL P. O. Box 15313, Las Vegas, NV 89114
DESTINATION FRANCE 521 Fifth Avenue, New York, NY 10017
DICARLO TOURS, INC. 151 West 40th Street, New York, NY 10018
DISCOVERY TOURS 628 N.W. Sixth Avenue, Portland, OR 97209
EAST COAST PARLOR CAR TOURS 1730 K Street, N.W., Washington, DC
    20006
EASTOURS, INC. 1140 Avenue of the Americas, New York, NY 10036
EMEX TOURS 915 Eighth Avenue, New York, NY 10019
EMPIRE TOURS 605 Market Street, San Francisco, CA 94105
EMPRESS TRAVEL 293 Madison Avenue, New York, NY 10017
EUROPA BUS (OVERSEAS) INC. 11 East 44th Street, New York, NY 10017
EUROPA CAR TOURS 3 E. 54th Street, New York, NY 10022
EUROPE-BY-CAR 45 Rockefeller Plaza, New York, NY 10020
EUROPE ON SKIS, INC. 49 West 57th Street, New York, NY 10019
EUROPEAN HOLIDAYS 500 Fifth Avenue, New York, NY 10036
EXPRINTER INTERNATIONAL 500 Fifth Avenue, New York, NY 10036

FINLAY FUN-TIME TOURS 11306 Burbank Blvd., North Hollywood, CA 91601
FLYFAIRE, INC. 300 East 42nd Street, New York, NY 10017
FOREIGN TOURS, INC. 1140 Avenue of the Americas, New York, NY 10036
FOREMOST INTERNATIONAL TOURS 1255 Post Street, San Francisco, CA 94109
FORLOW TOURS 17W620 14th Street, Oakbrook Terrace, IL 60181
FOUR WINDS TRAVEL, INC. 175 Fifth Avenue, New York, NY 10010
FOURWAYS TRAVEL 950 Third Avenue, New York, NY 10022
FRAMES TOURS N.Y. LTD. 185 Madison Avenue, New York, NY 10016
FRENCH CARIBBEAN ADVENTURES 475 Fifth Avenue, New York, NY 10017
FRENCH NATIONAL RAILROAD 610 Fifth Avenue, New York, NY 10020
ARTHUR FROMMER INTERNATIONAL 380 Madison Ac., New York, NY 10017
FUN IN THE SUN TOURS 1 East 57th Street, New York, NY 10022
FUNWAY HOLIDAYS 152 West Wisconsin Avenue, Milwaukee, WI 53203
GARZA TOURS 4256 North Milwaukee Avenue, Chicago, IL 60641
GATEWAY HOLIDAYS 8 South Michigan Avenue, Chicago, IL 60603
GENERAL TOURS, INC. 49 West 57th Street, New York, NY 10019
GERMAN FEDERAL RAILROAD 630 Fifth Avenue, New York, NY 10020
GIBSON TRAVEL 3258 Wilshire Blvd., Los Angeles, CA 90010
GLOBUS TOURS 8 South Michigan Avenue, Chicago, IL 60603
GOGO TOURS P.O. Box 457, Paramus, NJ 07652
GRAMERCY TRAVEL SYSTEM 444 Madison Avenue, New York, NY 10022
GRAY LINE SIGHTSEEING COMPANIES ASSOCIATED 7 W. 51st St., New York, NY 10019
GREEN CARPET TOURS 345 N.E. Eighth Avenue, Portland, OR 97232
GREYHOUND WORLD TOURS Greyhound Tower, Phoenix, AZ 85077
GROUP JOURNEYS INC. 5550 Main Street, Buffalo, NY 14221
GROUPS UNLIMITED 15 Central Park West, New York, NY 10023
GWV TRAVEL 1320 Central Street, Newton Center, MA 02159
HALEY CORPORATION 711 Third Avenue, New York, NY 10017
HAWAIIAN HOLIDAYS 711 Third Avenue, New York, NY 10017
HEMPHILL TRAVEL CORP. 1910 West Sunset Blvd., Los Angeles, CA 90026
HENDERSON TOURS 931 Hunter Street, N.W., Atlanta, GA 30314
HILL TOURS P.O. Box 413, St. Petersburg, FL 33731
HOLYLAND TOURS 444 Madison Avenue, New York, NY 10022
INCLUSIVE TRAVEL CORP. 685 Fifth Avenue, New York, NY 10022
INTERCONTINENTAL TOURS 609 South Grand, Los Angeles, CA 90017
INTERNATIONAL INCENTIVES 10600 West Higgins Road, Rosemont, IL 60018
INTERNATIONAL TRAVEL SERVICE 104 South Michigan Avenue, Chicago, IL 60603
INTOURIST (USSR) 45 East 49th Street, New York, NY 10017
ISLAND HOLIDAY TOURS OF HAWAII 2222 Kalakaua Avenue, Honolulu, HI 96815
ISLANDS IN THE SUN 2400 West Coast Hwy., Newport Beach, CA 92660
ITALIAN STATE RAILWAYS 500 Fifth Avenue, New York, NY 10036
JAPAN NATIONAL RAILWAYS 45 Rockefeller Plaza, New York, NY 10020
JAPAN & ORIENT TOURS, INC. 250 East 1st Street, Los Angeles, CA 90012
JAPAN TRAVEL BUREAU INTERNATIONAL, INC. 45 Rockefeller Plaza, New York, NY 10020
JET & CRUISE 32-03 Broadway, Astoria, L.I., NY 11106
JOHANSEN ROYAL TOURS 1410 Vance Bldg., Seattle, WA 98101
KNEISEL TRAVEL, INC. 348 N.E. 8th Avenue, Portland, OR 97232
KOMPAS 630 Fifth Avenue, New York, NY 10020
KUONI TRAVEL, INC. 11 East 44th Street, New York, NY 10017

LE BEAU TOURS, INC. 6 East 43rd Street, New York, NY 10017
LINDBLAD TRAVEL, INC. 133 East 55th Street, New York, NY 10022
LISLIND INTERNATIONAL 5 World Trade Center, New York, NY 10048
LOTUS ORIENT TOURS, LTD, 244 East 46th Street, New York, NY 10017
LOYAL TRAVEL, Greyhound Tower, Phoenix, AZ 85077
LYNNOT TOURS, INC. 350 Fifth Avenue, New York, NY 10001
E. F. McDONALD TRAVEL COMPANY 112 S. Ludlow Street, Dayton, OH 45402
MACKENZIE TOURS, HAWAII P.O. Box 2561, Honolulu, HI 96804
MACPHERSON TRAVEL BUREAU 500 Fifth Avenue, New York, NY 10036
MAGGIORE INTERNATIONAL RENT A CAR 535 Fifth Avenue, New York, NY 10017
MAGIC CARPET TOURS 1406 Beacon Street, Brookline, MA 02146
MARITZ, INC. 1325 North Highway Drive, Fenton, MO 63026
MARRIOTT WORLD TRAVEL 1651 Old Meadow Road, McClean, VA 22101
MARTIN EMPIRE TOURS 711 Third Avenue, New York, NY 10017
MAUPINTOUR, INC. 900 Mass. Street, Lawrence, KS 66044
MELIA TOURS, INC. 580 Fifth Avenue, New York, NY 10036
MERCATOR TOURS 720 Fifth Avenue, New York, NY 10019
MEXICO TRAVEL ADVISORS 1717 N. Highland Avenue, Los Angeles, CA 90028
MILLER TOURS, INC. 1100 Jorie Blvd., Oak Brook, IL 60521
MURRAY'S TOURS 740 West Santa Barbara Avenue, Los Angeles, CA 90027
NAWAS INTERNATIONAL TRAVEL SERVICE 20 East 46th Street, New York, NY 10017
NEW ORIENT EXPRESS, INC. 375 Park Avenue, New York, NY 10022
NILESTAR TOURS 9720 Wilshire Blvd., Beverly Hills, CA 90212
NILI TOURS 18 East 48th Street, New York, NY 10017
OLSON—TRAVELWORLD ORGANIZATION 6922 Hollywood Blvd., Los Angeles, CA 90028
ORBIS POLISH TRAVEL OFFICE 500 Fifth Avenue, New York, NY 10036
ORBITAIR INTERNATIONAL, INC. 20 East 46th Street, New York, NY 10017
OSBORNE TRAVEL SERVICE, INC. 3379 Peachtree Road, N.E., Atlanta, GA 30326
OVERSEAS CHARTER A COACH, INC. 10 Rockefeller Plaza, New York, NY 10020
OVERSEAS TRAVEL COMPANY 2 West 45th Street, New York, NY 10036
PACIFIC DELIGHT TOURS 3 Pell Street, New York, NY 10013
PACIFIC INTERNATIONAL TOURS, INC. 560 Sutter Street, San Francisco, CA 94102
PACIFIC PATHWAYS 442 Post Street, San Francisco, CA 94102
PARAGON TOURS 678 Pleasant Street, New Bedford, MA 02741
PARK EAST TOURS 1841 Broadway, New York, NY 10023
PASSPORT HOLIDAYS, LTD. 40 East 49th Street, New York, NY 10017
PELTOURS, INC. 70 West 40th Street, New York, NY 10018
PERCIVAL TOURS Cont'l. Nat'l. Bank Bldg., Fort Worth, TX 76102
PERILLO TOURS 30 N. William Street, Pearl River, NY 10965
PERSEPOLIS TRAVEL, LTD. 667 Madison Avenue, New York, NY 10021
PIERBUSSETI, INC. 2 Penn Plaza, New York, NY 10001
PINK HOLIDAYS 2630 Flossmoor Road, Flossmoor, IL 60422
PLEASURE BREAK TRAVEL 104 South Michigan Avenue, Chicago, IL 60603
PLEASANT SCANDINAVIA TOURS 444 Madison Avenue, New York, NY 10022
PORTUGUESE TOURS, INC. 321 Rahway Avenue, Elizabeth, NJ 07202
PRINCESS TOURS 1325 Fourth Avenue, Seattle, WA 98101
QUE PASA TOURS 1290 Avenue of the Americas, New York, NY 10019
QUESTERS TOURS AND TRAVEL 257 Park Avenue, New York, NY 10010

RAND McNALLY VACATIONS P.O. Box 6539, Chicago, IL 60680
ROGAL ASSOCIATES 97 Union Street, Newton Centre, MA 02159
RUSSIAN ADVENTURE TOURS, INC. 20 East 46th Street, New York, NY 10017
S & H MOTIVATION AND TRAVEL, INC. 5999 Butterfield, Road, Hillside, IL 60162
SARTOURS 610 Fifth Avenue, New York, NY 10020
SA TRAVELTOURS, INC. 25 West 43rd Street, New York, NY 10036
SCANDINAVIA OVERSEAS SERVICE, INC. 444 Madison Avenue, New York, NY 10022
SHARON TRAVEL ASSOCIATES, INC. 18 East 48th Street, New York, NY 10017
SIMBA SAFARIS 1113 Union Blvd., Allentown, PA 18103
SIMMONS GROUP JOURNEYS 205 East 42nd Street, New York, NY 10017
SITA WORLD TRAVEL, INC. 2960 Wilshire Blvd., Los Angeles, CA 90010
SKI TRAILS 134 North LaSalle Street, Chicago, IL 60602
SKYLINE TOURS, INC. 574 Fifth Avenue, New York, NY 10036
SPACIFIC TOURS, INC. 4029 Westerly Place, Newport Beach, CA 92660
SUNNY LAND TOURS, INC. 166 Main Street, Hackensack, NJ 07601
SWISS FEDERAL RAILWAYS 608 Fifth Avenue, New York, NY 10020
TALMAGE TOURS, INC. 1223 Walnut Street, Philadelphia, PA 19107
TAUCK TOURS, INC. 11 Wilton Road, Westport, CT 06880
THRU THE LENS TOURS, INC. 5301 Laurel Canyon Blvd., North Hollywood, CA 91607
TOP FLIGHT TOURS 132 State Street, Albany, NY 12207
TOTAL TRAVEL, LTD. 800 East Northwest Highway, Palatine, IL 60067
TOUR ARRANGEMENTS, INC. 82 Washington Street, Marblehead, MA 01945
TOUROPA 40 East 49th Street, New York, NY 10017
TOURSTARS 300 West 45th Street, New York, NY 10036
TOWER TRAVEL CORP. 380 Madison Avenue, New York, NY 10017
TRADE WIND TOURS OF HAWAII P.O. Box 2198, Honolulu, HI 96805
TRAFALGAR TOURS 30 Rockefeller Plaza, New York, NY 10036
TRAVCOA WORLD TOURS 875 North Michigan Avenue, Chicago, IL 60611
TRAVEL AMERICA CORP. 551 Fifth Avenue, New York, NY 10017
TRAVEL ARRANGEMENTS 435 North Michigan Avenue, Chicago, IL 60611
TRAVELCADE TOURS 46 W. 43rd Street, New York, NY 10036
TRAVEL DYNAMICS, INC. 964 Third Avenue, New York, NY 10022
TRAVEL—GO—ROUND 516 Fifth Avenue, New York, NY 10036
TRAVEL GUIDE 3660 Wilshire Blvd., Los Angeles, CA 90010
TRAVELINE, INC. 680 Fifth Avenue, New York, NY 10019
TRAVELPOWER 108 West Wells Street, Milwaukee, WI 53203
TRAVEL TOURS, INC. 25 West 43rd Street, New York, NY 10036
TRAVTOUR, LTD. 444 Madison Avenue, New York, NY 10022
TRAVEL AND TRANSPORT 3104 Farnam Street, Omaha, NB 68131
TRAVEL WORLD, INC. 6922 Hollywood Blvd., Los Angeles, CA 90028
T. V. TRAVEL, INC. 3085 Woodman Drive, Dayton, OH 45420
UNITED TOURING COMPANY 350 Fifth Avenue, New York, NY 10001
UNITOURS, INC. 1671 Wilshire Blvd., Los Angeles, CA 90017
UNIVERSAL/SKY TOURS, INC. 60 East 42nd Street, New York, NY 10017
VACATION VENTURES 55 East Monroe Street, Chicago, IL 60603
VENTURE TOURS 6007 18th Avenue South, Minneapolis, MN 55423
WALT DISNEY TRAVEL CO. 1150 W. Cerritos Ave., Anaheim, CA 92802
WESTERN SKI VACATIONS 3 West 57th Street, New York, NY 10019
WESTOURS 100 West Harrison Plaza, Seattle, WA 98119

WRIGHT WAY TOURS P.O. Box 6038, Glendale, CA 91204
YELLOWSTONE PARK CO. Wyoming, WY 82109

TRADE AND PROFESSIONAL ORGANIZATIONS

AAA—WORLD WIDE TRAVEL 8111 Gatehouse Road, Falls Church, VA 22042
AIR LINE EMPLOYEES ASSOCIATION 5600 S. Central Avenue, Chicago, IL 60638
AIR TRAFFIC CONFERENCE OF AMERICA 1709 New York Avenue, N.W., Washington, DC 20006
AIR TRANSPORT ASSOCIATION OF AMERICA 1709 New York Avenue, N.W., Washington, DC 20006
AMERICAN CAMPING ASSOCIATION Bradford Woods, Martinsville, IN 46151
AMERICAN CULINARY FEDERATION P.O. Box 53, Hyde Park, NY 12538
AMERICAN HOTEL AND MOTEL ASSOCIATION 888 Seventh Avenue, New York, NY 10019
AMERICAN HOTEL AND MOTEL ASSN. (Educational Institute) 1407 S. Harrison Rd., East Lansing, MI 48823
AMERICAN MEAT INSTITUTE 59 East Van Buren, Chicago, IL 60605
AMERICAN SIGHTSEEING INTERNATIONAL 420 Lexington Avenue, New York, NY 10017
AMERICAN SOCIETY OF TRAVEL AGENTS 711 Fifth Avenue, New York, NY 10022
ASSOCIATION OF AMERICAN RAILROADS 1920 L Street N.W., Washington, DC 20036
ASSOCIATION OF BANK TRAVEL BUREAUS 915 S. Clinton Street, Fort Wayne, IN 46802
ASSOCIATION OF INCENTIVE TRAVEL ORGANIZATIONS 312 Stuart St., Boston, MA 02116
ASSOCIATION OF RETAIL TRAVEL AGENTS 8 Maple Street, Croton on Hudson, NY 10520
ASSOCIATION OF LOCAL TRANSPORT AIRLINES 1801 K St., N.W., Washington, DC 20006
AVIATION MAINTENANCE FOUNDATION P.O. Box 739, Basin, NY 82410
AVIATION/SPACE WRITERS ASSOCIATION Cliffwood Road, Chester, NJ 07930
CARIBBEAN HOTEL ASSOCIATION 1120 Ashford Avenue, Santurce, PR 00907
CLUB MANAGERS ASSOCIATION OF AMERICA 7615 Winterberry Pl., Washington, DC 20034
COUNCIL ON HOTEL, RESTAURANT AND INSTITUTIONAL EDUCATION 11 Koger Executive Ctr., Norfolk, VA 23502
CRUISE LINES INTERNATIONAL ASSOCIATION 17 Battery Place, New York, NY 10004
FOOD SERVICE EXECUTIVE ASSOCIATION 508 IBM Building, Fort Wayne, IN 46805
GRAY LINE SIGHTSEEING COMPANIES ASSOCIATED, INC. 7 W. 51st St., New York, NY 10019
HOTEL SALES MANAGEMENT ASSOCIATION INTERNATIONAL 362 Fifth Ave., New York, NY 10001
INSTITUTE OF CERTIFIED TRAVEL AGENTS P.O. Box 56, Wellesley, MA 02181
INTERNATIONAL AIR TRANSPORT ASSOCIATION 1000 Sherbrooke St., W., Montreal, Canada

INTERNATIONAL ASSOCIATION OF AMUSEMENT PARKS AND ATTRAC-
TIONS 1125 Lake St. Bldg., Oak Park, IL 60301
INTERNATIONAL ASSOCIATION OF CONVENTIONS AND VISITOR
BUREAUS 702 Bloomington Rd., Champaign, IL 60820
INTERNATIONAL ASSOCIATION OF FAIRS AND EXPOSITIONS 500
Ashland Ave., Chicago Heights, IL 60411
INTERNATIONAL FESTIVALS ASSOCIATION 15 S. Fifth Street,
Minneapolis, MN 55204
INTERNATIONAL ASSOCIATION OF TOUR MANAGERS 198 York Street,
New Haven, CT 06511
NATIONAL AIR CARRIER ASSOCIATION 1730 M Street, N.W., Washington,
DC 20036
NATIONAL ASSOCIATION OF MOTOR BUS OWNERS 1025 Connecticut Ave.
N.W., Washington, DC 20036
NATIONAL EXECUTIVE HOUSEKEEPERS ASSOCIATION Business and
Professional Bldg., Gallipolis, OH 45631
NATIONAL INDUSTRIAL RECREATION ASSOCIATION 20 North Wacker
Dr., Chicago, IL 60606
NATIONAL INNKEEPING ASSOCIATION 1001 Virginia Avenue, Atlanta, GA
30354
NATIONAL INSTITUTE FOR THE FOOD SERVICE INDUSTRY 120 S.
Riverside Plaza, Chicago, IL 60606
NATIONAL PASSENGER TRAFFIC ASSOCIATION P.O. Box 5517, Grand
Central Stn., New York, NY 10017
NATIONAL RECREATION AND PARKS ASSOCIATION 1601 N. Kent Street,
Arlington, VA 22209
NATIONAL RESTAURANT ASSOCIATION, 1 IBM Plaza, Chicago, IL 60611
NATIONAL TOUR BROKERS ASSOCIATION 512 East Main Street, Lexington,
KY 40508
PACIFIC CRUISE CONFERENCE 311 California Street, San Francisco, CA
94104
SOCIETY OF AMERICAN TRAVEL WRITERS 1120 Connecticut Ave., N.W.,
Washington, DC 20036
THE TRAVEL RESEARCH ASSOCIATION P.O. Box 8066, Salt Lake City, UT
84108
UNITED STATES TOUR OPERATORS ASSOCIATION 2 Overhill Road,
Scarsdale, NY 10583
UNITED STATES TRAVEL DATA CENTER 1100 Connecticut Avenue, N.W.,
Washington, DC 20036
WORLD ASSOCIATION OF TRAVEL AGENCIES 37 Quai Wilson, Geneva,
Switzerland

TRAINING SCHOOLS AND UNIVERSITIES

Aviation

Because the schools and courses are too numerous to include here you are
referred to specific directories, available without charge, from the U.S. Department of Transportation, Distribution Unit, Washington, DC 20590

*Directory of Aviation and Transportation Majors and Curricula Offered by
Colleges and Universities*

This directory covers schools offering courses in Airline Flight Attendant
Preparation; Aviation Administration; Aerospace Operations Management;

Aviation Technology; Aerospace Sciences; Aviation Instrument Technology; Aeronautical Engineering; Flight Technology (career pilot); Aerospace Law; Agricultural Aviation; Meteorology (Atmospheric Science); Aviation Education and Air Transportation.

List of Certificated Pilot and Flight Ground Schools (Publication AC NO: 140-2H)

This publication lists courses and training programs for Airline Pilot; Flight Engineer; Flight Navigator and Aircraft Dispatcher.

Directory of FAA Certificated Aviation Maintenance Technician Schools (Publication AC NO: 147-2P)

Covers training schools for Airframe and Powerplant Mechanics.

Hotel and/or Restaurant Administration—four-year colleges

AUBURN UNIVERSITY Auburn, AL 36830
TUSKAGEE INSTITUTE Tuskagee, AL 36083
ARIZONA STATE UNIVERSITY Tempe, AZ 85281
CALIFORNIA STATE POLYTECHNIC UNIVERSITY Pomona, CA 91768
COLORADO STATE UNIVERSITY Fort Collins, CO 80521
UNIVERSITY OF DENVER Denver, CO 80201
FLORIDA INTERNATIONAL UNIVERSITY Tamiami Trail, Miami, FL 33144
FLORIDA STATE UNIVERSITY Tallahassee, FL 32306
MORRIS BROWN COLLEGE 643 Hunter Street N.W., Atlanta, GA 30314
UNIVERSITY OF HAWAII 1300 Lower Campus Road, Honolulu, HI 96822
UNIVERSITY OF ILLINOIS—URBANA-CHAMPAIGN Urbana, IL 61801
INDIANA NORTHERN UNIVERSITY Gas City, IN 46933
PURDUE UNIVERSITY Lafayette, IN 47907
IOWA STATE UNIVERSITY, Ames, IA 50010
UNIVERSITY OF MASSACHUSETTS Amherst, MA 01002
UNIVERSITY OF MARYLAND College Park, MD 20742
MICHIGAN STATE UNIVERSITY 425 Eppley Center, East Lansing, MI 48824
SOUTHWEST MINNESOTA STATE COLLEGE Marshall, MN 56258
UNIVERSITY OF MISSOURI Columbia, MO 65201
APPALACHIAN STATE UNIVERSITY Box 200, Boone, NC 28607
UNIVERSITY OF NEVADA Las Vegas, NV 89109
UNIVERSITY OF NEW HAMPSHIRE Durham, NH 03824
NEW MEXICO STATE UNIVERSITY Box 3470, Las Cruces, NM 88001
CORNELL UNIVERSITY, Ithica, NY 14853
PRATT INSTITUTE 215 Ryerson Street, Brooklyn, NY 14109
ROCHESTER INSTITUTE OF TECHNOLOGY 1 Lomb Memorial Drive, Rochester, NY 14623
OHIO STATE UNIVERSITY 1787 Neil Avenue, Columbus, OH 43210
OKLAHOMA STATE UNIVERSITY Stillwater, OK 74074
DREXEL INSITUTE OF TECHNOLOGY Philadelphia, PA 19104
PENNSYLVANIA STATE UNIVERSITY University Park, PA 16802
BRYANT COLLEGE 154 Hope Street, Providence, RI 02906
SOUTH DAKOTA STATE UNIVERSITY Brookings, SD 57006
UNIVERSITY OF HOUSTON 4800 Cullen Blvd., Houston, TX 77004
WASHINGTON STATE UNIVERSITY Pullman, WA 99163
UNIVERSITY OF WISCONSIN—STOUT Menomonie, WI 54751

Hotel and Motel Management and/or Food Adminstration—two-year colleges

BAKERSFIELD COLLEGE 1801 Panorama, Bakersfield, CA 93305
CITY COLLEGE OF SAN FRANCISO San Francisco, CA 94112
COLLEGE OF THE DESERT Palm Desert, CA 92260
COLUMBIA JUNIOR COLLEGE Columbia, CA 95310
LOS ANGELES TRADE-TECHNICAL COLLEGE 400 W. Washington Blvd., Los Angeles, CA 90015
LOS ANGELES VALLEY COLLEGE Van Nuys, CA 91401
MESA COLLEGE 7250 Artillery Drive, San Diego, CA 92111
MONTEREY PENINSULA COLLEGE 980 Fremont Avenue, Monterey, CA 93940
MOORPARK COLLEGE 7075 Campus Road, Moorpark, CA 93021
ORANGE COAST COLLEGE 2701 Fairview Road, Costa Mesa, CA 92626
PASADENA CITY COLLEGE Pasadena, CA 91106
WEST VALLEY COLLEGE 44 East Latimer Avenue, Campbell, CA 95008
COMMUNITY COLLEGE OF DENVER—AURARIA CAMPUS Denver, CO 80204
MANCHESTER COMMUNITY COLLEGE Manchester, CT 06040
SOUTH CENTRAL COMMUNITY COLLEGE 869 Orange Street, New Haven, CT 06511
BREVARD COMMUNITY COLLEGE Cocoa, FL 32922
BROWARD JUNIOR COLLEGE 3501 S.W. Davie Avenue, Fort Lauderdale, FL 33314
EDISON COMMUNITY COLLEGE Fort Myers, FL 33901
HILLSBOROUGH COMMUNITY COLLEGE P.O. Box 22127, Tampa, FL 33622
MARYMOUNT COLLEGE Boca Raton, FL 33432
MIAMI-DADE JUNIOR COLLEGE 1751 N.W. 27th Avenue, Miami, FL 33167
OKALOOSA-WALTON JUNIOR COLLEGE Niceville, FL 32578
PALM BEACH JUNIOR COLLEGE 4200 Congress Street, Lake Worth, FL 33460
ST. PETERSBURG JUNIOR COLLEGE St. Petersburg, FL 33733
VALENCIA JUNIOR COLLEGE P.O. Box 3028, Orlando, FL 32809
KAPIOLANI COMMUNITY COLLEGE 620 Pensacola St., Honolulu, HI 96814
CARL SANDBURG COLLEGE Galesburg, IL 61401
COLLEGE OF DuPAGE Glen Ellyn, IL 60137
DES MOINES AREA COMMUNITY COLLEGE Ankeny, IA 50021
SOUTHERN MAINE VOCATIONAL TECHNICAL INSTITUTE South Portland, ME 04106
COMMUNITY COLLEGE OF BALTIMORE 209 Liberty Heights Ave., Baltimore, MD 21215
MONTGOMERY COMMUNITY COLLEGE—ROCKVILLE CAMPUS Rockville, MD 20850
CAPE COD COMMUNITY COLLEGE West Barnstable, MA 02668
ENDICOTT JUNIOR COLLEGE Beverly, MA 01915
EDUCATIONAL INSTITUTE—AMERICAN HOTEL & MOTEL ASSN. (Home study courses) 1407 S. Harrison Rd., East Lansing, MI 48823
DELTA COLLEGE University Center, MI 48710
FERRIS STATE COLLEGE Big Rapids, MI 49307
GRAND RAPIDS JUNIOR COLLEGE Grand Rapids, MI 49502
HENRY FORD COMMUNITY COLLEGE Dearborn, MI 48128
KALAMAZOO VALLEY COMMUNITY COLLEGE Kalamazoo, MI 49009
LANSING COMMUNITY COLLEGE Lansing, MI 48914
OAKLAND COMMUNITY COLLEGE—SOUTHEAST Bloomfield Hills, MI 48013

SCHOOLCRAFT COLLEGE 18600 Haggerty Road, Livonia, MI 48151
WASHTENAW COMMUNITY COLLEGE Ann Arbor, MI 48106
RAINY RIVER STATE JUNIOR COLLEGE International Falls, MN 56649
UNIVERSITY OF MINNESOTA TECHNICAL COLLEGE Crookstone, MN 56716
CROWDER COLLEGE Neosho, MO 64850
FOREST PARK COMMUNITY COLLEGE 5600 Oakland, St. Louis, MO 63110
PENN VALLEY COMMUNITY COLLEGE 560 West Port Road, Kansas City, MO 64131
MISSOULA TECHNICAL CENTER Missoula, MT 59801
CENTRAL NEBRASKA VOCATIONAL-TECHNICAL SCHOOL P.O. Box 1024, Hastings, NB 68901
ATLANTIC COMMUNITY COLLEGE Mays Landing, NJ 08330
MIDDLESEX COUNTY COLLEGE Edison, NJ 08817
CULINARY INSTITUE OF AMERICA INC. Hyde Park, NY 12601
ERIE COMMUNITY COLLEGE Main and Young Road, Buffalo, NY 14221
JEFFERSON COMMUNITY COLLEGE Watertown, NY 13601
MONROE COMMUNITY COLLEGE 410 Alexander Street, Rochester, NY 14607
NEW YORK CITY COMMUNITY COLLEGE Brooklyn, NY 11201
SCHENECTADY COMMUNITY COLLEGE Washington Avenue, Schenectady, NY 12019
STATE UNIVERSITY AGRICULTURAL & TECHNICAL COLLEGE Canton, NY 13617
STATE UNIVERSITY AGRICULTURAL & TECHNICAL COLLEGE Cobleskill, NY 12034
STATE UNIVERSITY AGRICULTURAL & TECHNICAL COLLEGE Delhi, NY 13753
STATE UNIVERSITY AGRICULTURAL & TECHNICAL COLLEGE Morrisville, NY 13408
SULLIVAN COUNTY COMMUNITY COLLEGE Loch Sheldrake, NY 12759
VILLA MARIA COLLEGE OF BUFFALO Buffalo, NY 14225
WILKES COMMUNITY COLLEGE Wilkesboro, NC 28697
BISMARCK JUNIOR COLLEGE Bismarck, ND 58501
CUYAHOGA COMMUNITY COLLEGE 2214 E. 14th Street, Cleveland, OH 44115
HOCKING TECHNICAL COLLEGE Nelsonville OH 45764
PORTLAND COMMUNITY COLLEGE 12000 S.W. 49th Avenue, Portland, OR 97219
BUCKS COUNTY AREA COMMUNITY COLLEGE Newton, PA 18940
COMMUNITY COLLEGE OF PHILADELPHIA 23 S. 11th Street, Philadelphia, PA 19107
BRYANT COLLEGE Smithfield, RI 02917
UNIVERSITY OF SOUTH CAROLINA Columbia, SC 29208
MARTIN COLLEGE Pulaski, TN 38478
ROANE STATE COMMUNITY COLLEGE Harriman, TN 37748
DEL MAR COLLEGE 101 Baldwin Street, Corpus Christi, TX 78404
EL CENTRO COLLEGE Main & Lamar Streets, Dallas, TX 75202
COLLEGE OF THE VIRGIN ISLANDS P.O. Box 1826, Charlotte Amalie, V.I. 00801
NORTHERN VIRGINIA COMMUNITY COLLEGE—ANNANDALE Annandale, VA 22003
SEATTLE COMMUNITY COLLEGE 1625 Broadway, Seattle, WA 98122
DISTRICT 1—TECHNICAL INSTITUTE 620 Clairemont St., Eau Claire, WI 54701
GATEWAY—RACINE CAMPUS Racine, WI 53403

MADISON AREA TECHNICAL COLLEGE 211 N. Carroll Street, Madison, WI 53703
MILWAUKEE TECHNICAL COLLEGE 1015 N. 6th Street, Milwaukee, WI 53203
NORTHWEST COMMUNITY COLLEGE Powell, WY 82435

Travel, Transportation and Tourism—four-year colleges

ADELPHI UNIVERSITY Garden City, NY 11530
BRIGHAM YOUNG UNIVERSITY 55-220 Kulanui Street, Laie, HI 96762
FLORIDA STATE UNIVERSITY Tallahasse, FL 32306
PARKS COLLEGE OF ST. LOUIS UNIVERSITY Cahokia, IL 62206
UNIVERSITY OF NOTRE DAME, Notre Dame, IN 46656
UNIVERSITY OF HAWAII 2404 Maile Way, Honolulu, HI 96822
UNIVERSITY OF MASSACHUSETTS Amherst, MA 01002
MICHIGAN STATE UNIVERSITY Epply Center, East Lansing, MI 48824
UNIVERSITY OF NEVADA 4505 Maryland Parkway, Las Vegas, NV 89154
NIAGARA UNIVERSITY Niagara, NY 14109
UNIVERSITY OF WISCONSIN—STOUT Menomonie, WI 54751

Travel and Tourism—two-year colleges

JOHN C CALHOUN STATE TECHNICAL JUNIOR COLLEGE Decatur, AL 35601
FOOTHILL COLLEGE Los Altos, CA 94022
LOS ANGELES TRADE-TECHNICAL COLLEGE Los Angeles, CA 90015
MOUNT SAN ANTONIO COLLEGE Walnut, CA 91789
ORANGE COAST COLLEGE Costa Mesa, CA 92626
BROWARD COMMUNITY COLLEGE Fort Lauderdale, FL 33314
CENTRAL YMCA COMMUNITY COLLEGE Chicago, IL 60606
CARL SANDBURG COLLEGE Galesburg, IL 61401
BAY PATH JUNIOR COLLEGE Longmeadow, MA 01106
BECKER JUNIOR COLLEGE Worcester, MA 01609
ENDICOTT JUNIOR COLLEGE Beverly, MA 01915
COLUMBIA COLLEGE Columbia, MO 65201
MISSOULA TECHNICAL CENTER Missoula, MT 59801
GENESEE COMMUNITY COLLEGE Batavia, NY 14020
STATEN ISLAND COMMUNITY COLLEGE Staten Island, NY 10301
COMMUNITY COLLEGE OF ALLEGHENY COUNTY Pittsburgh, PA 15212
MARTIN COLLEGE Pulaski, TN 38478
EDMONDS COMMUNITY COLLEGE Lynwood, WA 98036
HIGHLINE COMMUNITY COLLEGE Midway, WA 98031
SPOKANE COMMUNITY COLLEGE Spokane, WA 99202

Private travel training schools

AIRLINE SCHOOLS PACIFIC 6043 Hollywood Blvd., Hollywood, CA 90028
ECHOLS INTERNATIONAL TRAVEL TRAINING COURSES, INC. 1390 Market St., San Francisco, CA 94102
PROFESSIONAL TRAVEL AGENT TRAINING SCHOOL 4501 Mission Bay Dr., San Diego, CA 92109
BRIARWOOD SCHOOL FOR WOMEN 2279 Mt. Vernon Rd., Southington, CT 06489
INTERNATIONAL TRAVEL TRAINING COURSES, INC. 4201 Connecticut Ave., N.W., Washington, DC 20008
ASSOCIATED SCHOOLS 9999 N.E. 2nd Ave., Miami, FL 33138

CENTRAL YMCA COMMUNITY COLLEGE 211 W. Wacker Dr., Chicago, IL 60606
INTERNATIONAL TRAVEL TRAINING COURSES, INC. 936 N. Michigan Ave., Chicago, IL 60611
ROBERTA FISHER TRAVEL TRAINING SCHOOL 133 W. Wing St., Arlington Heights, IL 60005
TRAVEL AGENT'S TRAINING SCHOOL 253 Northwest Hwy., Palatine, IL 60067
V.I.P. TRAVEL AGENT SCHOOL 333 E. Ontario, Chicago, IL 60611
TRAVEL SCHOOL OF AMERICA 1406 Beacon St., Brookline, MA 02146
McCONNEL SCHOOL, INC. 1030 Nicollet Ave., Minneapolis, MN 55403
HUMBOLDT INSTITUTE 2201 Blaidsell Ave., S., Minneapolis, MN 55404
EASTERN SCHOOL FOR TRAVEL AGENCY MANAGEMENT 721 Broadway, New York, NY 10003
THE SOBELSOHN SCHOOL 1540 Broadway, New York, NY 10036
INTERNATIONAL SCHOOL OF TRAVEL, INC. 21 S. 12th Street, Philadelphia, PA 19107
BRANIFF EDUCATION SYSTEMS, INC. P.O. Box 35001, Dallas, TX 75235
INTERNATIONAL TRAVEL INSTITUTE, INC. 6401 S.W. Freeway, Houston, TX 77036
WILMA BOYD CAREER SCHOOLS On the Plaza-Chatham Center, Pittsburgh, PA 15219

Correspondence travel training courses

ASTA TRAVEL CORRESPONDENCE COURSE 711 Fifth Avenue, New York, NY 10022
NORTH AMERICAN SCHOOL OF TRAVEL 4500 Campus Dr. Newport Beach, CA 92663

Merchant Marine training institutions

Officer training
CALIFORNIA MARITIME ACADEMY Vallejo, CA 94591
MARITIME INSTITUTE OF TECHNOLOGY 5700 Hammonds Ferry Rd. Linthicum Heights, MD 21090
CALHOON MEBA ENGINEERING SCHOOL 9 Light St., Baltimore, MD 21203
MAINE MARITIME ACADEMY Castine, ME 04421
MASSACHUSETTS MARITIME ACADEMY Buzzards Bay, MA 02537
GREAT LAKES MARITIME ACADEMY Traverse City, MI 48213
AMERICAN RADIO ASSN. 270 Madison Ave., New York, NY 10016
NEW YORK STATE MARITIME COLLEGE Forth Schuyler, NY 10465
RADIO OFFICERS UNION 225 W. 34th Street, New York, NY 10001
U.S. MERCHANT MARINE ACADEMY Kings Point, NY 11024
TEXAS MARITIME ACADEMY Galveston, TX 77550

Seaman training
MARINE COOKS & STEWARDS TRAINING PROGRAM 350 Fremont St., San Francisco, CA 94105
HARRY LUNDEBERG SCHOOL OF SEAMANSHIP Piney Point, MD 20674
SCHOOL OF MARINE STEWARDS 925 Summit St., Toledo, OH 43604

U.S. Coast Guard

U.S. COAST GUARD ACADEMY New London, CT 06320

INDEX

173